BETWEEN RACE AND REASON

BETWEEN RACE AND REASON

Violence, Intellectual Responsibility,
and the University to Come

Susan Searls Giroux

STANFORD UNIVERSITY PRESS

STANFORD, CALIFORNIA

Stanford University Press
Stanford, California

An earlier version of Chapters 1 and 3 originally appeared in *JAC* 29 (2009). An
earlier version of Chapter 2 appeared as an article in *College Literature* 33.4 (Fall
2006); reprinted with permission. Chapter 4 originally appeared as an article
in a special issue on academic freedom in *Works and Days* 26 & 27: 51/52, 53/54;
reprinted with permission. Chapter 5 originally appeared as an article in a special
issue on Lewis R. Gordon in the *C.L.R. James Journal* 14.1 (Spring 2008). An
earlier version of sections of Chapter 6 originally appeared in *Social Identities* 9:4
(December 2003).

Printed in the United States of America on acid-free, archival-quality paper

Library of Congress Cataloging-in-Publication Data

Giroux, Susan Searls, 1968–
    Between race and reason : violence, intellectual responsibility, and the
university to come / Susan Searls Giroux.
        p.   cm.
    Includes bibliographical references and index.
    ISBN 978-0-8047-7047-7 (cloth : alk. paper)
    ISBN 978-0-8047-7048-4 (pbk : alk. paper)
        1. Racism in higher education—United States.   2. Education, Higher—
Political aspects—United States.   3. Racism—United States.   4. United
States—Race relations.   I. Title.
    LC212.42.G57   2010
    378.73089—dc22

2009053222

Contents

For Henry

Acknowledgments

I left the United States in 2004 in order to begin a new job and the promise of a new life in Ontario, Canada. Physically, that is. Psychically, the move has been much slower. In spite of the change, I remain as concerned about the future of the country of my birth, as transfixed by its rapid changes, and as fearful of its faltering, though I now watch from a distance. As became clear to most everyone the world over when the global financial crisis of 2008 set in, our fates are linked regardless of borders. Poor decisions, bundled together and traded across the globe, have consequences, often tragic, well beyond their local origins. The hope that accompanied the election of Barack Obama to the White House that same year has quickly dissipated as two costly and likely unwinnable wars in Iraq and Afghanistan carry on unabated and everyday Americans continue to face unprecedented levels of home foreclosure, unemployment, impoverishment, the receding dream of universal health care, and a shattered educational system made worse by reforms that mimic the punishing inanities of No Child Left Behind. Bush may be gone, but the most reactionary (and indeed the most vocal) elements of the conservative counterrevolution of the last several decades still cast a foreboding shadow over the institutions, values, and social relations necessary for genuine democratization and peace in our time. Our actions have never been more weighted, and yet curiously our sense of responsibility never lighter—the reach and extent of it neatly bounded by our discrete, individual, highly privatized worlds. Personal responsibility remains the watchword; social responsibility, if media pundits are to be believed, is for socialists.

Only, I've never believed the new common sense, which inevitably fails when measured against the reality of a shared world. The eminent sociologist Zygmunt Bauman has written eloquently of the need to "take responsibility for our responsibility," which I have chosen to understand as a new and improved version of the Kantian project of Enlightenment. We're still being urged to transcend our "self-incurred immaturity," but the goal of autonomy has given way to the adult recognition of mutuality. There was a time when universities took this Enlightened project—the 1.0 rather than the 2.0 version—as central to its (civilizing) mission. But that moment, never secure and certainly never perfect, appears to have given way to the Economic Imperative, closely linked to the Military Imperative, of our contemporary moment, even as these have produced near-global catastrophe. But not for everyone. I have had the extreme good fortune upon my initiation into the academy to have met, to have been taught by, mentored by, and befriended by so many gifted and courageous intellectuals who have inspired me with an alternative vision of university possibility. Though I take responsibility for whatever limitations in argument and evidence my readers find in the following pages, I would like to express my deepest gratitude to those who have been so generous with their support, their criticisms, their time, and their unerring commitment to alleviate social injustice and the suffering of others.

Though an international border separates me from my family, they remain a daily, if technologically mediated, presence in my life. My gratitude to those who put up with me in moments of acute frustration and elation: my mother, Jessica Marlow, my aunt, Virginia Monet, my nephew, Benjamin Davis, and three young men of whom I couldn't be more proud, Brett, Chris, and Jack Giroux. I would like to thank those who, through the generous extension of their friendship, have made my transition to a new position, a new community, and a new country not only sane, but joyous: Tracy Wynne, Janice Hladki, Jasmin Habib, Wendy Simon, Maya Sabados, Antoinette Somo, and Lorraine and Gary Burch. Of the many people instrumental in my hiring at McMaster University, I am grateful most especially to Nasrin Rahimieh, then Dean of Humanities, whose leadership, wisdom, and compassion serve as daily reminders of how to "be" in the academy. I am told it is a most unusual circumstance, but I have had the experience of two deans from whom I've learned so much. I'm grateful for the opportunity here to express my gratitude as well to Carol Becker, who was my dean at the School of the Art Institute in Chicago, a woman of unsurpassed sophistication and always sage advice. I want to thank my many colleagues past and present who have helped me think through ideas and supported my work in ways I will never quite be able to repay: Elliott Gorn, Keith Gilyard, Elaine Richardson, Evan Watkins, Michael Payne, Roger Simon, Stanley Aronowitz, John Comaroff, Jeff Nealon, Donald Lazere, Deborah Britzman, Cary Fraser, who helped me find the right title, and Zygmunt Bauman, who graciously put up with my queries on the vicissitudes of liquid modern education. A very special thanks to Jane Gordon, who read chapters of this manuscript when she had absolutely no time and provided me with her unfailingly astute criticisms. And to my students, who also read parts of the manuscript, offered constructive feedback and would also remind me they had very little time (no thanks to me): Cathy Collett, Phanuel Antwi, Karen Espiritu, Jennifer Adese, Jenny Fisher, and Sonya Zikic. I owe them all for reminding me, when all our schedules feel harassed and we can hardly breathe, how much I love my work and what an honor it is to learn from them, to draw inspiration from their boundless curiosity and energy. I would also like to acknowledge that the inspiration for many of the lines of argument I develop here has come from editors who have graciously invited me to write articles for their journals or allowed me to work out ideas in conversation with them. For these opportunities, a heartfelt thanks to Paget Henry, Rob Reiman, Ed Carvalho, Michael Peters, Norm Denzin, and especially Lynn Worsham, who has encouraged and supported my work for over a decade. To be sure, this book would not exist but for the support of my editor at Stanford University Press, Emily-Jane Cohen, and her assistant, Sarah Crane Newman, both of whom have been graciously accommodating and ever so patient. My thanks to two reviewers, Zeus Leonardo and an anonymous reviewer, whose extensive critical commentaries on my manuscript have made the final version infinitely better for their more than generous efforts. And thanks to Ignacy and Stasys Eidrigevicius, who have graciously granted me permission to use the book's stunning cover art.

I owe an enormous debt of gratitude to three scholars in particular, who've not only exerted profound influence on my thinking but shown me great kindness over the years. Lewis Gordon, whose body of work, characterized by uncommon thoughtfulness, rigor, and breathtaking elegance, has been so very generative for my own. As I have gotten to know the man behind the work, I continue to be awed by the depth of his humanity, his astonishing erudition, and his keen sense of play. In his presence and that of his partner Jane and their gorgeous children, I feel, uncannily, home. David Theo Goldberg has most generously served as mentor over the last fifteen years, offering advice and instruction and graciously overlooking my moments of idiocy. I have learned as much from his meticulously crafted arguments and principled marshalling of evidence, always judicious, clarifying, and positively daring, as from his unwavering courage in the public sphere. Finally, my deepest thanks go to David Clark, dear friend and colleague extraordinaire, who has been unfailing in his support and solidarity since my arrival in Canada. I am daily humbled by his selfless generosity, intense brilliance, boundless integrity, and keen wit.

Miles and Kaya, my glorious Akitas and stalwart companions, have kept me company throughout; their bone-gnawing, their battling over favored squeak toys, and their endless, at times merciless, snoring have provided the soundtrack against which I write—offering me moments of acute levity when the weightiness of worldly events offered none. Their lessons have been elemental—reminding me to stretch, drink lots of water, take walks, and give and receive kisses. Most of all I thank my best friend and partner of nearly twenty years, Henry Giroux, the very figure of intellectual courage. The idea to extend my arguments into book form was his, and his unwavering faith in my abilities helped bring it to fruition. A more loving presence in my life I could not imagine. His genius and passion have influenced every page of this book; his patience and humor enabled us both to survive the writing of it.

Introduction: The University to Come

It is an idea that is probably bound up with the whole Western organization of knowledge, namely, the idea that knowledge and truth cannot not belong to the register of order and peace, that knowledge and truth can never be found on the side of violence, disorder, and war.

—MICHEL FOUCAULT, 1976

Now when we compare the technical mastery which man has over the world, with the utter failure of that power to organize happiness, and peace in the world, then we know that something is wrong. Part of this wrong is our conception of education.

—W.E.B. DU BOIS (1944?)

We ain't goin' study war no more.

—AN "OLD NEGRO SPIRITUAL"

This book engages an uneasy set of questions about the relationship between the university and public life at the dawn of the twenty-first century. The conditions that have prompted this investigation are all too obvious for those readers who number among humanistic or social scientific faculties, and perhaps only slightly less so for those who have acquired a passing knowledge of current events. For the past few decades, mainstream media have loudly disparaged the ongoing crisis of the university—a crisis the contours of which beg the widest possible interpretative dimensions, as pundits and critics from across the political spectrum can attest. My specific concern is in the ways in which this crisis can be said to be *racially predicated*, even as the prevailing common sense impatiently insists that race is now an irrelevance in national public life.

To be sure, African American intellectuals like Carter G. Woodson and W.E.B. Du Bois in the first decades of the twentieth century exposed the ways in which a democracy's self-assured and unambiguous allegiance to universal education could be perverted, producing generations of "miseducated" adherents to mythologies of racial superiority, nationalist provincialism, and techno-scientific idiocy, rather than inspiring an intellectually engaged, cosmopolitan, and democratic citizenry. Du Bois's magisterial *Black Reconstruction* delivers a clear rebuke to historians of the day, who sacrificed a faithful and accurate record of human action for "the most stupendous efforts the world ever saw to discredit human beings, an effort involving universities, history, science, social life and religion."[1] More recently, the work of postcolonial theorists such as Edward Said, Robert Young, Gayatri Spivak, and others has drawn critical attention to the relationship between modern European and American imperial adventures and forms of cultural invention and self-creation; between the university's transcendent quest for truth and knowledge and its role in the production of aesthetic, philosophical and scientific modes of legitimization that subtend liberal modernity's commitment to an utterly knowable, malleable, and ordered universe—to the task, in short, of mastery and so subjugation. Said's now classic *Orientalism* stands at the apogee of this tradition, tracing in meticulous and bracing detail how the backwardness, degeneracy, and inequality in scholarly and popular representations of the Islamic Orient—an imagined space standing outside of Western progress in the arts, science, governance, and commerce and hence requiring its "attention, reconstruction and even redemption"—derived from biologically defined analyses of racial inferiority fashioned by and circulated among the European intelligentsia for nearly two centuries.[2] Young concurs with this assessment in his study of racially fashioned disciplinary formation in the modern university in *Colonial Desire*. "Race became the fundamental determinant of human culture and history," he observes; "indeed, it is arguable that race became the common principle of academic knowledge in the nineteenth century."[3] Far from a premodern relic, race was a foundational force in this first wave of globalization, ranging from the age of insatiable exploration to enlightened enslavement, to imperial conquest and colonization, and finally to their formal, violent denouement. From the seventeenth century to the mid-twentieth century, race prompted and promoted, altered and refined forms of statecraft, population management, political economy, wartime strategy, scientific discovery, technological progress—the very content and condition of modern thought.[4]

Building on this vast and significant body of work, which focuses on the racially inflected period of Western modernization and its world-transforming consequences, my interest is in intellectual practices and institutional policies that have influenced the American university since the 1960s—a period defined by any number of epochal shifts ubiquitously yet ambivalently signaled by the prefixes "neo" and "post." In particular, I am concerned to examine intellectual complicity with a new "post-racial" politics that parallels the ascendancy of the latest phase of world capitalist development, or global neoliberalism. Whereas the racially shaped imperial politics of the modern era prompted intellectual discussion and analysis of the "white man's burden," the contemporary organization of intellectual labor in the academy, I hope to show, is in large part predicated on his *unburdening*. In contrast to the forms of racially patterned paternalistic imposition and oversight that accompanied glove-in-fist the various nation-building and empire-expanding projects of liberal modernity, the modes of racial management, control, and containment that mark the present moment, or what Zygmunt Bauman aptly calls "liquid modernity," seek more often than not to dissolve all forms of socially contracted responsibility. Neoliberal states, in other words, rush to dismantle the social safety nets on which citizens rely, alleging they promote dependency and sloth, dismiss as quaint cosmopolitan conventions that commit nations to observe the rights of others to move about the globe unharrassed and unharmed, and destroy preemptively in the name of national security threats to "*our* way of life"—threats, all of them, inevitably racially conceived though never identified as such. In a clear echo of Du Bois's analysis of the scholarly transformation of black Americans into a "problem people," Said asserted that Islamic "Orientals were rarely seen or looked at; they were seen through, analyzed not as citizens, or even people, but as problems to be solved or confined—or as the colonial powers openly coveted their territory—taken over.[5] So too in our "post-racist" present, blacks and Arabs, among other groups formerly and newly raced even where race is in denial, remain problem peoples—"rogue" populations, to borrow David Theo Goldberg's clever designation, who augur threat from within and without, as much economic as existential, political as physical.[6] The intellectual challenge, so to speak, is no longer (primarily) how to facilitate or justify the extraction of labor, the expropriation of lands, resources, and wealth, the monopolization of political power or militarized force. Rather, it is a question of how to dispose of—without being precisely seen or understood to dispose of, and so without accompanying forms of guilt or self-doubt—those populations whose culture or character is alien and alienating, whose patterns of work and consumption are neither required nor adequate, whose presence takes up too much valuable space, whose movement remains the source of too much unease, whose settlement threatens to drain once abundant and now dwindling economic and ecological resources, posing any number of risks to homeland security. In this new endeavor, race comes to assume an underground existence. Coded culturally or individually, targeted populations are "raceless," in that they are no longer racially identified in any traditional sense. What "naturalist" and "historicist" racisms were to the modern era, racelessness is to the contemporary moment.[7] The abiding faith in racelessness, Goldberg explains, is the "neoliberal attempt to go beyond—without (fully) coming to terms with—racial histories and their accompanying inequalities . . . to transform, via the negating dialectic of denial and ignoring, racially marked social orders into racially erased ones."[8]

The now-widespread belief that race no longer matters grew out of the civil rights victories of the 1960s, which dismantled the legal apparatus of racial segregation and conferred on the United States an officially post-racist or race-transcendent status. So too the biologically determined attribution of racial inferiority thought to legitimate such legalities fell into scientific and scholarly disrepute—along with the possibilities of a refashioned racism, appropriately privatized and deregulated, in keeping with a new free market edition of state sovereignty. If inequalities exist, they are the consequence of a culture of deprivation or a deficit in individual character, not the result of institutional injustice or its enduring legacy. Indeed the self-confident assertion that racism is part of America's past, slam-dunked in the dustbin of history, found its most potent symbolism in the November 2008 election of Barack Obama, now the forty-fourth president and the first African American to serve in the nation's highest office. My argument, however, is not that institutional policies and practices, or individual beliefs and attitudes, that govern and mediate how race is lived in America have not changed; it is rather to challenge whether recent changes necessarily signal social progress for all men and women of color—progress defined not by the acquisition of material wealth and middle-class comfort for a few but by full incorporation into and due influence upon the body politic. It is also to question whether the nation's post-racial pretensions ever correspond with robust forms of anti-racist commitment or represent merely their curtailment, when not their explicit repudiation.[9]

Although the electorate has found Obama "likeable enough," a clear majority appears to have neither the will nor the stomach to challenge and transform deepening racial disparities in employment, education, housing, health, and mortality—to say nothing of the existential crises to which such injustices give rise. It is both a tragic and an ironic commentary that the first African American in the Oval Office presides over the worst socioeconomic decline for blacks in recent memory—and the highest rates of incarceration ever recorded. As a result of the current recession, preceded by decades of post-industrial decline, Economic Policy Institute President Lawrence Mishel estimates that 40 percent of African Americans "will have experienced unemployment or underemployment in 2010 . . . increasing child poverty from one-third of African-American children to over half."[10] Since taking the oath of office, Obama has not addressed growing racial inequality and exclusion—a fact less reflective of personal indifference (I don't believe he is indifferent) than of his demonstrated ability to read painful political realities. Understanding the generalized ambivalence, where not open hostility, of most whites to any mention of race, Obama owes his electoral success in part to his efforts to ride the post-racial wave and to distance himself—generationally, politically, rhetorically—from civil rights advocates. So it remains to be seen whether the Obama administration will adhere to its commitment to change and usher in an era of purposive, collective action informed by sober reflection of the ongoing injustices that stem from the nation's racial past and a present commitment to serve in the interests of public freedom and human dignity—or whether it will inspire the symbolic unfurling of yet another gratuitous "mission accomplished" sign and feed the amnesiatic tendency of Americans to forget the past, and in so doing condemn the present to subtle and not-so-subtle forms of racist mimicry.

Another open question, and one which I hope the present study influences to some small degree, is the role that intellectuals in the academy play, will in fact choose to play, in this strange new phase of what Gunner Myrdal once called, in reference to the distance between the nation's democratic ideals and its racial realities, the "American dilemma." Aware of it or not, willing or not, intellectuals who devote their lives to studying, teaching, and writing about the human condition regardless of disciplinary location are acting with moral consequence, and often with political effect. Hence it is imperative to ask: What pressures will intellectuals in the academy bring to bear on the issues of our time? Which values and whose interests will they reflect in the identification of problems said to require scholarly attention, in the formulation of key concepts, in the choice of methodologies, and in the staging of solutions? And what pressures, in turn, will be brought to bear on them? The task at hand is, then, to assess critically the last forty years of academic allegiance to colorblindness and to theorize the possibilities for a much-needed reconciliation with a social reality that is highly and historically raced, as well as a rehabilitation of critical and creative thought.

This book thus investigates the emergence of, and effective responses to, the new racism, or raceless racism, in this officially post–civil rights era, which has prompted in turn new vocabularies, social sensibilities, and everyday practices reflective of contemporary colorblind consciousness.[11] More specifically it explores the impact of colorblind commitment on the academy, on the quality of intellectual thought therein, given the rise of the new forms of expertise, discursive strategies, analytic models, pedagogical practices, and institutional imperatives that are rhetorically nonracial and presumptively neutral. For Goldberg, colorblinding logics exact primarily three discursive prohibitions: a silencing of public analysis of what Philomena Essed calls "everyday racisms" in society; an emphatic denial of history such that it proves difficult to connect contemporary racial formations to past configurations of institutional power predicated on whiteness; and finally, a displacement of racially charged relations in the public sphere to the private, more or less out of reach of public policy interventions.[12] This triple effect is evident in the ways in which the discursive work of race obscures itself in—disappears into—the broad language of reified cultural or civilizational differences, or more narrow psychological assessments of individual prejudices or group instincts effectively silencing historical and structural analyses. Colorblinding imperatives, moreover, chamelionically assume the form of a contemporary cult of professionalism, a set of institutional pressures Edward Said identified that are often internalized by academicians in their pursuit of "objective," "specialized," and "non-political" research, which have been more recently buttressed by conservative calls for "balanced" scholarship that reflects a "diversity of views," regardless of their intellectual merit.[13] Putatively objective, nonpolitical, and noncontroversial research is particularly prized by increasingly corporatized universities, where scholars are urged to be "practical," particularly where practicality comes to mean not "effective social reform," as it once implied, but "efficiency" and "cost-effectiveness" in the bureaucratic monitoring and management of global flows of goods, information, and populations. Intellectual projects of merit, according to neoliberal logics, are essentially projects fundable via outside sources of revenue; their often specialized and piecemeal orientation are designed to garner clear results quickly before grant money runs out—without upsetting (racial) politics as usual.

These unambiguous institutional preferences have produced a shift away from qualitative and critical research to quantifiable and empirical data collection, one already exacerbated by the hierarchical arrangement of scientific over humanistic inquiry explored by C. P. Snow half a century ago, where the numbers are taken unproblematically to reveal more readily "social reality" and unmediated "truth." Such inputs, amassed in surveys or interviews or test scores, necessarily bespeak a "presentist" agenda rendering historical assessment irrelevant and thus in keeping with colorblinding protocols. The foci of data-driven studies are, moreover, narrowed to the particularity of time and place—all the better to control the play of variables. Such efforts, however, come at the expense of a false sense of pervasive social homogeneity—a condition which, despite its considerable normative appeal, renders investigators blind to social differences. The quest for neutrality and transparency thus reproduces the ideal of racelessness and the norms of whiteness they nonetheless express. Not only does this specificity preclude comparative assessments of outcomes, but structural or institutional changes that occur over time cannot be detected adequately; thus it becomes difficult in such instances to imagine alternatives to a present reality that appears immutable and fixed. Another victory for the established order. The predilection to analyze a singular factor among an assumed myriad of causal elements in the study of a social phenomenon, moreover, lends itself well to the always partial and inadequate reforms espoused of late by liberal and conservative politicians. Rather than engage the obvious racial and class disparities perpetuated by grossly unequal public school funding, for example, school administrators hip to the latest studies tinker with single-sex classrooms to bolster self-esteem or introduce pre-packaged commercial curricula into the classroom guaranteed to produce small spikes in standardized test scores among the chronically bored. Speaking at Teachers College in late 2008, Secretary of Education Arne Duncan, for example, criticized teacher education programs for failing to provide more hands-on classroom experience to new initiates and for failing to prepare them to use empirical data to inform and improve teacher preparation. Once the analytic value of history, social structure, and other increasingly suspect "theoretical" concepts is removed from the intellectual field, researchers have little recourse but to capitulate to the distinct tendency of the time to psychologize and hence depoliticize results, as I will elaborate further in the later chapters.

Significantly, the displacement of the discourse of race and the hermeneutic sophistication it requires finds its corollary in another order of displacement, with specific ramification for the university. Simultaneous with the redefinition of racism as a private and individual problem as opposed to a public and institutional one, we have witnessed a profound shift in conceptions of "good government." Specifically, the ideals that informed Lyndon B. Johnson's Great Society have been abandoned to a new civic common sense that is anti-statist, anti-political, and deeply anti-intellectual. Though in execution it proved a thoroughly compromised affair, in his memoir, *My Hope for America*, Johnson elaborated his vision. Succinct and to the point, he insisted that "the Great Society rests on abundance and liberty for all. It demands an end to poverty and racial injustice. But that is just the beginning. The Great Society is a place where every child can find knowledge to enrich his mind and to enlarge his talents."[14] A neoliberal society, strikingly, offers citizens an utterly opposed reality—point for point—delivering deeper poverty, more racial injustice, and radically diminished opportunities for thought, let alone intellectual growth. Not only has the gap between wealth and poverty grown exponentially, but economic standing is increasingly predicated on racial standing. The conservative mission to shrink "big government" has expanded, through a series of privatizing and deregulating policy shifts, the role of the market in circulation and control of various flows of commodities and peoples, and a singular logic of cost-efficiency has replaced the prior era's investment in expanding the rights and entitlements of citizens. As a result, public goods like education have been radically defunded at all levels—from elementary to postsecondary—leaving them open to "failure" or further privatization. The welfare state apparatuses that once provided social safety nets and a measure of security to all citizens (at least in theory) were condemned in racially coded language as too solicitous of so-called special interests, too inefficient in their reproduction of moral degeneracy and social dependency, and far too expensive, condemning taxpayers (understood as white) to foot the bill for tax recipients (understood as black). Thus, social progress has come to be measured exclusively in the language of economic growth—alleged to be transparent, morally neutral and, crucially, colorblind—even as growth nonetheless is procured only for the nation's wealthy and (mostly) white. The consequences for substantive democratization have been devastating, and especially so for children—the moral referent, ironically, of Johnson's social vision.

The recession that has come to define the latter half of the millennial decade has resulted from this perfect storm of deregulated system-wide market mendacity, greed, and corruption, an intellectual culture co-opted by forms of instrumental rationalization openly hostile to reason and reflection, and a distracted citizenry binging on a junk diet of spectacle, violence, apocalyptic harangue, and unapologetic idiocy. To failed health care, we have added failed schools, failed banks, even failed states such as debt-ridden California—and a booming prison-industrial complex. We should be deeply concerned at this point with the lingering faith in accounting figures that boast the robust health of a lending institution, the charts of improved test scores indicative of a child's or a school district's scholastic advance, the predictive acumen of the actuarial tables that point to victory ahead in the domestic wars on crime and drugs. Neither objective nor transparent, numbers can be made to say and do anything—particularly when the scale of a CEO bonus, or a teacher's salary, or a officer's promotion is made to depend on them. The temptation to manipulate the figures, however, stems not only from financial reward widely assumed in the neoliberal era to be the real motor of history, but also the concerted effort to resuscitate a waning sense of status and privilege formally accrued to whites. In each instance of recent or ongoing catastrophe—from the mortgage meltdown, to the collapse of financials, to the closure of failed schools, to states with no money for basic social services, to the ever-broadening drug and gun trade—it has been communities of color that have suffered the repercussions first, before the devastation spread outward and up the socioeconomic scale.

I do not mean, however, to suggest that as the pain spreads, all suffer equally; black and brown victims found themselves routinely blamed for their own unemployment, impoverishment, and homelessness. Culpability not assigned to corporate corruption abetted by political corruption, to large-scale downsizing or the flight of jobs, to collapsing social services or persistent racial exclusion is routinely redirected to individual failing and character flaw racially assigned—laziness or lack of work ethic, moral turpitude, sexual lassitude, drug dependence, and other forms of deviant behavior that betray contempt for mainstream American (white) values. Not only are poor men and women of color denied crucial forms of support and assistance, intensifying their existential grief, but also the public policy result of such pervasive and purposive regimes of misrepresentation has been the ongoing criminalization of social problems that plague poor and minority populations. According to a report released by the Pew Center in March 2009, one in every thirty-one U.S. adults resides in the corrections system; broken down racially, the numbers are: one in 11 is African American; one in 27 is Latino and one in 45 is white. This should not be surprising in a nation that has made closing "failed" schools (i.e., schools in poor, typically minority districts) and opening jails the signature of its domestic policy, where in fact states "even determine how many prison cells to build based on 4th grade reading scores and graduation rates."[15] The decision to invest in prison construction over—and at the expense of—already cash strapped schools reveals the degree to which investor returns on a hot growth industry like corrections far outweigh the social returns of an educated and engaged public. In an economy and society refashioned by a highly rationalized neoliberal logic, openness and freedom now characterize the movement of markets, not citizens.

What the culturalization of domestic and international conflict and the privatization of racist expression and exclusion share with equally reductive neoliberal market instrumentalities is an abiding commitment to scuttle modes of intellectual inquiry and analysis that foreground questions of structure, power, inequality, and history. The premise of this book is that consequences of the new racism for the academy as a site that once aspired to independent thought and critique have been particularly devastating. The institutional "repression of racial reference," or the rendering of race as "unspeakable" in public by reducing it to a past problem now resolved and best forgotten, has combined with an unquestioning faith in the neutrality of free market economics, short-circuiting not just our understanding of our past and our present, our political institutions, our national identity, and our international standing.[16] Most devastatingly, the commitment to colorblindness has also impaired our very capacity to think, to reason, to weigh and even be persuaded by evidence, to recognize error, to be reflective, and to judge. Yet, my argument is not that colorblind racism is "irrational," or even "unreasonable"; it is rather to claim that its adherents participate in radically reductive forms of rationality that make reason and reflection less likely and more difficult, where not impossible.

Of course my more conservative interlocutors would insist that humanistic inquiry over the last few decades has been unhealthily obsessed with race, or more specifically the mantra "raceclassgender" in ways that are only destructive and divisive—necessitating the very calls for colorblindness and race-neutrality in scholarly research, pedagogy, and (perhaps most viscerally) admissions policy in the first place. Yet even as the so-called campus "culture wars" of the 1980s and 1990s waned, national tragedy struck and revitalized the long-standing conservative critique of the academy. From the foot soldiers who waged war against forms of "political correctness" promulgated by campus "thought police" and intolerant liberals more generally came a new and ironically insistent cry for "patriotic correctness." Immediately following the catastrophic events of September 11, 2001, the university was pilloried by conservatives as the "weak link" in the War on Terror, and the professoriate were caricatured as a homogeneous mass of unpatriotic, pro-terrorist sympathizers by influential right-wing organizations with open access to the popular press—to conservative talk radio and news outlets like Fox as well as the more mainstream CNN, particularly programming anchored by Lou Dobbs or Glenn Beck (before he moved to Fox). In this bloody "clash of civilizations," the academy was, more often than not, guilty of siding with enemies both foreign and domestic. So began a period of intensive scrutiny, accusation, recrimination, even slander (as in the case of David Horowitz's ignoble *The Professors*) against progressive scholars, and middle-eastern scholars in particular, who were in turn passed over for academic positions, or denied the necessary visas to assume such posts once hired, or were denied tenure, or outright lost their jobs.[17] Perhaps no case received more national attention than that of Ward Churchill, whose "little Eichmanns" reference to the victims of 9/11 in a public lecture in 2005, led to the termination of his nearly thirty-year career at the University of Colorado and a heated court battle, which he eventually won, though the university refused to reinstate him just the same. Another highly visible case in point occurred in the denouement of the 2008 presidential election, during which some academicians were reviled as actual domestic terrorists, as in the now-infamous case of William Ayers, the 1960s radical turned University of Illinois at Chicago professor of education whose commitments to Chicago's public schools led him to share seats on a few boards with Barack Obama. When the Ayers story failed to produce poll results favorable to the McCain campaign, it was replaced by a "darker" tale featuring Rashid Khalidi, Edward Said Professor of Arab Studies and director of the Middle East Institute at Columbia University. Described as an associate and political ally of Barack Obama, Khalidi was alleged to have been a former spokesperson for the Palestinian Liberation Organization—a narrative undoubtedly meant to bolster rumors of Obama's Muslim faith, as it connected him indirectly with the most recent racially rendered "enemy" population. These highly publicized associations were meant to perform a double duty: first, they resurrected the culture of fear in order to alarm and/or inflame potential voters leaning toward the Democratic candidate (whose middle name was after all "Hussein") in the run-up to election day and second, they further cemented in the public imaginary a commonsense conception of the university as a hotbed of left-wing radicalism and anti-Americanism.

Liberal interests, on the other hand, also understand the academy to be in a state of crisis, but for an entirely different set of reasons. There has been a longstanding progressive challenge to the ongoing corporatization of the university—a transformation that has only accelerated in the last twenty years. Indeed, warnings were issued well before Big Pharma contributed millions toward named research chairs in prestigious medical schools who simultaneously ran their drug trials, before the Berkeley Free Speech movement of the 1960s railed against "the operation of the machine," before even Friedrich Nietzsche's 1872 lectures exposing the corruption of the university's educational mission by the dictates of political economy, back as far as Immanuel Kant, who in 1798 noted in the *Conflict of the Faculties* how "industrial-like" the academy was at that moment becoming. From this historical perspective, the university as a sacrosanct institution for both the preservation and production of knowledge has been less jeopardized by left-wing ideologues than by the relentless pressures of the market that seek not only to commodify knowledge, to invest in and so shape knowledge production in the interests of expanding profit over human need, but also to transform the academy itself from a democratic, egalitarian institution (in its best moments) into a corporate entity, hierarchically organized and overtly hostile to forms of thought that threaten its bottom line.

So too over time have scholars aspiring to intellectual autonomy warned of the university's ties to the state's war machinery, and by midtwentieth century, to the defense *industry*—now one of the primary (surviving) motors of the U.S. economy—fearing the inevitable militarization of the university and the weaponization of knowledge. The transformation of the university during the Cold War is by now a well-known story, but one that has lost its cautionary edge. Clark Kerr, chancellor of the University of California at Berkeley in the 1950s and early 1960s, was one of the first to recognize the significance for American universities of the war and the rapidly shifting economy, which had begun to shed its former industrial focus on raw materials in favor of the new post-industrial investment in expert knowledge. Kerr embraced forms of patronage from government, military, and corporate entities, even as these fundamentally altered—commercialized and instrumentalized—the "free" production and circulation of new knowledges. The emerging "postwar university was a wholly new institution, one that was uniquely responsive to the society of which it was now very much a part," writes Rebecca S. Lowen in her exemplary study, *Creating the Cold War University*. Advances in new military technologies such as ballistic missiles, guidance systems, hydrogen bombs, and radar now "required the expertise of highly trained scientists and engineers," expertise that it goes without saying could have been directed toward more peaceful, humane, and sustainable projects.[18] Of the approximately $10 billion the federal government—primarily, the Department of Defense and Atomic Energy Commission—was spending annually on research and development by the early 1960s, universities and university-affiliated centers received annually about one-tenth (or $1 billion). In turn, these universities came to depend on federal money for over 50 percent of their operating budgets. "As the organization and funding of science changed," Lowen observes, "so did the kinds of knowledges produced and taught."[19] Not only did new fields of study emerge, like nuclear engineering and Russian studies, but the ways that intellectuals actually thought, the way they conceived and diagnosed problems, also changed as the social scientists "shifted their emphases, stressing quantitative approaches over normative ones and individual behavior and cultural studies over sociological ones." What forms of censorship Senator Joseph McCarthy did not effect in his infamous purge of dissident intellectuals were otherwise produced by the intense financial pressures introduced by such dense webs of dependency between the government and the university.

Half a century later, post-secondary education found itself in dire straits indeed, facing even greater pressure to corporatize, to militarize, and to capitulate to conservative interests aflame over the alleged liberal fascists overtaking the university—a tripartite threat that has, in Henry Giroux's succinct phrase, "chained" the university.[20] This is to say nothing of those academics who—far from embracing progressive causes of their "liberal fascist" counterparts—have assimilated to the logic of the market, who are themselves *always* on the market, seeking ways to render their work more palatable to popular audiences, more commodifiable, more "sexy," more risqué, rather than risky. By the time the 2008 recession hit, even universities with heretofore-robust endowments suffered financially. So it is perhaps not surprising that today's academicians, seduced by the logic of efficiency and disinterested professionalism, are more often than not willing participants in wartime strategy—eager, in fact, to prove the utility of their invaluable expertise in exchange for funding from the few sources left open to them. In addition to the revenue streams available from the Department of Defense, the Pentagon, or various intelligence agencies, William Martin reported in 2005 that the Department of Homeland Security handled "a $70 million dollar scholarship and research budget, and its initiatives, in alliance with those of the military and intelligence agencies, point towards a whole new network of campus-related programs."[21] As a result:

The University of Southern California has created the first "Homeland Security Center of Excellence" with a $12 million grant that brought in multi-disciplinary experts from UC Berkeley, NYU, and the University of Wisconsin-Madison. Texas A&M and the University of Minnesota won $33 million to build two new Centers of Excellence in agrosecurity. . . . The scale of networked private and public cooperation is indicated by the new National Academic Consortium for Homeland Security led by Ohio State University, which links more than 200 universities and colleges.[22]

Some academics, however, have baulked. Quite recently scholars in fields such as anthropology and psychology have sought to challenge—through widely publicized pressure on professional organizations to revise their codes of ethics, as well as articles and books—government appropriation of academic research as well as government recruitment of various forms of intellectual labor in the interests of perfecting culturally specific methods of torture designed to crack enemy combatants in the War on Terror. A few prominent scholars such as David Price, Mary Louise Pratt, and David Gibbs have criticized the Roberts Program, the Human Terrain Project, the Minerva Project, and other attempts by the CIA and the Pentagon to enlist students and scholars in the service of intelligence gathering to be used against enemy combatants or, it can assumed, their sympathizers in the university. Even fewer have drawn much-needed critical attention to their racially inscribed conditions.[23]

But critique has been far outweighed by scandal of complicity, where not overt collusion, even when the enemy is domestically defined. Decades before the war on terror, the war on crime rose like a phoenix out of the ashes of Johnson's war on poverty, and it continues to this day. It began with the ratcheting up of militarized responses on the domestic front, and thus on *civilians*, to youth-led mass protests of the late 1960s—the antiwar movement, but also the black power and Chicano power movements that emerged out of civil rights disappointments which were effectively characterized as "street terrorism." As Ruth Wilson Gilmore has argued, "state, media and intellectuals of the late 1960s and early 1970s participated in the ideological production of 'moral panics' . . . to explain the social and political disorder sweeping the United States."[24] The resulting criminalization of politically dissident activity commenced a mass incarceration experiment that would see prison populations expand from less than 180,000 in the early 1970s to over 2.3 million behind bars and over 7.3 million in total in the correctional system by 2008. Over 70 percent of those currently in prison are people of color, though they make up about 24 percent of the general population. The devastation to black communities as a result of the prison binge in the form of spiraling poverty, unemployment, and (ironically) crime has been well documented by Glenn Loury, Angela Davis, Mark Mauer, Meda Chesney-Lind, and Paul Street, among other scholars and writers. But Gilmore also observes its specific—and staggering—impact on universities.

As California became home to the "largest prison building program in the history of the world"—the knotted result of "tough on crime" and antiurban strategies as well as Progressive-era rehabilitation efforts that sought, nonetheless, to maintain racial hierarchies—greater and greater portions of the state appropriations, and new opportunities for capital investment, went to the California Department of Corrections (CDC).[25] Like the cold war and later the war on terror, the war on crime dramatically influenced the production and circulation of knowledge in the academy, lending intellectual heft to policy decisions and providing the technical expertise for military adventures at home and abroad. The massive size and flexible budget of the CDC in turn prompted waves of critical studies by the state's universities. The focus of these, however, was not to challenge the political exploitation of an electorate whose fears of crime were fueled by ever-increasing media reportage, even in periods when crime rates stabilized or fell, nor was it to raise ethical or philosophical questions about the shifting nature of incarceration from "rehabilitation" to "punishment," nor to raise sociological or criminological questions about shockingly disproportional rates of poor and minority youth behind bars, or even the effectiveness of incarceration among a range of criminal justice responses that are demonstrably cheaper and reduce recidivism. Rather, it was the "pitched competition" between the CDC and all other state agencies dependent on the general fund that "seems to have prompted the university to criticize the CDC in such a way that the university itself would become a necessary player in the CDC project as a supplier of efficiency expertise, while freeing up funds for other productive state activities."[26] In other words, the engineers who conducted these studies did so in the interests of placing themselves in direct line with the CDC's massive funding steam. Gilmore's conclusion is revealing: not only did the university refuse to question the identification of crime itself as the central problem, as opposed to, say, the unprecedented expansion of the criminal justice bureaucracy in an era of "shrinking government" no less, it was posed as a problem for engineering in the interests of cost reduction, sacrificing its obligation to a much more capacious and critical form of thought and reason on the altar of rationalized efficiency:

As with earlier studies, the central problem remained crime and its mitigation through imprisonment, and the solution turned on cost-effectiveness in the design-bid-build sequence for prison construction—rather than any reevaluation of, for example, the relation between crimes (old and new), education, and recidivism. . . . *The unspoken power of these studies lies in the way the university presents itself, via its sober, analytical engineering faculty, as an eminently efficient institution.*[27]

The studies thus become emblematic of the ways in which the contemporary university seeks to break with older models of itself as an autonomous institution devoted to the singular pursuit of truth in efforts to advance its new self-image as "a competitive knowledge factory increasingly responsive to market forces." To this end, Gilmore notes with no small irony that "in 1995 the Regents of the University of California formally shed affirmative action over the objections of faculty, staff, students, and senior administration at the university's nine campuses, because, in the race-neutral language of racism, affirmative action is an inefficient (nonmarket) mode of resource allocation."[28] Thus, the rise in so-called "street terrorism" affected those disciplines that deal directly or indirectly with the criminal justice system and its expanding prison complex. Expertise is required not only in the construction and maintenance of prisons, but in the training of a vast range of personnel—from police and prison guards to specialized forensics teams and IT experts to criminal attorneys and judges. Gilmore notes that community colleges throughout the state rushed to offer associate degrees in correctional science to meet the needs of the immediate new labor market of new prisons. Of course professional training in such challenging terrain could be a very positive development, but the logic of corrections remains singularly focused on uniformity, efficiency, and cost effectiveness—rationalized commitments that seldom work in humane interests. The Merton P. Stoltz Professor of the Social Sciences and economist Glenn Loury has spoken with a humility and grace rarely found in the academy of the limits of social scientific inquiry in this instance: "Science may be necessary, but it is certain to be insufficient here. . . . [N]o cost-benefit analysis of our world-historic prison build-up over the past 35 years is possible without specifying how one should reckon in the calculation the pain being imposed on the persons imprisoned, their families and their communities."[29] The criminogenic effect of mass incarceration has been documented by social scientists, to say nothing of the effects on communities plunged ever deeper into poverty as a result of punishment policies, as I have already mentioned, but Loury is right to emphasize the suffering of the most vulnerable in our society and pose the most challenging of moral and ethical questions: "*Just what manner of people are we Americans? And, what then must we do?*"[30] Tragically, the influence of the law and order obsession that drives the mass incarceration experiment does not end here.

The war on crime also altered fundamentally American public school education and so teacher training and programs in administration offered by colleges of education across the nation. The Safe Schools Act of 1994 was patterned, revealingly, after the landmark 1968 Omnibus Crime Control and Safe Streets Act, observes Jonathan Simon in his study *Governing Through Crime*, through which Congress "appropriated significant new funds, conditioning eligibility for this funding on the adoption by states and local school districts of techniques of knowledge and power calculated to focus more governance attention and resources on crime in schools, while assuring a more rapid and punitive response toward it."[31] To qualify for federal money under the Safe Schools Act, schools must demonstrate that they have a serious problem with crime, violence, and student discipline, as well as strategies for resolving it. School administrators are thus required to develop their own forms of data collection about crime, as well as assess what kinds of incidents constitute criminal activity—under conditions that provide every incentive to make such judgments as broad and expansive as possible. Moreover, effective measures and techniques for dealing with the problem of school crime, which Simon calls "penal pedagogies," have been lifted directly from criminal justice settings—zero tolerance policy, the implementation of school uniforms, in-school detentions, and the like. The result, notes Simon, is total transformation of what now constitutes effective school reform. Whereas the ideals of racial equality and racial justice once generated massive intellectual (if not quite financial) investment in school integration and modernization, the problem of crime and crime prevention has now "recast much of the form and substance of schools" nationwide.[32] As in prison settings, youths marginalized by race and class are primarily targeted by the new zero tolerance policies. Simon's conclusion ominously highlights the degree to which the intellectual energies that fuel public policy are increasingly operationalized in the interests of disposing of problem populations:

If schools today are again coming to seem more and more like prisons, it is not because of a renewed faith in the capacity of disciplinary methods. Indeed prisons and schools increasingly deny their capacity to do much more than sort and warehouse people. What they share instead is the institutional imperative that crime is simultaneously the most important problem they have to deal with and a reality whose "existence"—as defined by the federally imposed edict of ever-expanding data collection—is precisely what allows these institutions to maintain and expand themselves in perpetuity.[33]

The challenge facing intellectuals today is thus to understand how the mid-twentieth century global economic and political crises—to which neoliberalized social, economic, military, and educational agendas are a response—are also racially predicated, manipulated, massaged, and maintained. Such controversies invite a number of troubling questions this book seeks to explore: Does the university, an institution revered for its perceived commitment to truth and reason untainted by worldly interest, have a relationship with—a role to play in—politics, or violence and war? How would we thus characterize such a role? On the one hand, does the Jeffersonian ideal of the university not create the very conditions for thoughtful action to the degree that it could be said to produce an informed and reflective democratic citizenry engaged in the struggle for social justice and equality? Is the university not a beacon of truth and peace in the face of weakening conditions of reasonable exchange among men and women? Yet, on the other hand, has it not earned a reputation as a force for repression and war, producing the very discourses, methodologies, strategies, technologies, and modes of legitimation and justification that have long accompanied Western exploitation and violence wielded against racially defined and managed populations? Was it not a force for the production of knowledge in the interests of wealth and whiteness, particularly in relation to those historically colonized, enslaved, or aboriginal populations dispossessed of their land, as well as those various others rendered "internal" enemies, as in the case of European Jewry? Various egregious examples come to mind—the infamous Tuskegee experiments or Martin Heidegger's tenure as Rector at the University of Freiburg—but this is perhaps to overlook the very mundane collusion of disciplinary knowledges with racial definition, imposition, management, and containment. What determinative role does the university presently play in the lives of those rendered "illegal," "criminal," or "terrorist"—categorical alibis for an otherwise racially rendered threat to national and global security? Might we say that the university works in all of these disparate interests, to the degree that the imposition of such binary logics undercuts the complexities and contradictions definitive of the project of liberal—and liquid—modernities?

Both W.E.B. Du Bois and Michel Foucault, two towering intellectuals of the twentieth century cited in this Introduction's opening epigraphs, reflect on an apparent contradiction between the staggering accomplishment that is the Western world's technical mastery, its ordered canons of truth and knowledge on the one hand, and its unabated proclivity toward "violence, disorder and war" on the other.[34] It is not often remarked that Foucault situates his 1976 lectures on the university within a broader discussion of what he terms a history of European "race war," the dreadful culmination of which is fascist domination and genocide. Du Bois's lecture, probably given about 1944 though the exact date is unknown, is similarly reflective about the mid-twentieth-century European fascism and murder as well as the triumph of the peculiarly American version of racial dictatorship. Yet the tension, as each intellectual frames it, is not really to be understood in terms of the order and mastery associated with peace being threatened by some external force for evil that seeks to promote the chaos of war, but rather in terms of the incitement to violence born of modernity's very (racially) reasoned investment in order and mastery. The clamor for order itself, as the distinguished sociologist Zygmunt Bauman has shown, generates its own fear of ambivalence, dictating the necessity of force wielded in the interests of certainty and security.[35] According to David Goldberg, the concept of race emerged in modernity precisely to provide definition, clarity, predictability, and so certainty in the Western capacity to contain the threat of populations newly "discovered."[36] What is at stake, then, for those of us in the university who purposively attempt to enact, however variously understood, a "university responsibility"? And what is at stake in shifting our understanding of that responsibility as grounded in the opposition order/disorder to that of order/peace? In this sense, the modern imperative of orderliness registers more aptly a repressive pacification that *undermines*—rather than creates or supports—the possibilities for intellectual dissent, for the negotiation of differences rendered racial or otherwise, or for real and sustainable peace.

Can the university stand thus for peace? The ambivalence of the question, which can be interpreted in at least two mutually exclusive ways, points to the paradox that lies at the very heart of thinking about the possible futures of higher education in a post–civil rights, post-9/11 era. Although the designation "post–civil rights" often signifies a colorblind or race transcendent triumphalism in the public imaginary, I have argued to the contrary that the present era is shaped by a new, persistent, more subtle but no less destructive, racism as well as permanent civilizational war. Indeed, this is the paradox that this book is devoted to elaborate and explore. On the one hand, the question asks, counter-intuitively, if the university, as the very institution of Enlightenment, can literally stand for, or tolerate—let alone undertake as its very mission—a commitment to justice, to peace, to free and equal democratic coexistence. Can it tolerate, let alone nurture and develop, modes of difference and dissension that mark the agonistic dimensions of a substantively democratic polity, the necessarily multiple understandings of its constitutive justice? Michel Foucault investigates the university's formidable influence on the production of knowledge, pedagogy, and power, in efforts to "outwit the problematic of the Enlightenment," which invariably *assumes* a history of successive victories in "the struggle of knowledge against ignorance, of reason against chimeras, of experience against prejudices, or reason against error"—victories understood, metaphorically, literally, and viscerally, of light over dark.[37] And, like Du Bois, and later Said, who queried the ways in which scholars were able to transform whole populations into "problem people," he prompts us to ask: In what ways is the university—historically and presently—complicit with modes of intellectual reification and instrumentalization that inevitably lead to violence, humiliation, torture, and war? And beyond this, an even larger question: For what purposes and for whom is knowledge pursued and "advanced"?

Are there alternative intellectual traditions, modes of university organization, and visions of university leadership that might subvert such inclinations? On the one hand, each chapter in this book explores and engages the work of diverse intellectuals located within modernity's canonical and counter traditions who challenge the academy's ongoing collusion with racism, violence, militarization, and war as well as the complicity of scholars—historically and currently—in the perpetuation of the same. Thus, on the other hand, this book undertakes to imagine what it would mean to answer the question "Can the university stand for peace?" in the most affirmative sense, in the interests of humanity and its survival. How can the university be reconceived, as Kant and others imagined it, as a uniquely privileged site for critique in the interests of those imperatives for peace and justice that are so immanent and urgent today? What would doing so entail pedagogically—in the classroom but also in public, on the lecture circuit, in policy meetings, or on government oversight committees? What responsibilities for social justice, for peace, and for democracy can those who constitute the university assume in a time marked by the resurgence of racially predicated inequality, exclusion, and violence at home and a catastrophic, ongoing civilizational war abroad? What conditions undermine such efforts? Can we, as scholars, students, or citizens supportive of the university and its commitment to critique, defend what is loudly denounced as a kind of poisoned partisanship, a "culture war" in its own right? On what grounds—political, ethical, intellectual—do we challenge the noisy and dismissive insistence that intellectuals "Save the World on [Their] Own Time," as Stanley Fish has recently insisted, and assume our responsibility?[38] Fish's declaration is indeed a telling sign of the times, a literal repudiation, in fact, of one of the most robust affirmations of academic intellectualism in twentieth-century letters by one of its most esteemed luminaries, C. Wright Mills. In the penultimate chapter of *The Sociological Imagination,* Mills makes an impassioned plea for academics to differentiate reason from bureaucratic rationalization in efforts to combat the former, to take risks in public, to present deliberately controversial theories and facts—and to encourage actively such controversy—in the interests of challenging official definitions of reality that are all too frequently narrow, misleading, and inadequate. He writes:

Attempts to avoid such troublesome issues as I have been discussing are nowadays widely defended by the slogan that social science is "not out to save the world." Sometimes this is the disclaimer of a modest scholar; sometimes it is the cynical contempt of a specialist for all issues of larger concern; sometimes it is the disillusionment of youthful expectations; often it is the pose of men who seek to borrow the prestige of The Scientist, imagined as a pure and disembodied intellect. But sometimes it is based upon a considered judgment of the facts of power.

Because of such facts, I do not believe that social science will "save the world" although I see nothing at all wrong with "trying to save the world"—a phrase which I take to mean the avoidance of war and the re-arrangement of human affairs in accordance with the ideals of human freedom and reason.[39]

To paraphrase Mills, if there are ways to survive the multiple crises that mark our present moment by means of intellect, is it not our responsibility to speak to them? And, if there is no peace without struggle, the question for intellectuals is not how to remain neutral and impassive, but how to distinguish, with due consideration and care, the kinds of battles in which they can and should engage.

The present book participates, broadly speaking, in conversations begun at least two decades ago. First, it complements, even as its focus on racially prompted exclusion and violence departs from, important work done on the politics of higher education that has examined the consequences of university corporatization and bureaucratization, and, rather belatedly and to a lesser degree, its militarization. There is also a historical component to this quite present crisis of the university, which understands the academy as an institution of liberal modernity and asks difficult questions about its role in relation to historical and ongoing *racially motivated and legitimated* economic exploitation, militarism, and war. It looks to the role of higher education in both perpetuating and potentially arresting cycles of violence and counter-violence. Second, it challenges the "cultural turn" in race theory and the critical gaps and lacunae to which the decades-long fascination with difference and identity have led, as well as the recent retrenched interest in narrow social scientific assessments of class-driven inequality. The critical focus here is on *both* the role of the state's post–civil rights legal apparatus and a neoliberalized economy in the perpetuation of raceless racism, or racial privatization, and the forms of intellectual, symbolic, and material violence these unleash. In other words, the analytic emphasis here is on both highlighting and challenging the refashioned racism of the post–civil rights era, which imagines itself to be "beyond race" and colorblind, all the while enabling modes of conservative reaction, the consequences of which are race-specific and radically unequal. The quest for racial and social justice that defined civil rights era struggles has been replaced by a new, intense, and individualized zeitgeist of security—financial and personal and national—whatever the social cost.

The subtitle of this book, a tribute to Jacques Derrida's influential and evocative notion of a university *without condition*, a university *à venir*, or "to come," emphasizes this radical openness with the regard to the university and its post–civil rights futures, as well as the inescapable—simultaneously without condition and conditioned—responsibilities to which humanistic faculties in the university are and should be held.[40] Given the devastating consequences of the last several decades of colorblindness on the academy and on thought more generally, I ask whether the university "to come" will be able to recognize, let alone assume, its unique and difficult responsibilities—or will it become an irrelevant institution for those stubbornly committed to thinking. This stark and disturbing query is the singular axis around which each chapter turns, looking to various archives—the canonical and the counter-modern, the distant past and present—debating the purpose and promise of higher education, and the responsibilities of intellectuals housed therein. Implicit, then, is also the question of complicity, a question that haunts Derrida's meticulous reading of Martin Heidegger's "The Self-Assertion of the German University" and other works dating from the period of his rectorship at Freiburg (1933–34), texts that are taken rhetorically and philosophically to align the university with the project of National Socialism. In *Complicities*, Mark Sanders has asserted that Derrida's achievement in these analyses is "to bring the deconstructive motif of complicity into proximity with an ethico-political discourse on complicity—claims and counterclaims swirling, in this case with renewed intensity, around the political career of Heidegger and his complicity with the National Socialist movement."[41] Derrida's reminder—that any profession of responsibility, whether in the name of justice or battling injustice, as a gesture of solidarity or stark opposition, carries with it the possibility of doing injustice—is of central importance to Sanders' own rich analysis of the intellectual in the context of South African apartheid. That ambivalence also marks the present study. "After apartheid," Saunders asserts, "the question of complicity is unavoidable."[42] And yet, as the following pages will reveal, it is precisely this question of intellectual complicity and willful collusion with past and present racisms in the post–civil rights American university that is today anxiously and aggressively avoided, refused, denied, misperceived, and misdirected by most. But, as I will also show, not by all.

The book is divided into two sections. The first section examines the consequences of the last several decades of colorblind racism and the various forms of anti-intellectualism they have inspired both within the university and outside it. Chapter 1 looks to complicate the state of the "dream" in Obama's America, alluding here not only to Martin Luther King's dream but also to the much vaunted, and now much endangered, American dream and the ways in which these dreams' realization (or rather nightmarish transformation) is entwined. In doing so, I trace my own experience of the demise of public commitment to collective struggle for civil rights and social justice (organized in the main around the right to literacy and educational access), which has been the result of nearly four decades of conservative counter-revolution predicated on relentless racial backlash and the ascendancy of neoliberal social and economic agendas. As a kind of heuristic device, I look to Dr. King's last speeches invoking dreams as well as a short story written by Delmore Schwartz in similarly dark times in 1937, entitled "In Dreams Begin Responsibilities" and attempt to think through the complexities of coming of age, of assuming self and social responsibility, in an era predicated on the evisceration of the social, its forms of mutuality and reciprocity, its elevation of self-interested individualism and communal homogeneity. I look to the crucial role of the university in securing the very conditions for socially responsible thought and action—even as I explore, through my own experiences within it, the ways in which the educational mission of this institution is being actively undermined.

Chapter 2 explores in more specific terms the most recent conservative assault on the university and the relative silence on the part of progressives in response to its challenge. In part, I argue that this apparent retreat is a consequence of vulnerabilities and anxieties of workers in the academy that result from the ongoing corporatization of the university as well as the pervasive culture of fear that permeates the United States in the wake of 9/11, and tends to punish critique as "anti-American." As important as such factors are, however, the current analysis focuses more inwardly on processes of internalization and normalization of the very ideals that marked the university's "multicultural turn." I suggest that the institutionalization of multicultural commitment is, with rare exceptions, an extension of, rather than a progressive alternative to, the privatizing impetus of the neoliberal era. Further, the often uncritical endorsement and bland acceptance of principles such as "nondiscrimination," "diversity," and "openness" *in the abstract* are precisely what enabled the Right's ruthless appropriation and simultaneous divestment of the vision and language of civil rights-era struggles.

Chapter 3 engages the general suspicion of intellect, and hence distrust of the university, in the United States, proposing yet another dimension of American anti-intellectualism given scant attention in Richard Hofstadter's unparalleled 1963 analysis and in more recent treatments of this tragic theme: the preeminent role that race plays in defining, delimiting, and at times derailing morality, reflectiveness, and reason itself—and most emphatically in an era that has come to define itself as post-racial. Few ideas have been exposed—over and over—as quite so empty and analytically void, and yet have continued to hold such passionate attraction, even for some of the most learned minds, as the concept of race. The question remains how racially rendered and radically unequal social relations are able to survive even the dismantling of formal apparatuses of segregation and exclusion, how race is so persistently able to structure and define in such compelling ways, transforming configurations of social relations. One place to begin is with an examination of the very contours of contemporary thoughtlessness and its routinization. Thus, in addition, and more specifically, Chapter 3 examines the role of race in the ongoing drama of American anti-intellectualism in what may seem like an unusual venue: the university. What role do academics play therein? How do they intervene in and challenge this peculiar dimension of American anti-intellectualism? I take up two anti-intellectual tendencies—in Hofstadter's sense of the term, not unintellectual, but committed to outmoded or rejected ideas advanced in stridently absolutist tones—that participate in the colorblinding logic of the post–civil rights university. Highly amenable to the mythology of a new post-racial or colorblind society, the first asserts itself under the mantle of neutrality and professionalism; the second presumes a lonely crusade for the now-forgotten working classes, whose interests fail to register in the miasmas produced by the university's gratuitous and deeply misguided infatuation with diversity.

The book's second section assumes a political landscape in which racism in its new, "neoliberalized" edition perpetuates, however invisibly, forms of violence and exclusion and looks to the ways in which the university might productively respond.

If "political theology" was a term seldom heard in wider academic debate prior to 9/11, mainstream scholarly indifference quickly abated after that tragic day as questions about the relationship between religion and violence, politics and force, legally sanctioned war and acts of terror, and what are, in essence, "morally good and morally evil ways of killing" in the new global world order became more insistent, contradictory, and often crudely ideological.[43] Chapter 4 thus explores the complex intersections among political theologies, liberal modernity, and the racial states—a conception of states that recognizes their racially conceived histories and the raced exclusions to which they have given rise. Recent intellectual exercises in distinguishing between just war and terrorism based on levels of cruelty inflicted or even the threat posed to entire ways of life have foundered on a review of historical evidence that favors neither and reveals that it is quite often the alleged "civilizational status" of the actors involved that proves decisive in the designation of legality and thus legitimacy. Thus I also look to various traditions that offer theoretical responses to the problem of "legal" violence enacted by the state, and the possibility of a non-violent counter violence or "educating" violence in the now classic work of Walter Benjamin as well as of the Jamaican-born philosopher of race, Lewis R. Gordon, who draws on an archive of black Atlantic writers extending from Frederick Douglass to C.L.R. James to engage these questions.

Continuing this meditation on violence and counterviolence, Chapter 5 offers much-needed historical depth to what are all-too-frequently presentist analyses of the challenges that the university has long confronted and continues to confront in relation to truth, knowledge, commerce, militarism, and war. The focus here is on one of the modernity's most influential philosophers, Friedrich Nietzsche, and his early lectures *On the Future of Our Educational Institutions,* which, unlike subsequent treatments of similar themes, grant singular attention to the question of youth, though this aspect is virtually ignored in the scholarly assessment of the lectures. In our post-Virginia Tech, post-Columbine era, in a time of permanent warfare when youth are variously seduced, cajoled, and conscripted to one side or the other of a global war on terror, the trigger-happy, gun-toting youths who are central characters in the drama are surely haunting. Yet, equally disturbing, given the presumptive focus on the peaceful, sanctified halls of higher education, is the scholarly indifference to the pervasive language of war—of battles, enemies, war cries, soldiers, military service, and, most unsettling, national, even civilizational, defense against "degeneration" in the interests of "purifying" the German spirit—in the unfolding narrative of education's futurity. Nietzsche's is an unmatched theoretical contribution, but, nonetheless, it seems necessary, in light of his analysis of the university's alleged freedoms, its commitment to youth, and its futurity, to reevaluate and complicate the institution's "peaceful" pursuit of truth and knowledge as part of its broader educational mission. I will argue that there is a deepening crisis of thought in the university, and so a crisis of academic freedom, which has implications for the future of the institution and for the sustainability of democratic futures more generally.

Finally, Chapter 6 examines the legacy of W.E.B. Du Bois, as both scholar and activist, at a time when the university's civic mission has been imperiled by four decades of corporatization and post–civil rights back-lash. Focusing on his magnum opus, *Black Reconstruction*, as well as lectures and speeches he penned during Roosevelt's New Deal, it elaborates in particular on the pedagogical implications of Du Bois's reading of the post-Reconstruction era for progressives caught in the contradictions of the current post–civil rights era and prospects of a new New Deal under the Obama administration—both of which suffer from what Du Bois calls the racial blindspot. Drawing on Du Bois's insistence that education is central to the functioning of a nonrepressive and inclusive polity, and most insistently so in times of recession and war, the chapter reflects on the current crisis of schooling at all levels, as well as the relentless attacks on the university's commitment to humanistic inquiry. In so doing, it explores the role that educators might play in linking rigorous scholarship and critical pedagogy to progressive struggles for securing the very conditions for thought itself—an active commitment to which determines the very survival of political democracy.

Section I

CHALLENGING THREE DECADES
OF COLORBLIND RACISM

CHAPTER ONE

Notes on the Afterlife of Dreams:
On the Persistence of Racism in
Post–Civil Rights America

Whose recovery is more doubtful, that of him who does not see or of him who sees and still does not see? Which deception is more difficult, to awaken one who sleeps or to awaken one who, awake, dreams that he is awake?

—SØREN KIERKEGAARD

One of the great liabilities of history is that all too many people fail to remain awake through great periods of social change. Every society has its protectors of the status quo and its fraternities of the indifferent who are notorious for sleeping through revolutions. But today our very survival depends on our ability to stay awake, to adjust to new ideas, to remain vigilant and to face the challenge of change.

—MARTIN LUTHER KING, JR.

In 2007 the Dutch journal *Nexus* invited a number of young professionals and intellectuals, myself included, from various fields the world over—each of us then under forty years of age—to respond to a short story entitled "In Dreams Begin Responsibilities" by Delmore Schwartz, originally published in the *Partisan Review* in 1937. The young Schwartz, heralded as an up-and-coming voice of his generation, penned a narrative describing an epiphanic moment in young man's life. The protag-

onist, upon waking from a dream about his parents' disastrous courtship and marriage, recognizes the necessity to assume responsibility for
his own actions in the world. We were asked, in a similar vein, to ponder
the world we were inheriting, the conditions of our own moral and political "awakening," our vision of and dreams about the future, the reach
and content of our responsibilities. And in light of this, we were asked to
account for what we had done thus far, and what, crucially, we would do
in the decades to come. As I look back on it, the assignment seems uncannily prescient, recapitulating many of the themes—of inheritance, of
forefathers, of dreams and responsibilities, and of change—that have been
a central preoccupation in the autobiographical writings and campaign
speeches of both presidential candidates in the run-up to the 2008 U.S.
general election.[1] In anxious efforts to stake special claim on some version
of the vaunted American dream, each man produced a highly romantic
and carefully differentiated *bildungsroman*—of self and nation—as well
as, in decidedly more vague terms, the past and future challenges both entities confronted.

One would have thought that, given my years of experience teaching English, I was in familiar territory; not only were the canonical and
counter-canonical texts I typically taught alive to such questions, but the
insistent self-reflectivity and conceptual care required to negotiate these
"big issues" lie at the heart of the pedagogical encounter. Yet, the more
I have thought about these questions, the more difficult and ambivalent
the very terms have become. As a woman born in northern Virginia, just
outside of Washington, D.C., in September of 1968, my interpretation of
"dreams" and "beginnings" and "responsibilities" is undoubtedly shaped
by my status as an American of the post–civil rights era. To be sure, the
richly heterogeneous experiences of my generation and the generation I
teach preclude the possibility of a singular, representative voice—least of
all mine. Nonetheless it seems reasonable to assume that the post–civil
rights generations share, by accident of birth, a common frame of reference, as they came of age in the wake (in both the temporal and funereal
sense) of a mass movement for civil rights, the political and spiritual leadership of figures like the Kennedys and Martin Luther King, Jr., and the
promise of the Great Society. They bore witness instead to a conservative
counter-revolution, a new time of turbulence that arcs between the demise

of Jim Crow and the birth of the carceral state, between the quagmire of Vietnam and the quagmire of an increasingly unpopular (if not also unwinnable) war on terror currently staged in Iraq and Afghanistan, between the infamous administration of Richard Nixon and that of George W. Bush, which will undoubtedly add war crimes to its own unique constitutional transgressions, and between the OPEC oil crisis of 1973 and the crisis of free market deregulation that spawned the global financial collapse of 2008. Those are some of the broad contours; the specificities of these epochal events, for the vast majority of my generation and the millennial generation that followed, have translated into a narrative of disinheritance. For them, the everyday is increasingly marked by volatility, instability, and precarity. It has meant and continues to mean, for most, the decline of the American dream and downward mobility; as well as "the dissolution of the family; growing child abuse and domestic conflict; drug and alcohol abuse; sexually transmitted diseases; poor education and crumbling schools; and escalating criminalization, imprisonment and even state execution."[2]

Now as the inspiring rhetoric of the campaign season gives way to the hard realities of governance, one wonders if the era's conservative ascendancy is indeed over. With the historic election of Barack Obama in November 2008 comes no small degree of hope for the many millions, unprecedented millions, who were moved to join his campaign and organize for change. And change we desperately need. As Americans headed to the polls, the nation confronted a mind-numbing series of crises—protracted economic recession, a financial sector reliant upon a trillion-dollar taxpayer bailout, two wars costing billions more per month, cash-strapped states unable to repair crumbling infrastructure and dilapidated public schools, spiraling tuition costs and diminished student aid to universities, everwidening unemployment, the plunging value of the family home, and retirement plans shrinking faster than polar ice caps—all of which threaten not only its immediate future, but also its very viability. Upon surveying the vast wreckage wrought by the past forty years of "colorblind" racial backlash and neoliberal rule, one hears again Dr. King's insistent query "Where do we go from here?" What America tolerated as the norm for the majority of its black citizens, who not only were dealt out of FDR's New Deal but also were among the first to suffer the bitter consequences of post-industrial decline—creeping poverty, higher unemployment, stagnant or depreciating home values, no or minuscule health care, pension plans, or job security, and deplorable schools—has now spread to the nation's once-robust middle class.[3] And, as a result, the nation as a whole suffers forms of social dislocation and dissolution, once arrogantly assumed to be a special preserve of black dysfunction, that nonetheless accompany these shockingly inadequate conditions—broken marriages, broken families, shattered communities. Our capacity to transcend this inglorious epoch and achieve an American dream in keeping with King's vision of pervasive peace, social justice, and equality will largely depend not only on new leadership, but on the ways everyday citizens understand *how we got here* and adjust accordingly. That means understanding that America's futurity rests on the capacities of her citizens to recognize the weight of the historical evidence: to see that the freedom and dignity of one population cannot be ruthlessly sacrificed for the perceived improvement of another and to acknowledge that reciprocity is the key to our responsibility. Thus the challenge we face is *educational* as much as it is economic, political, or cultural; our future rests on our capacity to learn collectively from our past, a past that remains utterly embattled, and, to paraphrase Dr. King, remain awake and responsive in rapidly changing times.

What follows is my attempt to respond to the difficulty of the questions posed to me in 2007. It is an examination of the place where personal biography and national politics intersect in the formation of individual consciousness and public memory. In recapitulating the marital prehistory with which Schwartz commences his own narrative search for agency, I attempt to offer another discourse of self and social responsibility—and the inescapably *pedagogical* conditions of their possibility.

My father has his back to the camera. I don't see his face, just a dark suit and the familiar wavy hair, cut short to keep the unruliness in check. My mother, in white lace profile, tentatively delivers the customary forkful of wedding cake upward to the groom's lips. The pretty divorcee with two children smiles her curious upside-down smile. Head bent forward and down, his gray eyes, flecked with gold, hidden from me, appear fixed on her fingers. Concentrating on the tender task at hand, her eyes, warm brown and soft, are also elsewhere. Slightly out of focus and mellowed with age, the photograph beckons the observer into its gilded reverie. The seduction might well have worked, but for the presence of a third face in this intimate yet ubiquitous scene, still and stoic, staring back at me. Dressed in a crisp white tuxedo, his dark skin becomes darker still, his black eyes seem to take in everything. In the background I recognize the dining room of my uncle's estate where this peculiar triad is assembled. The couple is conscious only of each other, while the server pours champagne for the indifferent menagerie of distant, faded relatives and polished recent acquaintances, old back-slapping buddies and important Washington contacts. The guests have been assembled to witness both a new bond, ceremoniously enacted and spiritually sanctioned, and a very old one, deprived of dignity and unholy. A private dream and a social perversion. The young black server is there and not there, unacknowledged and yet vital to the unfolding fantasy of a perfect union—of future prosperity, security, and propriety—for both family and nation. A conscript in a collective refusal to take heed of shifting contexts.

Such was Georgetown in July 1965. But really such was the nation. A citizenry in a state of denial—save for those caught in reality's crosshairs. Several blocks in one direction from the marital scene we find the famed Washington Mall, the Capital building, and the White House, then home to Lyndon B. Johnson and "the Great Society." But that wasn't the society it was; neither its domestic nor its foreign commitments approached such lofty idealism. Several blocks in the other direction lies one of the poorest, most segregated districts in the nation. Its young became prison fodder— in a burgeoning mass incarceration experiment that by 2008's season of hope would jail nearly one in three black men in the nation's urban centers—or cannon fodder, in successive imperial wars fought in the name of democracy that would eventually become the shame of the nation. It occurs to me, as I'm drawn back to this four-decade-old photograph, that it has no present tense; it conjures both a fading past and not too distant future. A paroxysm of nostalgia and an ill-fated prophecy, it recalls the genteel side of southern segregation as it simultaneously forecasts a future morality, so-called, predicated on the pulverization of society into isolated, men, women, and their families, responsible for themselves alone.[4] The denial of humanity that once ordered the world's variegated populations in rigid hierarchy would be reimagined and refashioned into the very denial of society, and so too its networks of social obligation, responsibility, reciprocity, and solidarity. Only recently have I come to understand these, consequentially speaking, as very similar if not quite the same thing.

Throughout the decade of the 1960s, worldwide transformation was occurring in ways seen and unseen by everyday people. A series of progressive social and political revolutions held the promise of freedom and a full schedule of rights for historically oppressed groups, but there were also technological and economic revolutions that, when tethered to narrow nationalist agendas or profitable market expansion, augured a less egalitarian and less just future. "Improved means to unimproved ends," Thoreau once said, in a suggestive phrase that effectively sums up the era. By 1968, the year of my birth, the national mood had turned less hopeful and more militant. Before his assassination in the spring of that year, Martin Luther King, Jr., wrote an essay titled "The World House" that addressed the challenges facing a rapidly evolving new world order. He announced that the day had arrived when civilization was "shifting its basic outlook," the very presuppositions upon which society was structured were being interrogated, challenged, and transformed. "For several centuries," he wrote, "the direction of history flowed from the nations and societies of Western Europe out into the rest of the world in 'conquests' of various sorts. That period, the era of colonialism, is at an end. East is moving West. The earth is being redistributed."[5] He warned that "nothing could be more tragic" than for men and women who lived in such revolutionary times to fail to "achieve the new attitudes and the new mental outlooks that the new situation demands." And he retold the tale of Rip Van Winkle, who failed to remain awake during a period of great social change, insisting that we as a nation must work "indefatigably" to "bridge the gulf between our scientific progress and our moral progress," to meet the challenge of our vast material wealth and our moral and spiritual impoverishment. Against the terrible propensity for procrastination, he warned that "there is such a thing as being too late" and invoked, famously, "the fierce urgency of now." "The large house in which we all live," King maintained, "demands that we transform this world-wide neighborhood into a world-wide brotherhood. Together we must learn to live as brothers or together we will be forced to perish as fools."[6]

Somewhere along the way, however, the nation's citizenry seemed to fall asleep—or only dreamed that they had awakened to King's moral vision. Indeed, the times took a great many by surprise. Neither of the unions frozen in the four-decade-old photograph would last for very long. The first was over in a few years. The groom, trapped in the basement of his own imagination, would survive scarcely a decade more before drinking himself to death. The bride, alone, facing financial hardship and responsible now for three children, would work until nervous collapse prevented her from ever returning. In a cold new world where, as Margaret Thatcher insisted, "there is no such thing as society," a world short on social provision and long on personal responsibility, hers would prove an unforgivable weakness. The poor were poor, after all, because they made bad decisions. The second union was, of course, doomed from the very beginning. Upon challenging centuries of overt repression and paternalistic imposition, the nation's black citizenry were eventually expelled from the American family romance, only to be recast as a primary threat to familial hearth and home. No longer a people victimized by the indignity and brutality of second-class citizenship under Jim Crow, they became a predatory population to be feared and contained at all costs. Technological advancement had rendered a significant part of that once-crucial labor force redundant, but young black men and women were called upon once more to perform another task for the nation, to enact yet another kind of fantasy. If by the 1980s it was clear that the American family, and its vaunted middle-class dream, was in danger, so this cheap and tawdry tale told, it was because of the ominous threat of "thugged out" young black males and "welfare queens," abetted by a government given over to special interests, living *la dolce vita* on the taxpayers' dime when not stealing from them directly. The avatars of individual choice, endowed with media omnipotence, denounced the taxing and spending abuses of "big government." But far from dismantling government or "drowning it in a bathtub," as Grover Norquist once promised, it was dramatically refashioned. If the mid-century social welfare state had been concerned, at least in theory, with citizens' social well-being in its performance of certain caretaking functions, including the funding of education, healthcare, and public housing—a set of commitments the civil rights struggles of the 1960s were meant to expand to all citizens—the neoliberal state that succeeded it grew more intrusive and more repressive, as resources drained from social safety nets were reallocated toward the police, military, prisons, border patrol, intelligence agencies, and an expanding homeland security apparatus. And, as fear overtook reason, personal safety trumped collective security—all the better for those who manipulated world markets and induced volatility into every aspect of daily life, who sought to inflame the apparently antagonistic interests of disconnected individuals to the detriment of the vast majority of humanity. According to the militarized metaphysic of the new American century, the malefactors have only increased.

This vast and violent apparatus, forty years in the making, eventually overtook the very site and role of responsible governance, and the consequences have resonated globally. Indeed, by the fall of 2008, the world had been brought to its knees by the devastation wrought by an American-led global financial collapse. Though now in crisis, these racially driven neoliberal policies hardly disappeared, as if by some miracle, after Obama's inauguration. Coming to the rescue of a besieged middle class, Obama pledged a new era of responsible and responsive governance. He spearheaded an economic stimulus package to put Americans back to work in decent and well-paying jobs that couldn't be exported, along with an investment in green energy sources to end the nation's dependence on foreign oil. He put forth a bold (if vague) vision for urgently needed health care reform, extending coverage to the over 45 million uninsured. Yet the promised improvement in the daily lives of most Americans failed to materialize by mid-summer 2009 in spite of successive waves of bailouts for banks and other industries, as everyday people continued to lose jobs and health care benefits, default on mortgages, car loans, and credit card debt, and drag down the all-important consumer confidence index. After receiving a substantial portion of an initial $800 billion infusion from the U.S. treasury, banks and other financials held tightly to their cash flow, inflating already-high interest rates and redoubling user fees. After three decades, trickle-down still failed to trickle down—and black Americans once again have been the ones to take the brunt of the recession, facing disproportionately higher unemployment and foreclosure. They are also the ones taking the brunt of white racial resentment—once the centerpiece of the infamous southern strategy that swept Republicans (and some southern Democrats) into power and kept them there for nearly forty years—now unleashed, if not unhinged, by the election of a black president, as I elaborate in Chapter 3.

Upon entering office, Obama promised to end the illegal and immoral practices embraced by the Bush team in the war on terror, but the new administration has fallen far short of this goal. Enemy detainees—the negated element of Bush's state of exception—are still held at Guantánamo, for no clear exit strategy was offered by the present administration once closure had been announced, and several legal loopholes remain pertaining to the Army Field Manual, the guidebook for U.S. interrogators, leading critics to charge that Obama's order was more symbolic than actual reversal of Bush administration policy. In spite of the condemnation of torture, "enhanced interrogations" continue and have even been given legal sanction under Obama. Most disappointing has been the president's opposition to the demand by various legal and human rights organizations for a full investigation of and prosecutions for the war crimes committed with impunity by Bush administration officials—a decision Obama bases on the pragmatics of "looking forward," as if to transcend the apparent bad faith and obfuscation buried in efforts to be attentive to and responsible for the mass violence and shocking brutality of our recent past.

Change, despite the campaign rhetoric, rarely comes from the top down—at least the kind of change that works to secure and dignify the lives of ordinary people. Democratic transformation requires the hard work of a committed and organized citizenry willing to take responsibility for themselves and their collective future. Thus, we are left individually and together to ponder this troubling bequest, this inescapable set of contexts that creates the conditions for the narration of self and social responsibility. The meaning and legacy of the 1960s have proven a vexing moral and political problem not only for the United States, but also for the West more generally (as the 2007 elections in France attested). King correctly foresaw the revolutionary transformation of the worldwide economy. East did move West. Global redistribution did take place—not as he predicted, but rather in ways that merely mimicked former colonial relations. Wealth and poverty, health and sickness, mobility and immobility, sustainable environments and devastated ones, life and death—material resources and life chances have been reallocated in dramatically unequal and tragically predictable ways. In the absence of open and meaningful public debate, the turbulent decade of the 1960s is quickly reduced to a clichéd set of images—of tear gas, water hoses, dogs, no-knock, napalm, and carpet bombs that repeatedly fails to incite reflective action, even as those memories morph into a troubling new montage—of rampant racial profiling, mass incarceration, the PATRIOT Act, Gitmo, and Abu Ghraib, depleted uranium, and precision bombs. What is the relationship between Then and Now? In a contemporary moment of free-roaming individuals, liberated from social commitment and reciprocity, is such a question still warranted? If society no longer matters, does history? How does one give an account of oneself at a time when the very constitution of the question of responsibility is so hotly contested?

The young literary critic and poet Delmore Schwartz faced a similar set of questions when he penned "In Dreams Begin Responsibilities" in 1937. Reflecting in this famed short story upon his own parents' courtship and marriage, he mapped a normative context that pre-dated him and in the production of which he had no role, yet through and against which his own choices could be made intelligible to himself. Schwartz attempted, in short, to narrate himself into a world in which the very codes of morality and legality were themselves immoral and unjust. In 1937 Nazism and fascism were spreading across much of Europe. That year alone, Franco took power in Spain, and Hitler in Germany successfully revoked the citizenship of its Jewish population—while Stalinism in Russia and a depression-racked United States demonstrated the utter corruptibility of state versions of communism and capitalist democracy. Published in the first issue of a re-launched *Partisan Review*, Schwartz was among a generation of young, gifted intellectuals and artists who grappled with the failures of an alternative socialist vision to arrest an unfolding worldwide catastrophe.

In the story, the young narrator dreams that he sits in a theatre where the events of his parents' courtship and eventual marriage unfold on the silver screen. He grows anxious; he repudiates his parents' parochialism, bourgeois sensibility, and social indifference. He suffers the pain of disinheritance. Hysterical, unable to contain himself, the protagonist eventually jumps to his feet and screams at the celluloid couple at the very moment of their betrothal: "Don't do it. It's not too late to change your minds, both of you. Nothing good will come of it, only remorse, hatred, scandal, and two children whose characters are monstrous." Eventually an usher seizes his arm and drags him away, scolding "What are *you* doing? . . . Why don't you *think* of what you are doing?"[7] But then he realizes in his dream that he is dreaming. His initial effort to assume responsibility for himself, he comes to understand, was really an evasion of himself in the guise of parental judgment. In the denouement, the young narrator confronts his own arrogance and hypocrisy; he resolves to focus on the problem of his own agency. Though how he will act upon the world, how his newfound responsibility will manifest itself, is not revealed. His triumph is relayed to us in individual terms. In a curious yet revealing real-life sequel to this fictional and autobiographical double narrative of youthful promise, Schwartz, in the years that follow his initial public celebrity, lost his way, descending into alcoholism and insanity. The lesson is clear: Beyond the challenge of awakening is the challenge of staying awake; beyond the necessity of singular commitment is the necessity of "acting in concert," as Hannah Arendt would insist.[8]

The decade of the 1930s and the present decade might be said to share something in common. Some of the challenges that defined Schwartz's generation bear resemblance to those of the post–civil rights generations, and some are entirely new. Authoritarianism, in its various forms, seems afoot in each era. War, ethnic conflict, even genocide, have killed hundreds of thousands and displaced millions. Fundamentalisms in (new) market and (old) religious guises are on the rise, spawning in each era global financial crisis. A permanent war on terror has picked up where the red menace receded, and ecological crisis now threatens global devastation. Yet among the most terrifying aspects of authoritarian societies, past and present—and upon which successive chapters will focus— is the inevitable war on social reality: evidence loses its persuasive value and language is emptied of meaningful content. As such, it is a war on thought itself.[9] In such contexts, concepts like "dreams," "beginnings," and "responsibilities" lose their referentiality; their positive meanings are no longer given. As Dr. King reminds us, "The stages of history are replete with the chants and choruses of the conquerors of old who came killing in pursuit of peace. Alexander, Genghis Khan, Julius Caesar, Charlemagne, and Napoleon were akin in seeking a peaceful world order, a world fashioned after their selfish conceptions of an ideal existence."[10] The twentieth and twenty-first centuries have only added several more names to the list, men who dreamed of ideal societies, of perfectly ordered worlds and fresh new beginnings. They all talked of peace while preparing for war. For the authoritarian, the responsibilities of leadership are lonely, the approval of an electorate an irrelevant luxury. For the thoughtful, such questions are infinitely more difficult. How can one be sure, in such contentious times, that one's dreams won't become the nightmare of others? What constitutes one's own moral awakening? What role must others play in the consciousness of oneself, or the consciousness of a nation? What struggle is involved, what vigilance, in order to avoid being seduced back to sleep?

With the November 2008 election of Barack Obama to the Oval Office, thus marking the official end of the Bush regime, the world heaved a collective sigh of relief. But more than that—amid global financial collapse and military malfeasance—there was a brief moment of jubilation, as the world caught a glimmer of the beacon of hope and possibility that America, in its best moments, used to represent. After the election, London's *The Guardian* ran an editorial entitled "Welcome Back," which literally welcomed the United States back to the world community, anticipating a new era of collective and cosmopolitan global democratic experimentation, even as it noted the "elephant traps that lie in the path of each step" Obama must take not only to assist in stabilizing the world economy but also to address the challenges of climate change and international security.[11] The stakes could not be higher for the new administration; indeed, but for the hope it represents such expectations might be said to approach the absurd. The kind of change the Obama campaign sought to deliver, and the world indeed craves, can happen only with the ongoing—and widening—personal and political commitments of the many millions who organized to make it happen. Invoking the legacy of King, Obama reminded us repeatedly on the campaign trail of the "fierce urgency of now." If the vast crowds who assembled in Grant Park, Chicago, and across the globe to witness history on the night of November 4, 2008, are not to take on the stagy and shallow contours of a massive rock concert—a one-off event followed by the return of business as usual, as some critics fear—it will require the persistent and unswerving commitment of an engaged citizenry to think, to reflect, and to act collectively.

Challenging the kind of somnambulism that pretends to political judgment, Bertolt Brecht once quipped that immaturity is blaming your parents for the world's ills and maturity is blaming the next generation.

The post–civil rights generation, the post-industrial generation, or what rapper Mos Def most presciently called the "fallout generation," and now the post-9/11 generation, the most vulnerable generation—each has been the subject of collective derision and scorn. They constitute, at present, the abandoned generation, a generation whose future has been literally sold out from under them.[12] And yet it is with them that futurity and possibility lie. In a departure from the demonizing rhetoric politicians have directed toward the nation's youth since the 1960s, Obama has urged us to

come together and say, "Not this time." This time we want to talk about the crumbling schools that are stealing the future of black children and white children and Asian children and Hispanic children and Native American children. This time we want to reject the cynicism that tells us that these kids can't learn; that those kids who don't look like us are somebody else's problem. The children of America are not those kids, they are our kids. . . . [13]

Much has been made of Obama's status as a member of the post–civil rights generation, indeed its first president, but the responsibility for the Obama administration's success or failure will rest on the actions of the people who have decided to reject the neoliberal thesis that "there is no such thing as society" and act in the interest of a peaceful and sustainable future for all. And that may prove a most difficult task. As Chris Hedges and others have argued, those who immediately surrounded the new president, "from Madeline Albright to Hillary Clinton to Dennis Ross to Colin Powell, have no interest in dismantling the structure of an imperial presidency or the vast national security state. They will keep these institutions intact and seek to increase their power."[14] Our choice couldn't be more starkly defined: survival and futurity, or war.

"Let us be our brother's keeper, Scripture tells us," Obama reminded us in his March 2008 speech on race, invoking the black prophetic tradition of Dr. King and a commandment that is in fact upheld by all the world's great religions. And so we, in adhering to this ethic of social responsibility and reciprocity, would do well to recall its spiritual antecedents as well as its place in the American protest tradition, of which King was a central protagonist. King's words calling us to consciousness as they condemned U.S. involvement in Vietnam—a war brought to an end by a mass movement of everyday people—are striking for their relevance today:

Our involvement in the war in Vietnam has torn up the Geneva Accord. It has strengthened the military-industrial complex; it has strengthened the forces of reaction in our nation. . . .

It has played havoc with our domestic destinies. This day we are spending five hundred thousand dollars to kill every Vietcong soldier . . . while we spend only fifty-three dollars a year for every person characterized as poverty-stricken in the so-called poverty program . . .

. . . it has put us in a position of appearing to the world as an arrogant nation. And here we are ten thousand miles away from home fighting for the so-called freedom of the Vietnamese people when we have not put our own house in order. And we force young black men and young white men to fight and kill in brutal solidarity. Yet when they come back home th[ey] can't hardly live on the same block together. . . . [15]

What lessons are we to learn from this? Tragically, once again, our unilateral decision to go to war in Iraq, to expand the theater of war beyond Afghanistan, has greatly diminished our standing in the world community. And our military presence in these regions, and the scores of civilians dead as a result of our presence, has not rid the world of terrorist organizations but rather increased their recruitment efforts. The Geneva Conventions have been dismissed as quaint, and the constitutionally guaranteed rights of citizens have been repeatedly violated with impunity. And we still do not have our house in order. President Obama has not yet made good on the promises made by candidate Obama. Not only has the gap between the wealthy and the increasingly racially defined poor become a vast canyon, but the poor have been rendered a disposable population, like the victims of Hurricane Katrina, like the millions rotting in the nation's jails and prisons—all disproportionately men and women of color.

The collateral damage of the wars abroad and at home has been all too obvious. In the wave of national and international protest before the Iraq War began in 2003, children in Seattle and other cities marched with banners aloft demanding "Books, not Bombs." Now, seven years into that war and nine years into an Afghani war with no end yet in sight, the nation's public schools, bankrupt where not broken, are dealing with unprecedented homelessness, poverty, and malnutrition among youth.[16] Much vaunted university systems, particularly in the state of California, now find themselves in similarly dire circumstances facing near ruinous cuts in funding. In confronting the educational impoverishment of our time, King's words suggest that we must not only demand better schools as a matter of national priority, but become critical students of our own educational history, press our elected representatives to learn from it as well, and act thoughtfully and collectively:

There comes a time when one must take the position that it is neither safe nor politic nor popular, but he must do it because his conscience tells him it is right. I believe today that there is a need for all people of good will to come with a massive act of conscience and say in the words of the old Negro spiritual, "We ain't goin' study war no more." This is the challenge facing modern man.[17]

And in so doing, King reminds us, pithily and persuasively, that the capacity of citizens to think and act in good conscience is predicated on *pedagogical* conditions—inescapably moral and political in nature—that privilege "nonviolent coexistence" over "violent coannihilation."

I too believe, as an article of faith rather than a clear reflection of the historical record, that just and sustainable societies are well-educated societies—and societies that look after their children, all of them. For this reason I have devoted much of my adult life to the classroom. I have taught youth in poor urban middle schools whose distrust of the educational system was matched by the indifference with which the institution often met them, as well as teens in wealthy suburban high schools who harbor the general expectation for entrance into the nation's ivy leagues and exciting, lucrative careers. But the vast majority of that time, I have spent in universities, teaching literature and social theory in large and small, Midwestern and urban, U.S. and Canadian academic contexts. I have moved across diverse borders between nations, institutions, disciplines, and classroom configurations with more or less the same open set of pedagogical commitments: to expand students' critical capacities, intellectual curiosity, and sense of agency in the interests of a more socially just world—what John Dewey simply and yet capaciously described as "growth," which, despite his critics, was never directionless. But the specificity of context that greets each pedagogical encounter inevitably requires a radical rethinking of what it means "to act" on one's principles. The enabling and constraining particularities of context—from student histories, needs, interests, learning styles, the popular/cultural mediated spheres they inhabit, the socio-political environment in which they live and study, to the technical and material resources at one's disposal, the institutional mediation of curricular content, the time restrictions that frame classroom interaction as well as students' study habits when most are financially burdened and must resort to at least part-time labor—all of these necessarily define and delimit what I can do as a teacher.

And yet, the vast majority of policy makers and university administrators of late have become as indifferent to student needs as they have been inhospitable to humanistic inquiry more generally. It is enough to know how to assemble and advance exciting new technologies—medical or military, capable of redefining the human or obliterating it altogether—we no longer need to be able to talk about them, it seems, or question them, much less be required to think about them. But as philosophers, historians, artists, and other apparently antediluvian intellectuals would remind us, we should be wary of the time when knowledge and thought part company "for good."[18] Such pressing pedagogical contexts as I have outlined above are rendered irrelevant, and teaching, as a moral and political practice, is reduced to a fixed set of skills or methodologies through which one more or less efficiently delivers a stripped-down, standardized curriculum to students, in ways that can be empirically tested according to the latest measures of accountability in the institutional pursuit of "excellence." There are crude and sophisticated articulations of such premises, to be sure, but the upshot is more often than not a mandate for "teaching" that often substitutes training for education and the acquisition of marketable skills for critical thinking and ethical accountability. Such an alienated concept of teaching and learning should offend—if not outrage—parents, politicians, and concerned citizens. But it is more often praised for its smooth patriotism. Yet, as I will demonstrate later in greater detail, it offers no moral or political vision that connects education to the everyday lives of students, enabling different visions of the future or, more broadly, to the responsibilities associated with participation in a democratic, let alone a humane, society. Of course, this may well be the point—institutional memory of the student activism of the sixties perhaps remains too vivid.

Severing questions of learning from questions about how to enlarge the capacities of young people to imagine, reflect, value, and act in ways that expand their sense of agency, instrumentalized and technicalized versions of university education rarely engage students, let alone establish the conditions for independent, creative, and rigorous thinking. The consequences of this failure cannot be overestimated. As the current president of Harvard University, Drew Gilpin Faust, recently inquired,

As the world indulged in a bubble of false prosperity and excessive materialism, should universities—in their research, teaching and writing—have made greater efforts to expose the patterns of risk and denial? Should universities have presented a firmer counterweight to economic irresponsibility? Have universities become too captive to the immediate and worldly purposes they serve? Has the market model become the fundamental and defining identity of higher education?[19]

Citing the dramatic decline in liberal arts and science majors and the corresponding popularity of business degrees, Faust acknowledges that the pressure to vocationalize is only likely to intensify. But it is a pressure, she argues, that must be resisted, affirming that "higher learning can offer individuals and societies a depth and breadth of vision absent from the inevitably myopic present." Although I do not agree that such pressures come primarily from students, or that corporatization is the only danger confronting higher education (as I elaborate in the next chapter), I do think it crucial that, in Faust's words, we "ask more than this from our universities" and in so doing challenge the many anti-intellectual and reductive conceptualizations of higher education and pedagogical relationships that these presuppose.

The pedagogical encounter has a crucially philosophic, existentially unsettling, and semiotic nature; as an educator, I am implicated in the construction of narratives about the social world and horizons of possibility I articulate for myself, my students, and the communities we inhabit. My central task as a teacher—creating the conditions for opening up the critical and responsive capacities of students—necessitates introducing to students and exploring with them various intellectual traditions that offer structured, systemic models of social analysis that reflect the complexities of a linguistic universe that simultaneously unsettles and disrupts common sense. It is all too easy to lose sight of human reality, to not see suffering even when it is shown, to confuse victims with perpetrators, particularly in the contemporary context of institutionally encouraged indifference—or, indeed, (color)blindness. By challenging the taken-for-granted nature of students' own linguistic horizons and the often enormous parochialism that informs them—the suspicion of others, the contempt for difference, the seduction of social homogeneity—the pedagogical space I hope to open up encourages a confrontation with, and the challenge of being open to, radical difference—to the discomfort of recognizing that one's own scheme of intelligibility is never adequate, never complete, not nearly so commonly shared, and often closes down the possibilities of engaging if not quite understanding otherness in a more open and capacious way. Assuming such response-ability, the precondition for intellectual and moral growth, can never take root in a soil free of surprise, conflict, contingency, ambivalence, and doubt. The struggle with this commitment and all that is entwined with it—students' fears and anxieties with difficult language, with difference, with uncertainty (as well as, of course, one's own)—necessarily remains a unresolved and irresolvable preoccupation in meaningful and effective pedagogical exchange.

The precariousness of the world young people stand to inherit—the result of global wars, ecological catastrophe, exacerbated economic inequality, and racisms in old and new, colorblinding modalities—multiplies daily. And in the cruelest of ironies, they have been afforded neither the resources nor the guidance of their elders to aid them in their transition to adult responsibility. As we shall soon see, such pedagogical gestures as I have outlined above within the context of, ironically, "higher education" are often met with withering critiques of academic "radicalism" or roughly dismissed as an imprudent surrender of professional standards of instruction. As a consequence of our devastatingly misguided priorities and our negligence, our children's future—and perhaps our own—hangs in the balance. In spite of the bellicose religiosity sounding from the far corners of the globe, we have failed to hear Gabriel's trumpet. A complex metaphor, as James Baldwin once noted: "Poor Gabriel is not only responsible for when we dead awaken—heavy enough—but he must also blow that trumpet to wake the children sleeping. The children are ours, every single one of them, all over the globe; and I am beginning to suspect that whoever is incapable of recognizing this may be incapable of morality."[20] It is without question time to wake up, and time to stay awake.

CHAPTER TWO

Playing in the Dark: Racial Repression and the New Campus Crusade for Diversity

I concluded Chapter 1 with reference to the now-ubiquitous charges of "academic radicalism" which sound not only in the popular press but also on the floor of the U.S. Congress. I do so with a kind of chagrin; these days to write about the conservative attack on the university, even in its newest incarnation, runs the risk of opening oneself to charges of over-kill, even a kind of vapid self-indulgence. Like the discovery of corporate greed. In truth, what motivates me to engage this issue, in spite of the pit-falls, has less to do with questions of why the assault is taking place, or the conditions that give rise to it. What puzzles me most about the retooled right-wing assault on the university in the aftermath of 9/11 is the relative silence of progressive voices in response to this challenge, as compared to the cacophonous "culture wars" of earlier decades. In part, the crippling quiet seems to be a function of the vulnerabilities and anxieties of workers in the academy that result from the ongoing corporatization of the university—its increasing hierarchical organization, the rise of a managerial class and reduction of faculty to mere advisory capacity in hiring, tenure, and promotion as well, as its commitments to the casualization of the labor force with the disappearance of tenure-track lines, the hiring of fixed-term contract employees, the introduction of post-tenure review, and the continuing difficulties, post-*Yeshiva,* of organizing faculty (i.e., the curtailment of collective bargaining rights among faculty now legally defined as management). Or, perhaps the hush is part of the culture of fear that permeates the United States in the wake of the terrorist attacks in New York and Washington, exacerbated by efforts of the Right to silence progressives who dare to critique foreign policy, or any policy of the former Bush administration, by characterizing such commentary as anti-American, even pro-terrorist sympathizing. The mounting victories on behalf of well-orchestrated campus crusades for "patriotic correctness" not only in university classrooms, but in state legislatures, the courts, and the major media appear to have left many progressives stunned, disoriented, and utterly disorganized.

Of late, however, I find myself resisting the value of crushing economic vulnerabilities and insecurities that mark the rise of fixed-term laborers who constitute the new majority of workers in the academy, or the "everything has changed" rhetoric of the post-9/11 era in providing a comprehensive explanation for the apparent progressive retreat. Cataloguing external, repressive forces "from above" all too often serves to impede a necessary gaze inward, to consideration of the less visible, more prickly processes of internalization and normalization of the tenets of professionalism and (neo)liberalism in the post–civil rights American academy. And so, I find myself returning again to the "culture wars" of the 1980s and 1990s, locating part of an explanation for such confounding quiet in the ideals that marked the university's "multicultural turn." I contend that such commitments, in hindsight, proved much more difficult to materialize than their advocates were willing to recognize—and required far more than many, if not most, were willing to concede. The limp endorsement and bland acceptance of principles such as "nondiscrimination," "diversity," and "openness" *in the abstract* enabled the Right's ruthless appropriation of the vision and language of multiculturalism, turning fact and history on their heads.

Thus we begin.

The decades of the 1980s and 1990s have generally been associated with the ascendancy of multicultural education in American universities. Although embattled, progressive thinkers in the liberal arts invested in notions of "tolerance," "diversity," and "inclusiveness" appeared victorious in the first round of battles in what came to be known as the "culture wars."

In some instances, even radical interventions in modes of pedagogical exchange, the nature of critical engagement, and the role of the university in
democratic public life could find their way in the "marketplace of ideas,"
though these were often marginal to the university's well-rehearsed commitments to "excellence," "efficiency," and "standards." The outgrowth
of student agitation in the late 1960s and early 1970s, new disciplinary
formations emerged in the form of programs and (much) later departments in fields such as women's studies, African American studies, Latino
studies, or simply "ethnic studies," reflecting the shifting demographics
of college campuses across the nation. Equally influential were new theoretical discourses that mapped the contours of the emergent conditions of
postmodernity in areas as diverse as continental philosophy, postcolonial-
ism, race theory, feminism, revisionist historiography, queer theory, and
media studies, to name but a few. Their impact on traditional courses of
study such as English, history, and philosophy proved decisive, motivating
both change and retrenchment and reinvigorating—for a time—a waning
interest in the humanities.

Though hardly across the board, the liberal arts seemed to offer in
those years a space for teachers and students to quicken a democratic society's necessary commitment to rigorous self-questioning, to open yet
scholarly debate, and when necessary, to ameliorative change. It is difficult
not to look back, for example, on the year 1992 as a watershed moment in
American letters. That was the year that *Playing in the Dark: Whiteness
and the Literary Imagination*, a collection of lectures by the soon-to-be
Nobel laureate Toni Morrison made its way into print. An eloquent and
provocative challenge to the historical tendency of literary criticism and
education to ignore the centrality of race to any understanding of the
national culture, Morrison offered a theory of the American canon to rival
such venerable classics as Vernon Parrington's three-volume *Main Currents
in American Thought* (1927–30), F. O. Matthiessen's *American Renaissance*
(1941), Leslie Fiedler's *Love and Death in the American Novel* (1960), Leo
Marx's *Machine in the Garden* (1964), and Richard Slotkin's *Regeneration
Through Violence* (1973). Countering the conventional wisdom of literary
historians and critics that the four-hundred-year presence of Africans and
then African Americans "had no significant place or consequence in the
origin and development" of American literature, Morrison suggested that

the "major and championed characteristics of our national literature—individualism, masculinity, social engagement versus historical isolation; acute and ambiguous moral problematics; the thematics of innocence coupled with an obsession with figurations of death and hell" are in fact responses to a "dark and abiding Africanist" presence.[1] Through a writerly investigation of black characterization, narrative strategies, and idiomatic expressions in the fiction of white American writers such as Willa Cather, Edgar Allen Poe, Herman Melville, and Ernest Hemingway, Morrison gathered persuasive evidence for her compelling thesis. Had it not been for the "willful critical blindness" of scholars in the field, she argued, such commentary on American literature's encounter with racial ideology would have been commonplace. Yet, she contended, silence and evasion have historically ruled literary discourse:

When matters of race are located and called attention to in American literature, critical response has tended to be on the order of a humanistic nostrum—or a dismissal mandated by the label "political." Excising the political from the life of the mind is a sacrifice that has proven costly. . . . A criticism that needs to insist that literature is not only "universal" but also "race-free" risks lobotomizing that literature, and diminishes both the art and the artist.[2]

Political agendas, she argued, cloaked in appeals to objectivity and universalism—further complicated by the problematic liberal assumption that ignoring race is a "graceful, even generous" gesture—have shut down scholarly inquiry into the very processes by which American culture distinguishes itself as a coherent entity through an excluded racially defined population.

Morrison's political and pedagogical objectives far exceeded the typical demand for the expansion of the canon, a remedy-through-inclusion of different voices in American arts and letters. She also challenged the triple effect of the official colorblinding rhetoric of the Reagan-Bush era with its insistence that "race no longer matters," effectively used to silence any serious discussion of everyday racisms, its tendency toward historical denial precluding any connection between past and present inequality, and its subsequent displacement of racially charged relations to the relatively invisible realm of the private.[3] Morrison insisted on nothing less than a radical rethinking of American intellectual history and its role in the perpetuation of racist exclusions within and beyond the ivory tower.

Hers was a project in keeping with what some (though certainly not most) progressives in the university saw as nothing less than their intellectual and social responsibility. Indeed, Morrison offered a glimpse at what might have been possible if rigorous critical engagement with the national culture and history had been allowed to unsettle and challenge the official narratives of post–civil rights America as a classless and now raceless society, what changes in culture and consciousness might have enabled a real experiment in economic and social justice, in substantive democracy.

The contributions of Morrison and others associated with more insurgent versions of multiculturalism, however, were seldom met with the spirit of intellectual courage and thoughtfulness that they were meant to inspire. Rather, conservatives who described themselves as "independent thinkers" yet were covertly backed by well-endowed think tanks such as the Olin and Heritage foundations or the American Enterprise, Cato, and Hoover institutes came out in force to claim that the academy had become the privileged site for the dissemination not of truth or excellence, but rather of left-liberal political propaganda that sought to unravel the very fabric of American civilization. Conservatives in the academy cast themselves as the last vestiges of Enlightenment rationality, before the barbarians took over. The Sterling professor of humanities at Yale, Harold Bloom, for example, responded to multiculturalist critiques of sustained efforts to maintain European hegemony in the world of ideas, "its special monopoly of access to scientific, ethical or aesthetic modernities," in the following terms:[4]

We are the final inheritors of Western tradition. Education founded upon the *Iliad*, the Bible, Plato, and Shakespeare remains, in some strained form, our ideal, though the relevance of these cultural monuments to life in our inner cities is inevitably rather remote. Those who resent all canons suffer from an elitist guilt founded upon the accurate realization that canons always do indirectly serve the social and political, and indeed the spiritual concerns and aims of the wealthier classes of each generation of Western society. It seems clear that capital is necessary for the cultivation of aesthetic values. . . . This alliance of sublimity and financial and political power has never ceased, and presumably never can or will.[5]

A bloodless pronouncement to be sure, but candid in its conclusions that the fruits of Western civilization (1) appear to require capital growth and investment; (2) serve the interests of wealth and whiteness, as he insists, (3) on the irrelevance of canonical knowledge to those in remote reaches on the other side of America's great racial divide. Of course, the Left has made similar claims, more as an object of critique than a statement of supposed fact or legitimation. But there we have it: a point of agreement. Canonical knowledge serves power; and power—financial and political—was indeed on Bloom's side. In the 1980s and 1990s, conservatives, for all their rhetoric about liberal media and radicalized college campuses, were neither weak nor isolated. With Democratic party hegemony, in place from FDR's New Deal to the Great Society of the 1960s, now eclipsed, the Right enjoyed greater representation in government and increasing visibility in a variety of public forums and mass media from television (MSNBC, Fox), talk radio, newspapers (*Wall Street Journal, Washington Times*—as well as op-eds in the *Washington Post* and *New York Times*), and smaller journals of opinion (*National Review, Commentary, The American Spectator, The New Criterion*), to carefully orchestrated and well-endowed advertising campaigns in the realm of publishing, prior to obtaining their own houses. Consider the push for such classic screeds as *The Closing of the American Mind, Illiberal Education, Tenured Radicals, Cultural Literacy,* and *The Western Canon,* among others. Out they came—Harold Bloom, William Bennett, Roger Kimball, E. D. Hirsch, Phyllis Schafly, George Will, Dinesh D'Souza—to expose and castigate the "liberal fascism" permeating universities across the nation, attacking political correctness and campus hate speech codes, sexual harassment, "femi-nazis," the decline of standards, affirmative action for overly advantaged and under-appreciative minorities, "reverse racism," black separatism, white guilt, moral relativism, postmodernism, and, of course, Jacques Derrida and Paul de Man. (Pomophobia, we call it.) And so the Right was able to redefine the national conversation about postsecondary education on pretty much the only leg they could—by ruse of rhetoric—stand on: cultural values. Issues of paramount concern to students themselves and what should have been an ongoing critical conversation across the nation—questions not only of the kind and quality of education but of access, the nodal point where racist exclusion and neoliberal privatization meet in the form of declining public funds, spiraling tuitions, and the ever-expanding student loan racket—were effectively scuttled. Luckily for conservatives, as this is precisely where the right-wing agendas could been effectively unmasked and challenged.

But conservatives weren't alone in their derision of the university's multicultural turn, an argument I explore more fully in Chapter 3. Suffice it to say for now that by the mid-1990s a number of progressives such as Todd Gitlin and Michael Tomasky were in retreat and denounced the cultural left for "its divisive obsession with race and sex, its arcane 'elitist' battles over curriculum, its penchant for pointy-headed social theory and its aversion to the socially and sexually conservative values most Americans uphold."[6] In his *Professional Correctness* (1995), Stanley Fish took to task the literary critic who would conclude his analysis of *Sister Carrie* or the *Grapes of Wrath* with a commentary on homelessness rather than with an assessment of literary realism, while assuming her critique will find its way to the policy makers at the Department of Housing and Urban Development. Exposing as fallacious and insipid any academic pretense to social change, Fish advocated—and continues to advocate—a return to the practical and professional criticism associated with the New Critics of the 1940s and 1950s. That same year, Richard Rorty suggested, in his "The Inspirational Value of Great Works of Literature," that the then-current academic fervor for literary analysis of the "knowing, debunking, *nil admirandi* kind" drains the possibilities for enthusiasm, imagination, and hope from scholars and students alike. In place of critical analysis, Rorty urged an appreciation of "great" works of literature; by which he means seeking inspiration from works of literature that "inculcate . . . eternal 'humanistic' values."[7] What such an appeal to transcendent truth means coming from a philosopher once committed to the notion of cultural relativism remains unclear, but the universalizing gesture has a profoundly Eurocentric pedigree. Decrying the rise of particular forms of cultural critique in English departments and its cult of knowingness, Rorty contended that "you cannot . . . find inspirational value in a text at the same time you are viewing it as a product of a mechanism of cultural production."[8] Pitting understanding against the romantic values of awe, inspiration, and hope, Rorty advocated a kind of intellectual passivity among readers in the name of "hopefulness," though it might be described more aptly as a kind of helplessness. So much for the concept of a unified, left-leaning academy.

What many liberals share with conservative critics of the humanities then and now is a desire to narrow the field of intellectual inquiry, to reduce the productive work of English departments to what makes it most "distinctive": its capacity for formal aesthetic appreciation. Such a call is a retreat from the political in the name of professional survival. The moral and ethical imperative to engage the social implications of what and how students learn to read is traded for either a breathless romanticism (Rorty) or a cool-headed pragmatism (Fish). Edward Said rightly associated the call for such limited notions of professionalism (or what he calls, after Burton Bledstein, the "cult of professionalism") and its attendant demands for specialization and expertise with intellectual inertia and laziness. In the study of literature, Said argued, "specialization has meant an increasing technical formalism, and less and less of a historical sense of what real experiences actually went into the making of a work of literature." The result was the inability to "view knowledge and art as choices and decisions, commitments and alignments, but [instead see them] only in terms of impersonal theories or methodologies."[9] The specific target of Said's animus was the renewed impetus to return to the new critical formalism of a bygone era, which divorced texts from any contextual consideration and, of course, writers from their respective publics.

Needless to say, this was not the conversation Toni Morrison had in mind. As for the deleterious, disuniting impact of a radicalized university on the national culture, I want to return us, briefly, to 1992 for a cursory glance at other events that year which would seem to temper any claims about the academy's precarious influence on the nation in its pursuit of radical anti-racist and anti-sexist "agendas." In fact, 1992 proved a banner year for the nation's criminal justice system, which reached the halfway point in its incarceration of over a million Americans (By 2009, 2.3 million citizens were serving time, 70 percent of whom are black and Latino in spite making up only 24 percent of the nation's population). The U.S. carceral apparatus at that point was approaching an average rate of arrest for young black males of one in three between the ages of 20 and 29, a ratio it would meet and surpass, with that statistic becoming almost one in two in the nation's capital by 2004. What is less known is the impact of mass incarceration of black women, which increased more than 859 percent in the decade of the 1990s. The year 1992, for instance, saw the incarceration and sentencing of Cornelia Whitner "for endangering the life of her unborn child," a judicial decision in a landmark case that would spark a media-manufactured "crack baby epidemic" and lead to the criminalization of pregnancy among young black and Latino women—as well as conditions, not unlike those produced under chattel slavery, of black women giving birth in chains only to have their babies forcibly removed from them by the state.[10]

The year 1992 was notable for the fact that while the "get tough" movement remained popular with Washington ideologues and much of the electorate, even as its impact on actually reducing crime was mixed, (one is tempted to say) its only demonstrable "successes" were in sending more young black males to prison than to college and in escalating tensions between police and the minority communities they were to serve and protect. By mid-year, one community in South Central Los Angeles was aflame after the jurists at the Rodney King trial returned a verdict declaring the four police officers accused of beating King innocent of the charge of excessive force. But get tough policies had also succeeded in another way, quite literally by "bankrupting the states," according to the Connecticut corrections commissioner attending a high-profile Washington conference that same year.[11] In other words, the pressure that this mass incarceration experiment had put on state coffers had sunk them well into the red, which translated into deeper cuts in the nation's health care, K-12 education, and, most profoundly, higher education—funding for which is seen as "discretionary," thus hardly a guarantee to begin with. The upshot has been spiraling tuition rates and dwindling government-sponsored student loan programs, which have pushed middle-class parents to the financial edge for the last two decades, saddled most students with enormous debt as a result of new predatory private lending services, and placed college well out of reach for youth of poor and minority families. Though bankrupt by the end of the first Bush administration, the devastating consequences of state impoverishment wouldn't be seen until the second term of Bush Jr. when Hurricane Katrina blew apart New Orleans and other coastal cities of the south, leaving citizens to their own wretched devices for days and weeks on end.

After two terms of Reagan and one of Bush Sr., the nation's social services by 1992 were already decidedly lean, as was repeatedly exposed in Jonathan Kozol's *Savage Inequalities*, which would make its paperback appearance that year. What Kozol revealed in that now-classic study of

American schooling, however, was not only the staggering—indeed savage—disparity in access to quality education in poor and minority communities in contrast to their wealthy counterparts, but the ongoing and deeply entrenched segregation that still wracked public schooling four decades after *Brown v. Board of Education*. As Clarence Thomas, a vocal opponent of the *Brown* decision, replaced Thurgood Marshall, its chief architect, in the Supreme Court—a kind of supreme irony—remedy via the courts proved an increasingly remote possibility. In fact, in 1992, Thomas's first full year in office, the *Freeman v. Pitts* decision enabled once-segregated school systems to dismantle their desegregation plans without ever having desegregated their faculty or providing equal access to educational facilities. It was quite a year.

So, to recapitulate my claims thus far, on the one hand, we have conservatives who insist on an end to campus radicalism and in its place a value-neutral, race-free education as they support "colorblind" public policies favored by a largely white electorate that have resulted in the maintenance of pervasive residential and school segregation, mass criminalization and incarceration of populations of color, with tacit approval of police surveillance, harassment, and profiling (if not brutality and murder), along with the attendant consequences of exacerbated unemployment, increasing poverty, alienation, and dislocation. And on the other hand, we have an academy at least nominally committed to multiculturalism (though hardly unified, especially on the Left), accused of foisting a politicized debate about race, among other issues, onto discussions of national culture and consciousness (where, the implication is, none is needed) and pushing a value system onto impressionable students—at public expense—that transgresses, for the most part, those mainstream beliefs that their taxpaying parents uphold. What conclusions can be drawn, then, about the relative success (or threat, as more conservative-minded would insist) of academic multiculturalism, given the broader political and cultural climate in the United States, when the principles of racial justice and equality are not only imperiled but excised from mainstream public discourse?

If we assent, for the moment, to the conservative view of the university as a hotbed of radical thought, we would have to admit that thus far it's been devastatingly ineffectual. If this is the case, why? Perhaps there is an *unwillingness*, or a refusal, on the part of liberal intellectuals in the university to translate their research in scholarly yet rhetorically effective ways to the broader public. (It does seem, at times, that the choicest rewards accrue to scholars with the tiniest of audiences—but that's a topic for another essay). Or perhaps it reflects an *inability* of intellectuals to do so, not because they are a particularly slow-witted lot, but because they are *unable*, given the transformation of the university into a more corporate entity in both its structure and its interests. Like the tale spun about the liberal media, the public secret about the university is not its overreaching radical influence, but rather the radical downsizing of humanistic faculties, with efforts either to assimilate disciplines to corporate interests (as the proliferation of business writing courses in English, for example, in the drive for more service-oriented learning) or to render them into an entirely ornamental, if not irrelevant endeavor, as Stanley Aronowitz has comprehensively examined in his uncompromising and erudite volume *The Knowledge Factory*. The latter disposition has translated into the near-collapse of federal funding and into the increasingly selective interests of granting institutions, the nonrenewal of tenure track faculty lines, and the diminishing emphasis on liberal arts requirements for undergraduates. For all the public concerns over academic freedom and its abuse, consider that in the United States currently over 60 percent of undergraduate teaching is performed by graduate students and fixed term faculty, who teach from six to eight courses a year, with no guarantee of contract renewal, and with no say about the conditions under which they work. The introduction of precarity, a kind of generalized insecurity that paralyzes political agents, is hardly the context for producing either provocative scholarship or inspiring pedagogical praxis.

We must also consider, too, the slipperiness of the concept of multiculturalism itself as we take the measure of the success of university's allegedly left-leaning agenda. In their more insurgent moments, I do think advocates of multicultural education like Toni Morrison, Cornel West, David Theo Goldberg, and many others successfully challenged the contemporary authority of Western canons of thought and aesthetic value, interrogated the organization of scholarly disciplines, opening up promising routes to new knowledge formations, as they more broadly critiqued the notion of a "common culture," a national identity based on homogeneity—and hence the repression or exclusion of difference—as the primary principle for social cohesion. At the same time, we would do well do consider what Paul Gilroy calls that "fateful prefix" *multi-*, drawing our attention to the concept's stubborn capacity for reinvention, such that it can be abused as "the new racism" by the Right, or enthusiastically endorsed by a contingent of cultural brokers from the corporate sector hoping to establish themselves as "the hip vanguard in the business of difference."[12]

With the ascendancy of the "welfare queen" to public enemy number one in the Reagan-Bush era, it would seem, at first blush, that the university did offer one of the few spheres (outside of *Oprah*) where a woman of color could be accorded some respect. After the "discovery" of the black woman writer in the 1970s, the works of Alice Walker, Toni Morrison, and Zora Neale Hurston—and later, the self-conscious additions of Sandra Cisneros, Barbara Kingsolver, and Maxine Hong Kingston—became a ubiquitous part of the college curriculum by the 1990s, with many departments and programs proudly pointing to an "integrated" curriculum, as "diversity" became the dominant code word of the day. The triumph of the last leftist redoubt? Seems doubtful. The university, upon closer inspection, could be said to follow in its embrace of multiculturalism a corporate logic akin to the promotion of a new niche market. Or, in keeping with the conservative tenor of the times, an investment in a kind of symbolic racial diversity, if not the actual—and more costly—racial and ethnic diversity of its faculty or student body. Yale literary theorist Hazel Carby suggests that

we need to ask why black women, or other women who are non-white, are needed as cultural and political icons by the white middle class at this particular moment? What cultural and political need is being expressed, and what role is the black female subject being reduced to play? I would argue that it is necessary to recognize the contradictions between making the black female subject in the classroom and failing to integrate the university student and faculty bodies on a national scale. Instead of recognizing these contradictions, the black female subject is frequently the means by which many middle-class white students and faculty cleanse their souls and rid themselves of the guilt of living in a society that is still rigidly segregated. Black cultural texts have become fictional substitutes for the lack of any sustained social or political relationships with black people in a society that has retained many of its historical practices of apartheid in housing and schooling.[13]

Against the victory of whiteness purged of collective guilt and self-doubt (through a process Barthes called "inoculation") in an officially colorblind era, Carby points to the actual, ongoing conditions of segregation in post–civil rights America. "Inclusive" curricula perpetuate the illusion of a post-racist, or nonracial, new world order. In contrast to the financial drain of an actual commitment to an inclusive student body, the costs of curricular expansion are insignificant to the university and its interests in terms of either money or power sharing, while serving to pacify new student-consumers of color.

I want to expand on Carby's insights about the university's multicultural commitments by drawing attention to further implications of such policy that I think are central to understanding the new conservative attack on the university in the wake of September 11. As colorblind public policy gives way to a lexicon of bland corporate multiculturalism and ethnic diversity, the academic marketplace rushes to quash lingering guilt and responsibility as it satisfies consumer demand for exotica or "authentic" insider information about nonwhite others. In an era marked by colorblind politics, race is, at long last, an officially irrelevant category, officially removed from the discourses of politics, power, and history; and yet in the private sphere, racial differences seem to proliferate endlessly: thus, a movement from absolute homogeneity to absolute difference. The university's often weak endorsement of pluralism and diversity may not function simply to mystify the operations of white guilt or efforts to attract ethnic markets (which I think it does do), but also to consciously rearticulate contemporary racial reason, now reconceived as a matter of private discrimination. The university's embrace of multiculturalism is not necessarily in contrast to, but rather in concert with, the colorblinding policy commitments of the Right. Rather than understand, for example, the academy's enthusiastic inclusion of women of color in literature and the arts (as against their exclusion or denigration in every other social sphere), we might read their presence in the liberal arts as part of the process of the privatization of racial discourse, in keeping with the neoliberal push to privatize the university and every other public sphere in the United States.

As Robin D. G. Kelley (1997), Arif Dirlik (1999), David Theo Goldberg (2002), and others have noted, there has been a silent migration of critical race theory from the social sciences to fields in the humanities in keeping with the "culturalist turn" of the last few decades—for better *and* for worse. Liberalism's flirtation with race relations at the mid-century had given way to a full-blown infatuation with racial identities by the dawn of the new millennium. It seems that the progressive possibilities of that turn, as Goldberg suggests, "have run their course. Time . . . to move on."[14] Moving on, though, requires looking back at the consequences of such disciplinary transit—the critical blind spots and bothersome gaps resulting from the displacement of structuralist analyses of racially defined relations of power and inequality manifest in schools, housing, medical care; the evasions concerning the role of the state in the formation of its citizenry, its conceptualization of order through homogeneity, its power to include or exclude, endow or withhold rights, construct enemies or grant protections. In short, we must ask: What happens when African American history becomes literary history? When analyses of state sovereignty, or more recently market sovereignty, and their powers of exception give way to the romance of hybridism, the claims of identity, and the reputedly transgressive possibilities of race traitorhood? My argument is not opposed to the study of African American, Latino, or Asian American cultural texts, but rather it is against certain de-historicized, de-politicized engagements that have all-too-frequently lent themselves to brash essentialisms and cultural reifications, a dubious priority of culture over history. Without recourse to a language of modern state power, shifting historical conceptualizations of race, and exploitative economic relations that have translated into public policies governing racially rendered populations, we are left to examine (not altogether unfruitfully) private, individual experiences and the formation of particularized identities. Then follows another unsettling question: How might the privatization of racial experience reproduce, as opposed to challenge, the neoliberal emphasis on privatization, individualization, and its depoliticizing effects? Does it not help us to understand how students can read and appreciate Toni Morrison in the classroom and return home to redlined, market-segregated neighborhoods without ever making the connection? It seems necessary to acknowledge that the upshot of an often narrow focus on the politics of identity is, rather ironically, in keeping with the ideology of colorblindness and its commitment to historical denial. Moreover, by reconceptualizing racism as a private—as opposed to a deeply social and structural—phenomenon, a function of individual discrimination, colorblind ideology displaces the tensions of contemporary racially charged relations to the relative invisibility of the private sphere—safely beyond the reach of public policy intervention or the hope of social amelioration.[15]

But this may not be the most tragic legacy of the university's ambivalent commitment to liberal multiculturalism, cultural diversity, and ethnic pluralism. Its often depoliticized and dehistoricized expression, I want to argue, has enabled the ruthless appropriation of left-liberal discourse by the Right for starkly reactionary, often racist ends at the dawn of the new millennium. I want to fast-forward now from 1992 to 2002 and talk about the new conservative assault on the university in the wake of 9/11.

Following the terrorist attacks on the Twin Towers and the Pentagon, the academic left found itself in a state of accelerated crisis—its intellectual energies dispersed in debates over the relative evil or merit of postmodernism versus a renewed interest in economics; critique of the politics of Empire vs. concerns about anti-Americanism in the ranks; the inevitably political nature of education versus the need to bid a hasty return to aesthetic formalism. And these only to name a few, as such wrangling always takes on the peculiarities of region, institution, and personality. If, as a result, the university's—or more precisely the humanities'—perceived influence on the pressing issues of the day appeared more and more tenuous, particularly in a climate of rapidly escalating corporatism and authoritarianism, neoconservatives rushed to construct an opposing image of the university as a vast and powerful repository of radical groupthink poised to infect the nation's youth.

It would become an image endlessly reproduced in the mass media, from talk radio to the editorial pages of the *Wall Street Journal* to prime-time on CNN. In a characteristic depiction, journalist Jeff Jacoby, relating such horrors to the readers of the *Boston Globe,* warned that "today campus leftism is not merely prevalent. It is radical, aggressive, and deeply intolerant. . . . " To support his claims, Jacoby cited research based on a sample of nineteen universities published in *The American Enterprise* in 2002 that alleges to reveal the near-complete liberal stranglehold on the university, a situation rendering ideological diversity on college campuses nonexistent. The study based its finding on the tabulation of voter registrations, such that a professor's being registered as a Democrat would prove that (1) her politics were decisively on the left and (2) that radical propaganda was given free rein in her classroom, to the profound detriment of students. The study found that

> at Cornell, of the 172 faculty members whose party affiliation was recorded, 166 were liberal (Democrats or Greens) and six were conservative (Republicans or Libertarians). At Stanford the liberal-conservative ration was 151–17. At San Diego State it was 80–11. At SUNY Binghamton, 35–1. At UCLA, 141–9. At the University of Colorado-Boulder, 116–5. Reflecting on these gross disparities, *The American Enterprise*'s editor, Karl Zinsmeister, remarked: "Today's colleges and universities . . . do not, when it comes to political and cultural ideas, look like America."[16]

Jacoby concluded that such "one-party domination" of any major institution is deeply troubling. He charged: "In academia it is scandalous. It strangles dissent, suppresses debate, and causes minorities to be discriminated against. It is certainly antithetical to good scholarship."[17] To cinch his case, Jacoby cited a survey conducted by the American Council of Trustees and Alumni which was designed to measure student perceptions of faculty partisanship. (This is the same group that organized and sent to university boards of trustees across the nation the McCarthyite list of 117 professors and students who were said to constitute the "weak link in the War on Terror.") They found, unsurprisingly, that "of 658 students polled at the top 50 colleges, 49 percent said professors 'frequently comment on politics in class even though it has nothing to do with the course,' 48 percent said some 'presentations on political issues seem totally one-sided,' and that 46 percent said that 'professors use the classroom to present their personal political views.'"[18] While I don't have time here to rehearse the various critiques of the deeply flawed character of the studies and surveys conducted by right-wing think tanks by Russell Jacoby (2005), Donald Lazere (2004), Robert Ivie (2005), John Wilson (2006), Michael Bérubé (2007), and others, suffice it to say that the sample for these studies selectively gleaned from top liberal arts schools and from six fields in the humanities and social sciences (excluding business schools and disciplines like engineering) produced an in-built bias—let alone the spurious presumption of leftism based on one's Democratic voting record. Consider that John Silber, for example, is a registered Democrat and one of the most radically conservative influences not only on Boston University, where he served as president for several decades, but on educational administration and policy across the nation. My point, however, is that conservative cultural warriors have managed to recreate themselves as champions of open debate, dissent, and the protection of oppressed "minorities." Ironically, the disabused "minority" in question happens to be conservative faculty and students "intellectually harassed" by the pressures of liberal groupthink.

Such studies and news articles, however, are only part of a much larger story. A series of books, right-wing campus organizations, and websites have taken up the cause against the alleged left-totalitarianism of the academy. Conservative think tanks provide $20 million annually to the campus Right, according to the People for the American Way, to fund campus organizations such as Students for Academic Freedom, whose credo is "You can't get a good education if they're only telling you half the story" and which boasts over 150 campus chapters. Providing an online complaint form for disgruntled students to fill out, the organization's website monitors insults, slurs, and allegations of more serious infractions that students claim to have suffered. Similarly, the Intercollegiate Studies Institute, founded by William F. Buckley, funds over 80 right-wing student publications through its Collegiate Network, which has produced such media darlings as Dinesh D'Souza and Ann Coulter. There is also the Leadership Institute, which trains, supports, and does public relations for 213 conservative student groups who are provided with suggestions for inviting conservative speakers to campus, help starting conservative newspapers, or training to win campus elections. Or the Young Americans for Freedom, which sponsors various campus activities such as "affirmative action bake sales," where students are charged variously according to their race or ethnicity, or announcements of "whites-only" scholarships. College Republicans at Penn State organized a massive Conservative Coming Out Day in which students were encouraged to show their support by wearing, of all things, blue jeans. Diverse and ever-expanding, these organizations share nonetheless the same four goals: training conservative campus activists, supporting right-wing student publications, indoctrinating the next generation of cultural warriors, and demonstrating liberal academic "bias" to justify conservative calls for aggressive intervention by university boards of trustees and concerned politicians.

Indeed, one of the most worrisome tactics of right-wing strategists has been to appeal directly to state and federal legislatures as well as the courts for various protections—typically a demand for external oversight in university hiring practices to achieve balance, a kind of conservative affirmative action that puts a candidate's ideology above questions of academic merit—as well as formal redress of grievances against individual members of a proselytizing leftist professoriate charged with "intellectual harassment." In 2002 David Horowitz penned the opening salvo of this campaign with his "Campaign for Fairness and Inclusion in Higher Education," which demanded that universities "adopt a code of conduct for faculty that ensures that classrooms will welcome diverse viewpoints and not be used for political indoctrination, which is a violation of students' academic freedom."[19] While much of the campaign has failed to make any impact, Horowitz's proposal for an "Academic Bill of Rights," which he hopes to pass into educational policy and law, has had a hearing in the U.S. Congress and in dozens of state legislatures across the nation. How do we make sense of the strange career of David Horowitz?

David Horowitz, for readers unfamiliar with him, is author of such screeds as *Hating Whitey and Other Progressive Causes; Unholy Alliance: Radical Islam and the American Left;* and most recently *The Professors: The 101 Most Dangerous Academics in America.* He made his big splash nationally in 1998, when he sued the University of California because it didn't hire Michael Savage (a right-wing talk show host now infamous for his incendiary racist remarks) as dean of the school of journalism, and again in 2001, when he raged against the reparation movement in a full-page advertisement in college newspapers nationwide. Typical of Horowitz's approach, the ad declared that African Americans benefited from slavery and pondered, "Where's the gratitude of black America?" This is the man—well-known for his bullying, belligerence, and inflammatory rhetoric—arguing in favor of a more diverse, open, and inclusive educational environment on college campuses. And either the bullying or (dare I say?) the bullsh*tting appears to be working for him, as he was given the honor of speaking at the 2008 Modern Language Association Convention.

Truth be told, Horowitz's current strategy is not so typically inflammatory or offensive as his past efforts to galvanize his right-wing base through appeals to anti-black racism. Capitalizing on both the culture of fear in the wake of the terrorist attacks as well as a few decades worth of conservative slander against the university, he developed—rather brilliantly—the concept of *student* academic freedom in an effort to undermine the academic freedom of faculty. As John Wilson notes, the question of academic freedom is, for Horowitz, "a useful rhetorical tool, not a principle he believes in."[20] Horowitz would appear to admit as much when he described his efforts to mimic, even satirize, traditionally progressive idioms in pursuing his conservative platform. He stated:

I encourage [fellow Republicans] to use the language that the Left has deployed so effectively in behalf of its agendas. Radical professors have created a "hostile learning environment" for conservative students. There is a lack of "intellectual diversity" on college faculties in academic classrooms. The conservative viewpoint is "underrepresented" in the curriculum and on the reading lists. The university should be an "inclusive" and intellectually "diverse" community.[21]

Horowitz's clever appropriation of various progressive touchstones has proven successful in state legislatures and the U.S. Congress, where politicians adopt over and over the same liberal rhetoric in the pursuit of nakedly right-wing ends.

Of course, some of what Horowitz proposes is unimpeachable: for example, that students should not be graded "on the basis of their political or religious beliefs." But the implications of much of the Academic Bill of Rights are quite dangerous indeed, as in the insistence that "faculty members will not use their position for the purpose of political, ideological, religious or antireligious indoctrination" but rather that their "curricula and reading lists should reflect the uncertainty and unsettled character of all human knowledge" and provide "students with dissenting sources and viewpoints where appropriate."[22] It sounds reasonable until one considers what Horowitz means by "where appropriate." Horowitz provides a list of abuses that includes an introductory Peace Studies and Conflict Resolution course, taught by George Wolfe at Ball State University, that excludes military approaches. A conservative student, Brett Mock, had claimed that the professor did not include an endorsement of war as a legitimate means of conflict resolution, or acknowledge that violence could be good. This exclusion constituted, according to Horowitz, a violation of Mock's student academic rights. By this logic a course on the Holocaust would have to include Nazi political philosophy or the viewpoints of Holocaust deniers; courses on evolutionary biology would have to give equal time to intelligent design; courses on contemporary theories of race and racism would have to include the positions of Charles Murray and Dinesh D'Souza, and so on. The American Association of University Professors (AAUP) rightly concluded that the bill "seeks to distinguish indoctrination from appropriate pedagogy by applying principles *other than* relevant scholarly standards, as interpreted and applied by the academic profession."[23] In short, academic freedom extended to students slides effortlessly into the end of freedom for teachers. In the name of diversity, debate, and openness, the bill is tantamount to a ban on politics in the classroom. And this is the point. In spite of the difficulties around discerning what exactly constitutes "politics" and who will decide such matters, the bill has already had much success. Horowitz's legislation has been proposed in no less than twenty-seven states. As John Wilson observes, Horowitz's Academic Bill of Rights passed the Georgia Senate on March 2004 by an astonishing 41 to 5 vote and Jeff Sessions, Republican from Alabama, has sponsored an academic bill of rights resolution before the U.S. Senate.[24] Moreover, several individual campuses have already enacted some version of the bill, such as Utah State University and Occidental College, with similar efforts at Cornell University, University of North Florida, University of Montana, Roger Williams University, and many other institutions. The recent controversy over the remarks of former University of Colorado professor Ward Churchill has spearheaded legislative proposals in Colorado, Florida, and other states.

Much important work has been done on the impact of 9/11 on the university, especially in terms of the neo-McCarthyite attacks on professors and students who raised critical questions about U.S. foreign policy, its militarism, its apparent contempt for international governing bodies like the UN, the policing of Middle East area studies, and the stepped-up surveillance and harassment of Islamic students and teachers from the Immigration Office—now folded into Homeland Security—to the hallowed space of the classroom. What I have attempted to demonstrate here is less along the lines of the now-trite assertion that "everything fundamentally changed" after 9/11, but rather to claim that the War on Terror, and the resultant backlash against the university, is not a radical departure into some unknown, uncharted political territory, but rather the culmination of political, economic, and cultural forces set into motion decades before. The context for the conservative "culture wars" waged against a "political correct" academy and its alleged race-class-gender fanaticism in the 1980s and 1990s was a broader domestic assault on people of color in the name of the war on drugs and the war on crime. The redoubled attack on the academy under the rubric of the War on Terror and its commensurate insistence on patriotic correctness invokes a racially coded international threat (a "clash of civilizations," in its public articulation) and retools its rhetoric to mimic, even as it silences, left-liberal critique.

With respect to both its domestic and international policy, it appears the United States is once again, to invoke Morrison's serviceable phrase, "playing in the dark."[25] As Morrison considered the major themes and presumptions of the national literature—autonomy, authority, newness and difference, absolute power—she arrived at a kind of epiphany that proved as relevant to George W. Bush's America as it had been more than a decade ago: "Autonomy is freedom and translates into the much championed and revered 'individualism'; newness translates into 'innocence'; distinctiveness becomes difference and the erection of strategies to maintain it; authority and absolute power become a romantic, conquering 'heroism,' virility, and the problematics of wielding absolute power over the lives of others. All the rest are made possible by this last . . . absolute power called forth and played against . . . a 'raw, half-savage world' . . . [savage because] peopled by a nonwhite indigenous population."[26] As rampant individualism hardens into alienation, isolation, and pugilistic arrogance, we are left to ponder: What is America always so insistently innocent of? What is the connection between American freedom and its passion for swaggering masculinist militarism? Its presumption of civilization against the annihilating threat of a dark other? In the name of student academic freedom, such questions could be purged from university classrooms, just as they are increasingly disappeared from mainstream media. "Through the simple expedient of demonizing and reifying the range of color on a palette," Morrison concludes, racialism "makes it possible to say and not say, to inscribe and erase, to escape and engage, to act out and act on. . . . It provides a way to contemplat[e] chaos and civilization, desire and fear, and a mechanism for testing the problems and blessings of freedom."[27] The "new" conservative assault on the university in the context of permanent war can fruitfully be seen as an expansion of, rather than a departure from, its domestic corollary and its racially coded recourse to cultural and civilizational differences, even as both lay claims to race neutrality. The recourse to colorblind rhetoric and its commitments to inclusion and diversity, purged of historical memory and material relations of power, has proven an effective bulwark against anti-racist organization and reform, as new educational and legislative demands shift accordingly "from redressing past and present racist exclusion to protecting the expression of private racial preference in the 'racial marketplace'" of ideas as it excises them from intellectual discussion and debate.[28]

Tragically, little may change with the election of the first African American to the office of president in 2008, in a time of skyrocketing unemployment, impoverishment, and home foreclosure that threatens the "destruction of the black middle class," to say nothing of the exacerbated suffering of the racial poor.[29] Although it is still early in his administration, Barack Obama has thus far steered clear of any plans for the redress of racial inequality and injustice historically or currently—nor for that matter has he organized an anti-poverty campaign. And although he has drawn much inspiration and insight from Dr. Martin Luther King, he has visibly distanced himself from every other living civil rights leader and much of the substance of that tradition. Of course, to have done otherwise, as David Roediger and others have argued, would have greatly strained his run for office and cooled his reception among white voters.[30] Reluctantly or willingly, Obama has chosen to capitulate to the nation's collective refusal to address race and, more shamefully, its willful denial of ongoing racist exploitation, exclusion, humiliation, and violence. He and his team of advisers have carefully constructed his public image as a "post-racial" president, insisting that race is no longer a central issue in American life, in spite of the racist iconography that inevitably accompanies the "tea-partiers," the "tenthers," the "patriots," and other right-wing grassroots movements that riveted media attention since the summer of 2009. With this refusal, as well as his decision to forgo legal investigation of war crimes against the key Bush administration officials in the interests of "looking forward," Obama has postponed indefinitely the kind of painful public conversation about past and present expressions of racist violence that Morrison insists is necessary for the very viability of a democratic nation—to say nothing of a peaceful and cosmopolitan new world order.

To be sure, Obama's presidency has come to be perceived as a national triumph against "prejudice" and "hate," among other psychologizing and reductive tropes for racism, as well as a form of redemption—one that affirmatively absolves the nation's centuries-long history of racial injustice. Long before election results were in, one reporter effectively summed up the mainstream media consensus: "If America actually nominates [Obama] and then votes for him for president and elects him, this will be a sign that we are a good and decent country that has healed its racial wounds."[31] But such a hastily drawn conclusion requires a profound theoretical conflation of two antithetical pedagogical and political commitments: "antiracialism," the desire to be done with race, to erase without redress the violence (still) done in its name, and "antiracism," the commitment to end racist exploitation and exclusion. In the *Threat of Race*, Goldberg elaborates on the crucial distinction:

Antiracism requires historical memory, recalling the conditions of racial degradation and relating contemporary to historical and local to global conditions. If anti-racist commitment requires remembering and recalling, antiracialism suggests forgetting, getting over, moving on, wiping away the terms of reference, at best (or worst) a commercial memorialization rather than a recounting and redressing of the terms of humiliation and devaluation. Indeed, antiracialism seeks to wipe out the terms of reference, to wipe away the very vocabulary necessary to recall and recollect, to make a case, to make a claim.[32]

Antiracism as a political commitment makes serious intellectual demands on a citizenry; it requires an attentiveness to history, to painful self-scrutiny. Antiracialism is a flight from memory and at times a flight from reality. In short, antiracism is an educational project; anti-racialism is anti-educational, and, I hope to make the case in the next chapter, an anti-intellectual one. Ironically, though Obama has capitulated to the fantasy of a colorblind or post-racist era in American politics, the Right has nonetheless made recourse to the language of left extremism, intolerance, and partisanship to describe the president's political commitments and policy initiatives. Nonetheless, Obama's position is entirely in keeping with neoliberalism's racial logic, even as he attempts, often unsuccessfully, to distance himself from its fetishization of the free market. As we shall see in the next chapter, efforts to smear Obama as a socialist or communist or worse began on the campaign trail, with the McCain/Palin camp insisting that the senator from Chicago "palled around with terrorists," who just happened to be in the academy.

CHAPTER THREE

The Age of Unreason: Race and the Drama of American Anti-Intellectualism

Anti-Intellectualism in American Life: The Resurrection

In late October 2008, just days before the U.S. presidential election, George Monbiot of London's *The Guardian*, caught perhaps in a mood of deepening anxiety and dread over the impending outcome, leveled an indictment against the American government and at least half of the electorate in the form of a question: "How did politics in the U.S. come to be dominated by people who make a virtue out of ignorance?" In a rather unkind primatological allusion, he invoked as evidence the eight-year reign of George W. Bush, the recent vogue of Sarah Palin—and before her, Dan Quayle, apparently to round out the VP wing of "gibbering numbskulls" past and present—as well as the "screaming ignoramuses" in attendance at Republican rallies who insisted that Barack Obama was both a Muslim and a terrorist. "Like most people on my side of the Atlantic," he ventured, "I have for many years been mystified by American politics. The U.S. has the world's best universities and attracts the world's finest minds. It dominates in discoveries in science and medicine. Its wealth and power depend on the application of knowledge. Yet, uniquely among the developed nations . . . learning is a grave political disadvantage."[1] A troubling observation to be sure. How exactly does one make sense of, let alone respond to, such an astonishing contradiction, such an ungenerous play on the concept of American exceptionalism? There are, of course, a number of possibilities. (a) Denial: reduce the charge to a hiccup of European arrogance tinged with a bit of resentment. (b) Dismissal: declaim as cynical the blanket condemnation of ineptitude among government officials and the fools who elected them. (c) Deflection: assert that the election results—and the resounding defeat handed to the McCain-Palin campaign, which ran primarily on emotional appeals to fear and patriotic fervor—vindicate the good sense of the voters and render Monbiot's judgment too quick. It would be tempting to answer "(d) all of the above" and continue to bask in the warm afterglow of the Obama victory and the ensuing worldwide celebration that marked the end of the Bush era. But, alas, we are not saved.

Indeed the pre-election antics appeared in hindsight little more than an opening prelude to the "delirium," as *The Economist* termed it, of the summer of 2009 debates on health care; the furor over the president's "indoctrination" of school children; the growing momentum of the "birthers," unchecked by repeated proof against their claims; and other crazed conspiracy theorists who showed up at town hall meetings armed to the teeth, leaving many to wonder why the nation surrendered public debate over the most pressing political issues of our time (to say nothing of media coverage) to the most extreme and unstable elements of the far right.[2] Even the esteemed journalist Bill Moyers, deeply unsettled by current events, couldn't resist a bit of uncharacteristic sarcasm: "So here we are, wallowing in our dysfunction. Governed—if you listen to the rabble rousers—by a black nationalist from Kenya smuggled into the United States to kill Sarah Palin's baby."[3] The peculiar degradation of these three fundaments of a substantive democracy—informed and judicious political discourse, intelligence, and education—in contemporary American politics to which Monbiot and others refer has had a long and storied career, extending back to the early days of the republic. The subject was given unparalleled examination in Richard Hofstadter's Pulitzer-prize winning volume, *Anti-Intellectualism in American Life,* published in 1963. It is important to note, however, that for Hofstader anti-intellectuals are neither the "gibbering numbskulls" nor the "screaming ignoramuses" that Monbiot and a growing chorus of journalists, scholars, and others criticize. Rather, Hofstadter viewed them as a far more effective enemy to the educated mind and to a vibrant, democratic political culture, which requires for its very survival an abiding commitment on the part of its citizenry to critical thought, moral judgment, the capacity for self-reflection, and an acute awareness of self-limitation. Neither uneducated nor unintellectual, anti-intellectuals constitute the ranks of the "half-educated," men and women who are "deeply engaged with ideas, often obsessively engaged with this or that outworn or rejected idea."[4] Hofstadter describes them as hardly indifferent or hostile to the life of the mind, but as "marginal intellectuals, would-be intellectuals, unfrocked or embittered intellectuals, the literate leaders of the semi-literate, full of seriousness and high purpose about the causes that bring them to the attention of the world."[5] Indeed, he notes, even the most rigorous thinkers are not immune to anti-intellectual moments. Writing in the immediate aftermath of McCarthy era, he locates among the anti-intellectual vanguard the following: highly intelligent and articulate evangelical ministers; religious fundamentalists of various sorts; politicians who inflamed populist and nationalist sentiment (including, he notes, some of the shrewdest); businessmen and other self-appointed spokespersons for practicality, utilitarianism, and free enterprise; right-wing editors with strong intellectual pretensions; anti-Communist pundits; and for that matter, Communist leaders, who held intellectuals in high suspicion, if not contempt. What such a disparate assemblage of characters share is a kind of militancy fueled by a severe, fundamentalist morality; he calls them "one hundred percenters," who brook no ambiguities, doubts, equivocations, reservations, and certainly no criticism. Such rigidity they consider evidence of their own toughness and strength—as well as, revealingly, a testament to their masculinity.[6]

Following Hofstader's logic into the present moment, we would add to these ranks latter-day market fundamentalists, such as Jim Cramer and other disciples of the brilliant and tragically myopic Milton Freedman, and their powerful and embittered friends in the conservative movement, such as the peerless Grover Norquist and Karl Rove, Bush's reputed brain; the intellectual denizens of highly partisan think tanks, from the American Heritage Institute to the Heritage, Olin, Schaiffe, and Coors foundations, like Charles Murray; as well as their learned counterparts in the academy, like Lawrence Mead or Samuel Huntington; the various crusaders of the Christian right, like Pat Robertson, who called for the assassination of a world leader, and others who rail against science and the rights of women and gays such as Bill McCartney, the founder of the Promise Keepers; demagogic populists like Patrick Buchanan and Rush Limbaugh; jingoistic patriots inspired by Newt Gingrich and Tom DeLay; and the impassioned, often inflammatory anti-immigration and anti-terrorist politicians and media pundits, of whom there are far too many, such as Tom Tancredo, Thelma Drake, Bill O'Reilly, Ann Coulter, Lou Dobbs, Glenn Beck. And we would acknowledge, as we do so, the continuing draw of masculinist posturing for both men and women. For nearly four decades, these "leaders of the semi-literate" have assisted in the transformation not only of all three branches of government but of the political culture of the nation as well, swaying the voting public through base appeals to our deepest insecurities and fears, most typically expressed and circulated through racially charged representational codes. In apocalyptic tones, they warned that "traditional American values" and "our American way of life" were on the brink of collapse as a result of some marauding horde—thugged-out young black men, welfare queens, overpopulating Latinos, illegal immigrants, radical Jihadists, or "gay married terrorists" (in economist Paul Krugman's satiric phrase). And most Americans went along for the ride. Even those who didn't buy the coded rhetoric (even as they enjoyed the privileges of a still-uneven playing field) complacently went about their lives, feasting on too-easy credit, flipping houses, or fixating on celebrity culture until all the consumer bubbles finally broke. Though the candidate who stood for change, for a restoration of democratic principle against a rising tide of fundamentalisms—market, military, religious—won the 2008 election by a respectable but not overwhelming margin, the legacy of the last forty years of conservative counterrevolution did not magically disappear after Inauguration Day.[7]

Nearly a half-century after it was written, Hofstadter's erudite volume remains essential reading for those troubled by the effects of anti-intellectualism, and the various fundamentalisms that inspire and inflame it, on democratic public life and political culture. In fact, his uncompromising analysis of the political climate in which Thomas Jefferson ran for president in the infamous 1800 election—an election that also signaled a revolutionary shift in the political direction of the nation—is particularly instructive in light of the 2008 campaign, which uncannily recapitulated many of the same themes. Jefferson was the first distinguished victim of a decisively anti-intellectual attack, and the assault on him (leveled principally by Federalist leaders and members of the established clergy) set a precedent for subsequent efforts to render an active, curious mind either trivial and ridiculous or evil and dangerous. The echoes of such efforts to sway the electorate on principles that violate reason, reflection, evidence, and judgment are heard to this day: intellect makes "men" timid and ineffectual; they are likely to vacillate rather than to act boldly in the face of crisis; their intellectual pursuits produce in general a suspicion of, or a hostility to, Christianity; and they are committed to abstract, radical, or even "foreign" ideas over the quintessential American values of God and country.

The capacity for reflective, creative, and critical thought, finely honed argumentation, and public persuasion—talents one might otherwise assume well recommend a candidate for the office of president—were transformed into the gravest of liabilities. Jefferson's critics assailed his philosophical training and literary talents, which they insisted made him unfit for practical tasks. Their eager acknowledgment of the elegance of his rhetorical style provided only further proof of the man's lack of political substance. Said one South Carolina congressman, William Loughton Smith:

The characteristic traits of a philosopher, when he turns politician, are, timidity, whimsicalness, and a disposition to reason from certain principles, and not from the true nature of man; a proneness to predicate all his measures on certain abstract theories, formed in the recess of his cabinet, and not on the existing state of things and circumstances; an inertness of mind, as applied to governmental policy, *a wavering of disposition when great and sudden emergencies demand promptness of decision and energy of action.*[8]

Thought, according to those suspicious of a critical and contemplative mind, inevitably got in the way of action. In addition to these offenses, Jefferson also stood accused of a lack of experience, particularly military experience—the very ingredient which had made his esteemed predecessor, George Washington, a patriot, a man of great character, and an effective, no-nonsense leader. Smith, contriving to portray Jefferson's astonishing and wide-ranging intellectual abilities as trivial and ridiculous, mocked his scientific interests and his inventiveness as "impaling butterflies and insects, and contriving turn-about chairs" adding that such merits "might entitle him to the Professorship of a college" but were utterly incompatible with the duties of the presidency and the command of the Western Army.[9]

Such charges should sound strangely familiar. Barack Obama's reflective capacities and rhetorical strengths have been frequently acknowledged by his opponents, who, interestingly enough, hailed from similar quarters: the religious right and Republican descendants of Federalist persuasion. But the praise, like that heaped on Jefferson, primarily served to underscore allegations of inexperience and unbridled idealism. Like its distant predecessor, the election of 2008 was framed as a choice between military experience and character—the strength of which seemed to rest on an ex-soldier's patriotic zeal and plain speech, on the one hand, and change—in the figure of a young cosmopolitan and former University of Chicago professor of law who represented new ideas, gifted oratory, and hope—on the other. Then, as now, when the bad news befalls the White House—whether by messenger on horseback or emergency phone call—at three o'clock in the morning, Americans are prompted to vote for a man of action, not intelligence, which is derided as inevitably naïve, "timid," "abstract," or "wavering." Whereas the former law professor was said to lack any military experience and have negligible foreign policy credentials, McCain emphasized his war record, his heroism, his endurance, as vouchsafed by his five-year imprisonment in a Viet Cong POW camp, and above all his patriotism.

Appeals to practicality and patriotism were not the only rhetorical weapons in the arsenal of Jefferson's opponents—or Obama's. Hofstadter regales his readers with various efforts to paint Jefferson as a dangerous scourge without faith or morals. His learning and speculation, it was said, made an atheist of Jefferson; he had not only challenged theologians about the age of the earth but opposed having school children read the Bible— vagaries that made him a threat to religion and society. Further proof of his alleged immorality was offered in a litany of accusations: that he was a coward during the Revolutionary War, that he started the French Revolution, that he harbored a secret ambition to become a dictator, another Bonaparte. And strikingly, though Hofstadter makes only a passing reference to the charge, the integrity of this white, patrician male was tainted by an association with race: it was asserted that he "kept a slave wench and sired mulattoes," a dishonor less to his wife than to his white blood—thus, according to the racial reasoning of the time, proof of moral depravity.

Obama was subject to similar demagogic efforts throughout the seemingly interminable two-year campaign cycle. While McCain played the role of the valiant soldier and patriot, Obama stood accused of "palling around with terrorists" like University of Illinois at Chicago professor Bill Ayers and other subversive intellectuals (a redundancy for conservatives). Moreover, Obama's Christianity was called into question repeatedly with insinuations of his secret Muslim faith, as if the espousal of such doctrines were adequate grounds to disqualify him immediately from political office. Indeed, it was Sarah Palin's very religiosity—in addition to other perceived assets including her folksy demeanor, her status as mother of five, her fascination with guns, and not so implicitly her whiteness as mirrored in the clean, white snows of the Alaskan wilderness—that made this contemporary Annie Oakley such an appealing vice presidential pick for the McCain team. She embraced the very commitments and values of the Republicans' most stalwart constituency: the Christian right. In contrast, much was made of Obama's middle name, "Hussein," which was chanted over and over again at Republican rallies, betraying similar efforts to associate him with the dangerous Middle Eastern dictator, if not quite claiming, as in Jefferson's case, that he aspired to become a despot. (That accusation, of course, would come within Obama's first six months of office, when during the summer of 2009, angry constituents at town hall meetings would tout images of the president with a Hitler moustache or feature him on placards with Stalin, Mao, or Che Guevara.) Such charges performed a double duty for the Obama's critics, casting "Barack Hussein Obama" as not only a threat to all Christians, but beyond the pale of whiteness, both as a man of African descent and as an alleged Muslim, a category that increasingly carries both religious and ethno-racial "civilizational" implication.

Just as Jefferson's intellectual disposition, his sensibilities, his tastes were pilloried as "foreign," a clear precursor to contemporary tactics designed to generate fear toward those characterized as "not American," Barack Obama was consistently characterized as alien. Of Jefferson, one

Federalist pamphleteer claimed: "It was in France, where he resided nearly seven years, and until the revolution had made some progress, that his disposition to theory, and his skepticism in religion, morals, and government, acquired full strength and vigor. . . . Mr. Jefferson is known to be a theorist in politics, as well as in philosophy and morals. He is a *philosophe* in the modern French sense of the word."[10] The anti-intellectual rejection of the candidate as a "theorist" and a "*philosophe*" anticipates accusations of anti-Americanism hurled at contemporary intellectuals, particularly those critical of the Bush administration, even as the charge ironically depicts thinking as a foreign, even subversive activity. Obama was not only educated in various regions of the world including Indonesia, Africa and the United States, but he was also of mixed-race heritage. Most definitely, it was implied, where not emphatically stated, he was "not one of us."[11] Of course, like Jefferson, Barack Obama did win the presidential election; but the rather shocking figure of the fifty-eight million (46 percent of the popular) votes cast for the McCain-Palin ticket, despite its many allegiances to the utterly corrupt and generally despised Bush administration, should give us pause. This brief engagement with the Jeffersonian legacy is all the more revealing for the decidedly ironic way in which Jefferson, and much of the iconography of the American Revolution, has been appropriated by the far right in post-election America—from "tea parties," to the incessant appearance of the Gladstone flag and other militia flags featuring rattlesnakes and often accompanied by the slogan, "Don't Tread on Me," to the "patriot movement" (and its various calls for revolution, succession, and state sovereignty), which has made Jefferson's quip that "the tree of liberty must be refreshed from time to time with the blood of tyrants and patriots" its rallying cry.

Historically speaking, the suspicion of intellect has for centuries spawned a variety of anti-intellectual commitments—the fetishization of folksiness, the cult of efficiency and practicality, jingoistic patriotism, militarized masculinity, and religious fervor. Whereas in the era in which Hofstadter wrote it was still possible to equate mainstream intellectual culture with the culture of liberalism, this is no longer the case. The below-the-radar conservative counter-revolution begun in the late 1960s, coterminous with a highly visible repressive law-and-order crackdown on various civil rights and anti-war protesters, and eventually displaced the liberal hegemony of mid-century America, as its advocates exploited and intensified the anti-intellectualism of the culture. The consequence of this ascendancy has been a crisis of liberal ideals and democratic values, of the very possibility of politics, which has generated a cottage industry of similarly themed tomes that commence where Hofstadter's probing analysis left off. Indeed, whereas Hofstadter believed anti-intellectual resentments were a pervasive rather than a dominant force in public life, current analyses of the post–civil rights era—which examine the ascendancy of consumerism, celebrity culture, and the sound-bite culture of media infotainment, as well as deepening cultural conservatism, militarism, and fundamentalist revivalism—would suggest otherwise. Susan Jacoby's *The Age of American Unreason* and Al Gore's *The Assault on Reason* are notable among the most recent analyses—and it is to the former that George Monbiot defers for understanding this strange dimension of American political culture. To be sure, in our efforts to come to terms with the contradictory nature of contemporary American politics, there is much to be productively assimilated from these works. However, my central thesis in this chapter is that another dimension of American anti-intellectualism, which is given only passing attention in Hofstadter's otherwise comprehensive analysis and in more recent treatments of this tragic theme: the preeminent role of that race plays in defining, delimiting, and at times derailing moral judgment, reflectiveness, and reason itself—and most emphatically in an era that has come to define itself as "post-racial."

Race and the Drama of American Anti-Intellectualism

In Richard Hofstadter's defense, at least until the mid-twentieth century racial thought still carried the imprimatur of scientific and social validity, such that its adherents might avoid charges of anti-intellectual investment. That moment has passed. I argue, in fact, that the anti-intellectual dimensions of racial thought emerge most strikingly not simply with the battalions of embittered and resentful "Angry White Men" that figures like Rush Limbaugh, Newt Gingrich, and Glenn Beck unleashed on the dominant media, but with the generalized and pervasive repression of racial memory and history, even of reference to race, associated with the ascendancy of colorblind consciousness over the past several decades. Consider Limbaugh's characterization of Obama's reaction to the news of the arrest of Harvard professor Henry Louis Gates in his own home as "a black president trying to destroy a white policeman,"[12] or the leap of logic in Limbaugh's depiction of "Obama's America: white kids getting beat up on school buses now. I mean, you put your kids on a school bus, you expect safety, but in Obama's America, the white kids now get beat up with the black kids cheering."[13] Or Beck's accusation that Obama is a racist, harboring a "deep-seated hatred for white people or the white culture,"[14] which one would have to assume includes most of his cabinet, his top advisors, and his own mother. But one doesn't dare call these folks racist. The specter of white victimization by a malicious black presence in the White House, who apparently has it in for the police, children, and all white people, is compounded by accusations of racism hurled at those who attempt to expose it. Even as Obama and his spokespersons invariably deny that racism is behind his critics' attacks, Limbaugh insists: "Today, it's all based in racism—the criticisms of Obama's health care plan or whatever." A pious Gingrich agrees, "I think it's very destructive in America to suggest that we can't criticize a president without it being a racial act."[15] Incensed by their own false allegations that the Obama administration "plays the race card," Beck, Limbaugh, and others spend hours on the airwaves cataloguing equally fictitious claims of bias against whites. What follows, then, is an analysis of the impassioned obsessions, absolutist pretensions, and forms of willful intellectual myopia (even purposeful misdirection) Hofstadter characterized as anti-intellectual, which I am here suggesting also drive contemporary colorblinding racism—both in mainstream national political debate and in the not-so-hallowed halls of academe. In relation to the last-mentioned charge, I should hasten to acknowledge that scholarly allegiance to colorblindness is not all of a piece. The refusal to "see race," as we saw in Chapter 2, is often presumed to be a "graceful" and "liberal" (if "lobotomizing") gesture, as Toni Morrison so keenly observed. But for others, such refusal is celebrated as a marker of the professional expert's detachment and objectivity, or it is more militantly defended as a form of *realpolitik* waged against pernicious forms of identitarian distraction.

In defining what I mean by colorblind racism—and what all of these positions share, however variously justified—I draw on the expansive work of David Theo Goldberg. The appeal to racelessness, or colorblindness, he concisely explains,

> is the neoliberal attempt to go beyond—without (fully) coming to terms with—racial histories and their accompanying racist inequalities and iniquities; to mediate racially classed and gendered distinctions to which those histories have given rise without reference to the racial terms of those distinctions; *to transform, via the negating dialectic of denial and ignoring, racially marked social orders into racially erased ones.*[16]

Given Goldberg's characterization, the leap from "Whites Only" signs to the anxiously insistent claims that "I don't see race"—from systemic forms of racial exclusion to systemic denials of the past and present consequences of racial exclusion—is perhaps not so great a leap after all. What we have "achieved" in post–civil rights America, if one wishes to call it an achievement, is not so much the "end of racism," as some (anti)intellectuals insist, but rather the end of racial referencing, the repressive silencing of the ongoing and determinant role that race plays in American life. What is publicly unspeakable has thus come to be privately embraced; if the state no longer discriminates, it remains open to the discretion of private citizens whom they will hire, or rent to, or admit, or provide professional services to. Call it, in good neoliberal fashion, deregulated racism. This is also what Goldberg terms, in keeping with the fundamentalist tenor of the times, "saved" racism or "born again racism." "Born again racism," he explains, is "racism without race, racism gone private, racism without the categories to name it as such." It is "racism shorn of the charge, a racism that cannot be named . . . ," a "racism acknowledged, where acknowledged at all, as individualized faith . . . rather than institutionalized inequality."[17] Not only, he points out, are such preference-based racist exclusions and privileges deemed acceptable in the private sphere, but they are also rendered immune from state intervention, and so from forms of official protection or legal redress.[18] Colorblind policy thus introduces a standard of justice focused on the protection of individual rights—preeminently the right to express one's own private racial preferences—with no regard for the consequential exclusion of an entire group, so long as such denials are neither created nor implemented by the state.

How do we account, then, for racism's astonishing durability, its "born again" status as America's civic religion—its treatment, in other words, as a set of privately held, religious-like beliefs with which the state dares not interfere? Few ideas have been exposed, over and over in the last fifty years, as quite so empty, quite so analytically void, and yet have continued to hold such passionate attraction, even for some of the most learned minds, as the concept of race. To be sure, racial logics and the racisms to which they give rise have been historically and presently driven by "rational" interests: power, resources, land, and labor. Even so, socio-economic, political, and sociological explanations of racism, as Goldberg has rightly argued, fail to account for its deeply compelling character, its ongoing persuasiveness for subjects.[19] The discourses of racism also participate in the drama of self-recognition and the recognition of (potential) group members; it defines not only otherness but subjectivity as well, and as such it is never merely an extension of economic exploitation. It constitutes an order of alterity invested with a high degree of ambivalence, uncertainty, and danger as well as deeply held, or (what Goldberg calls, following Sartre) "passionate" beliefs about dangers posed by Others as well as the perceived safety and predictability of sameness, the security of social homogeneity.[20] And the rationalities, technologies, and governmentalities that secure what Goldberg calls "states of whiteness" correspondingly shift in keeping with historically transforming social conditions, from the state imposition of legal segregation, to assimilative strategies, to those that aspire to nonracialism or "racelessness," even as "whiteness remains unquestioned as the arbiter of value, the norm of acceptability, quality, and standard of merit."[21]

Lewis Gordon extends the Sartrean analysis of racism as passion, illuminating the ways in which racists affectively invest in a form of evasion, in a "magic" world or a distorted reality. Racists, Gordon argues, insistently place the Other in the category of socially *inferior*, which "serves as a ready-made outlet for deeper, immediate efforts at self-evasion," an evasion that is, moreover, institutionally encouraged when for example material resources, labor, and power are at stake.[22] So, too, the same might be said for those who place the racial Other in the category of the socially *invisible*. The more racists indulge in the game of evasion, the more estranged and "serious" they become, propelling them (masochistically) further still into the make-believe world required to maintain this correlative "magical" evasion. Quite interestingly for our purposes, Sartrean "serious" racists bear a striking resemblance to Hofstadter's absolutist and obsessed anti-intellectuals; they are not "irrational," but rather "nonrational" or "unreasonable," in that they have chosen to adopt false beliefs—racial inferiority or racial transcendence—with the same emotional sense of urgency and the same disregard for evidence and logic. Neither incapacitated nor impaired, racists in this discourse are thus responsible for their choices, for choosing to reside in that region of reasoning consciousness that can accommodate contradiction, paradox, irony, and self-delusion. In Sartre's own words:

> Thus, man is always a wizard to man, and the social world is at first magical. . . . What happens, then, when the superstructures laboriously built by reason cave in and man finds himself once again abruptly plunged into the original magic? It is easy to guess; consciousness seizes upon the magical as magical; it forcibly lives it as such. The categories of "suspicious," of "alarming," designate the magical insofar as it is lived by consciousness, insofar as it urges consciousness to live it. The abrupt passage from a rational apprehension of the world to a perception of the same world as magical, if it is motivated by the object itself and if it is accompanied by a disagreeable element, is horror; if it is accompanied by an agreeable element it is wonder.[23]

Sartre is thus able to capture the intense emotional activity—the horror, paranoia, suspicion, gloom, and fear—that corresponds to the "magical world" that racists inhabit. To be sure, contemporary experiences of ever-increasing volatility, insecurity, fear, and violence create conditions conducive to such racist projections. Yet daunting questions remain in our "post-racial era" about how racially rendered and radically unequal social relations are thus "saved" and able to outlive the formal dismantling of legal apparatuses of segregation, exploitation, and exclusion, how race is so persistently able to structure and define in such compelling ways radically transforming configurations of social relations. How might we make sense of the new racism, discursively reconfigured as race transcendence or race-lessness, which provides its adherents with a refuge from a reality that remains determined by race, a "magic world" that undermines the critical capacities, to say nothing of the humanity, of democratic citizens at every turn—with deeply consequential, catastrophic effects? The following sections comprise an effort to think through these questions, albeit in a partial and incomplete way given the complexity of the task at hand, beginning with an examination of the individual beliefs and institutional forces being played out in national political debate that collaborate with the contemporary recoil from thought.

In the latter half of this chapter, my focus shifts to examine the discursive deployment of race in the ongoing drama of American anti-intellectualism in what may seem like an unusual venue—the university and the role that academics perform therein. It is worth recalling again, from this book's Introduction, Drew Gilpin Faust's assessment of the university's "crisis of purpose," and asking with her why the university and its resident intellectuals do not offer a firmer counterweight to our gross economic irresponsibility—or to our military misconduct, if not war crimes, or the expanding police state at home, to name only the boldest and baldest expressions of racially driven neoliberalization. Thus, I'm concerned to explore such questions as these: How are university educators complicit with the logic of what David Theo Goldberg effectively calls "racial neoliberalism," which underscores the deeply entwined and informing nature of the privatizations advanced by the new racism and neoliberal agendas? And how might educators, conversely, intervene in and challenge this peculiar dimension of American anti-intellectualism? In the 1950s, Joseph McCarthy did much to cement in the public imaginary the relationship between the university, as the very seat of intellectual culture, and the forces of subversion threatening the vaunted American way of life. But it was later, with the student revolts of the 1960s and then the culture wars of the 1980s and 1990s, that the university's fate was sealed. In Chapter 2, I examined the accusations of anti-Americanism and pro-terrorist sympathizing against those (relative few) in the university who challenged the Bush-era "clash of civilizations" thesis and the policies mandating the use of force that issued from it—pre-emptive military strikes, the use of torture, and racial profiling, among other transgressions of human and civil rights—by various reactionary watchdog groups bent on threats and intimidation. I also investigated the ways in which scholarly participation in the culturalization and privatization of racism have rendered such forms of state violence all but invisible. This studied indifference to questions of power and history in turn impoverished the very anti-racist policies that universities have advanced in the name of tolerance, diversity, and multiculturalism.

There are solid ethical grounds for challenging the various practices that go under these progressive-sounding headings—principally that they don't go nearly far enough in their alleged commitment to equality and racial justice. I have even challenged the viability of such terms as "diversity" and "balance" in favor of those that are less amenable to co-optation and more pointedly invested in anti-racist policy and power sharing. I remind readers of this in order to underscore the difference between my position and two variants of multicultural attack that have come to influence mainstream pedagogical practice of late and that participate, in my view, in the racially consequential anti-intellectual tendencies that have been the hallmark of the contemporary "colorblind" era. Again, I use anti-intellectual in Hofstadter's sense of the term; its adherents are not unintellectual, but rather "passionate" and "one hundred percent" committed to false or rejected ideas—which, in this case, I extend to the "magical" raceless logics of the post–civil rights university. Many educators, rather ironically, advance anti-intellectual modes of analysis and model "critical" dispositions that reproduce the make-believe world of a neoliberalized, "post-racial" society under the mantle of professional detachment, on the one hand, or a high-minded liberal crusade for the now-forgotten working classes, whose interests fail to register in the miasmas produced by the university's infatuation with racial identities and diversity, on the other.

Of course, it should have been otherwise. Given the ways in which the civil rights struggles of the 1960s tied the advance of both civil rights and human rights agendas most emphatically to the right to literacy as a democratic necessity, one should have expected the university, first among those institutions that take as their mission the shaping and educating of good citizens, to challenge and transform the anti-intellectual resentments that have driven right-wing, often fundamentalist agendas of the last forty years. Yet reactionary interests often cite the 1960s, and the progressive transformation of university curricula and modes of governance that were the fruit of student revolts, as the real source of the "closing of the American mind," as one critic infamously put it.[24] Often described in vivid, bellicose terms, the campus "culture wars" were never so dramatically pitched; the casual observer would have witnessed over the course of three decades a decidedly uneventful and one-sided match, featuring much more pandering and capitulation than robust challenge to the forces of racial reaction and corporate restructuring.

Race and the War on Reality 1.0:
The Southern Strategy

Although the verdict of Obama's first year in office has been decidedly mixed, few would disagree that the outcome of election cycles prior to 2008—accompanied by a paucity of intellectual leadership or debate, a fourth estate in high retreat, and voters generally distracted and disengaged—has been anything short of disastrous. Fueled by the terrorist attacks of September 2001, Bush and the Republican Party—infamously disdainful of ideas, reason, logical argumentation, evidence, or precise language in its single-minded pursuit of Empire—succeeded in selling the American public on the concept of permanent, "civilizational" war abroad, while it waged another, more covert war on the domestic front. The borderless War on Terrorism, of course, continues unabated (despite regime change at home) as Afghani caves are blown up in search of the ever-elusive Bin Laden and foreign-looking or foreign-sounding students in the United States are routinely surveilled, harassed, corralled, and interrogated. (In fact, Obama has sent tens of thousands more American troops to Afghanistan, as he proceeds with a formal drawdown from Iraq.) As the war in Iraq approached its seventh year with no clear end yet in sight, nearly 4,700 lives had been lost, tens of thousands of severely wounded soldiers had returned home often without limbs, often with brain damage, to an utterly broken medical system. Estimates of the projected cost of this war have reached upwards of three trillion dollars—a staggering price tag as we attempt to recover from global economic collapse and rising demand for multi-billion dollar bailouts. The massive human rights violations that Abu Ghraib and Guantanamo have come to symbolize have further cost the United States its world reputation as guardian of democratic freedom, human rights, and global justice. Such consequences were not exactly unforeseen; indeed, overwhelming opposition to the war came from constituencies less impervious to thought, as multiple and varied as "old Europe," the Pope, world leaders for peace like Nelson Mandela and Jimmy Carter, high-ranking military officials in the Pentagon, and literally millions of everyday people on six continents worldwide. And yet one still hears rumors of a coming showdown with Iran or North Korea, with the cost in human life and economic stability worldwide anybody's guess. But the Bush years in particular have been defined by a below-the-official-radar but no less comprehensive war within the nation's borders—that is, until events like Hurricane Katrina and three years later the "financial Katrina" blew into full view heretofore-invisible populations of the impoverished and disposable.[25] Criminalized and convicted with the guilt of their own exclusion, they make up the nation's ever-swelling ranks of the homeless, destitute, or incarcerated, with one of every hundred adults now sentenced to jail or prison.[26] But this war has proven more difficult to name. A race war? A class war? A war on children? Urban centers? Civil liberties? The Constitution? Women's right to privacy?

Compelling evidence for each interpretation abounds, but perhaps at bottom, driving all such expressions, has been a War on Reality. Like the wars in Iraq and Afghanistan, it has not been met without protest or challenge, however ineffectual. To such opposition, the usual ham-fisted techniques of censorship and intimidation have been applied, as again we saw in Chapter 2, in the context of right-wing assaults on the university, the alleged "weak link in the War on Terror." But, as Susan Jacoby notes, there are other ways of silencing the exchange of ideas and intellectual debate vital to democratic life. She recounts a conversation journalist Ron Suskind reported to have had with a senior Bush aide (widely believed to be Karl Rove). The aide informed Suskind that he and other members of the press were part of what the Bush administration liked to call "the reality-based community," which consists of those who "believe that solutions emerge from judicious study of discernible reality." However, the aide insisted, "That's not the way the world really works anymore. We're an empire now, and when we act, we create our own reality. And while you're studying that reality—judiciously, as you will—we'll act again, creating other new realities, which you can study too. . . . We're history's actors . . . and you, all of you, will be left to just study what we do."[27] As Jacoby's analysis of this exchange rightly concludes, the explicit distinction between those (only) fit for the task of "judicious study"—and as such, relegated to irrelevance—and those who "act" and in the process "make history" disparages those who require logic and evidence, rather than power and emotion, in the crafting and implementation of public policy.

How is it that such an audacious strategy would appear to have worked with a majority of the American public? And how is it that those who make their living as "judicious studiers" had indeed been moved, or moved themselves, ever more effectively to the margins of a putatively open and informed democratic polity? What sets of appeals would be so strong, so compelling as to render an electorate so indifferent or impervious to reality—and, it would appear, to thought itself? I would like to advance the claim that the most powerful and most emotional appeals of the last four decades have been racially predicated. Racist discourse associated with an earlier period of segregation occasionally finds overt expression in public debate—for example, in the association of racially rendered populations with contagion or threat—but such strategies of persuasion have come to carry their own risk in the aftermath of the civil rights movement. What has been called the "Southern strategy," however, provides the one of the best examples of a racial rhetoric that seldom invokes race explicitly and as a result has been able to shape quite successfully mainstream national political debate in the post–civil rights or "post-racial" period of contemporary U.S. history. In short, the Southern strategy presented a racially divided electorate, still reeling from the shocking violence as well as the hard-won socially transformative victories that resulted from civil rights struggles, with a new, coded reality: an abstract, racially evasive, yet racially charged depiction of the country's ills going forward and a rhetorically veiled set of policy "solutions" that nonetheless were understood by white voters to support their perceived interests.[28]

Lee Atwater, the infamous Republican strategist and advisor to Reagan and later to Bush Sr., provides the most succinct—and most brazen—account of how the Southern strategy worked. Alexander P. Lamis, in his *Southern Politics in the 1990s,* interviewed Atwater, engaging him in a quite revealing discussion of politics in the South that is worth citing at length:

Atwater: As to the whole Southern Strategy that Harry Dent and others put together in 1968, opposition to the Voting Rights Act would have been a central part of keeping the South. Now [the new Southern Strategy of Ronald Reagan] doesn't have to do that. All you have to do to keep the South is for Reagan to run in place on the issues he's campaigned on since 1964 . . . and that's fiscal conservatism, balancing the budget, cut taxes, you know, the whole cluster. . . .

Questioner. But the fact is, isn't it, that Reagan does get to the Wallace voter and to the racist side of the Wallace voter by doing away with legal services, by cutting down on food stamps . . . ?

Atwater. You start out in 1954 by saying, "Nigger, nigger, nigger." By 1968 you can't say "nigger"—that hurts you. Backfires. So you say stuff like forced busing, states' rights and all that stuff. You're getting so abstract now [that] you're talking about cutting taxes, and all these things you're talking about are totally economic things and a byproduct of them is [that] blacks get hurt worse than whites.

And subconsciously maybe that is part of it. I'm not saying that. But I'm saying that if it is getting that abstract, and that coded, that we are doing away with the racial problem one way or the other. You follow me—because obviously sitting around saying, "We want to cut this," is much more abstract than even the busing thing, and a hell of a lot more abstract than "Nigger, nigger."[29]

Taking up Atwater's astonishing admission about the Republican party's relentless—and veiled—appeal to racist whites, *New York Times* editorial writer Bob Herbert drew the appropriate conclusion from the above exchange: "Tired of losing elections, [the G.O.P.] saw an opportunity to renew itself by opening its arms wide to white voters who could never forgive the Democratic Party for its support of civil rights and voting rights for blacks."[30] And renew themselves they did, transforming in the process the role of government, economic relations, public consciousness, and political life. In the post–civil rights era, an "abstract" and exclusively economistic language of "tax cuts" and "less government" thus came to replace the language of vicious dehumanization. And yet with that seemingly more benign, less openly aggressive, and "raceless" discursive shift toward privatization, the conditions of violence—against people of color, the compassionate arm of the state, and the very concept of society—escalated as if invisibly.

The Southern strategy offered a more palatable reality, retooled and "recoded" by ex-movie actor Ronald Reagan to sell an embittered white citizenry—a mode of "reality governance" that transformed political culture in ways that prefigured the rise of "reality TV" and its impact on visual culture in the decades to follow. With Reagan, "effective governance," much like a popular televised game show, unleashed the free play of private interests, enjoining citizens—recast in the role of pleasure-seeking consumers and spectators—to find amusement not only in the contest of the fittest, but in the trouncing of the weak. Newly unbound by social obligation or common interest (because there was after all "no such thing as society" in this make-believe universe), the players, in real life and on TV, availed themselves of the new and fast-growing opportunities for violence, exploitation, humiliation, and exclusion that we've now come to associate with the era of economic Darwinism. This, as the very conditions—the time, the space, the civic capacity—for reasoned debate and argument radically diminished. Both government and media advanced a distorted and dystopian reality that hailed the most vile instincts in contemporary subjects—a winner-take-all competitiveness, a ruthless individualization that rendered social solidarities unthinkable, an exultation of mendacity and guile coupled with a disdain for perceived weakness or dependency (more often than not coded as "cultural deficiency," where not overtly criminalized), and a capacity to rationalize, if not take overt pleasure in, the violent exploitation and exclusion of others. Zygmunt Bauman has argued that as "the dividing lines between the 'news', the drama and the game" grew increasingly difficult to decipher, "reality bec[a]me in the process but one of many images, and not a particularly clear or interesting ('amusing') one at that. . . . "[31] Thus, he notes, we have come to find ourselves in Jean Baudrillard's world of simulacra, where images have a competitive advantage over reality, which by comparison seems toned down, if not flatly uninteresting, and technically flawed. But the consequences exceed even this diminishment of collective capacities to discern the "reality-based world" from make-believe. With the dissolution of the dividing line between reality and reality-effects, aesthetic criteria and entertainment value come to displace moral evaluation and responsibility, as evidenced by the success of the catchy advertising slogan for war "shock and awe." And our capacity to think and to judge, our ethical inclinations and our willingness to take responsibility for Others, thus unexercised are left to atrophy and weaken. In combination with a lethal new economic theory that promoted massive deregulation, downsizing, and privatization, the transformation in governance and the corresponding public policy shifts—in short, from welfare state to warfare state—were successful in the first instance because they were, of a piece, perceived to (and did) punish citizens of color. But they promoted, in the end, what

Bauman calls "a constant carnival of cruelty" for nearly all Americans—a funhouse metaphor that appropriately captures the willful public embrace of distorted realities and obscene pleasures that somehow spiraled out of control and turned unsparingly violent.[32] A "constant" carnival, he notes, is indeed no carnival at all.

The Southern strategy and all that it enabled is an example of what David Theo Goldberg ingeniously calls "make believe." Mapping the cultural contours of racial neoliberalism, he captures in this suggestive phrase the repressive capacities of the new market sovereignty in combination with the seemingly self-assertive, self-promoted, and autonomous belief in this most brutally conceived dystopian fantasy, driven by a post–civil rights racist backlash. The electorate was simultaneously persuaded and forced to abandon its one-time manifest support of the social state, in social safety nets, in provisions for those who fall on hard times (or merely grow old or weak or ill), in its participation in a collectivity much greater than the aggregate of its individual(ist) ambitions—in short, in its pursuit of the good society. And race was implicitly and at times explicitly invoked in national debates as the strategy of choice to fuel new anti-statist and anti-political agendas, accelerating the forces of neoliberal privatization and deregulation, as well as the depoliticization of the body politic. The raceless, or colorblind, commitments of the state enabled not only widespread racial backlash in ways gratuitously depicted by Atwater, but also the nearly unchecked ascendancy of neoliberal corporate power, the widening of the gap between the rich and the (increasingly racial) poor, the most regressive tax reform in the nation's history, and the wholesale dismantling of the welfare state, at a time when more citizens needed it than ever. Ongoing debates over who has rights under what conditions and who doesn't, who has the capacity to be productive and self-governing and who hasn't, who can meaningfully participate in public life and who can't, have been recoded in covertly racist terms that the general public often resists recognizing as such. Since the late 1970s, we have been told, for example, of the need to support victims' rights over criminals' rights, to cut taxpayers a break over tax recipients, to transform welfare into back-to-work programs, to end affirmative action in support of "race-transcendent" public policies, to end illegal immigration and protect "American" jobs, even to profile suspicious neighbors in the interests of homeland security. In each instance, reform is tacitly understood to improve the economic security and personal safety of a white electorate at the expense of people of color, while racist assumptions that equate criminality, poverty, and now terror with specific nonwhite populations remain, with few exceptions, unchallenged and unchecked.

To be sure the declining social and economic standing of lower- and now many middle-income whites and blacks since the late 1970s is real and a not-unanticipated result—at least for those who crafted the fantasy—of "free market" economics and racial backlash camouflaged as "colorblind" public policy, which enabled the dismantling of public goods and services as it criminalized the poor. Over the last four decades conservative rhetoric has consistently invoked the evils of state power (particularly the imagined abuses suffered by white taxpayers), the need to shift decision making from the federal to the local level to allegedly "rejuvenate" the public sphere, and the need to dismantle massive federal bureaucracy. The spate of starving and drowning metaphors applied in those years to "big government" references the desire of neoliberals and neoconservatives to disassemble a particular mode of governance that was represented as, and eagerly believed to be, too solicitous of blacks, Latinos, workers, women, environmentalists, and other groups dismissively referred to as "special interest" organizations. This, even as these same "big government" critics simultaneously expanded and strengthened the repressive apparatuses of the state through increased spending on homeland security, border patrol, the military, police, prison building, and various mechanisms for surveillance. Thus conservatives created, in the cruelest of ironies, popular support for policies that merely deepened racially predicated animosities and exclusions, economic disequilibrium, social dislocation, and generalized anxieties and fears among the nation's citizenry. The tax-cutting and privatizing avengers of "big government" aided and abetted a dramatic restructuring of the corporate economy that took every advantage of decentralization, deregulation, and privatization and has nearly bankrupted the federal government, rendering it unable to respond to citizens' needs when worldwide recession finally hit—all the while further deepening the immiseration and incarceration of minority populations. Astonishingly, even as a global economic collapse followed from these very deregulatory and privatizing policy decisions, Republicans continued to hammer home the virtues of the "free market"—accountability, family values, and rugged (or, in Palin-speak, "mavericky") individualism—as well as the inherent evils of the academy—in the 2008 election campaign and beyond.

Race and the War on Reality 2.0:
On "Academic" Anti-Intellectualism

How is it that such a corrupt version of reality gained so much traction for four decades? How was it not checked by the forces of critical judgment and reasonable, reflective consciousness, or even the straightforward demand for and assessment of evidence—a collective disposition, indeed a democratic duty, one would assume second nature for an educated citizenry, if not those for whom intellectual life is a vocation? What was the university's response to this protracted period of conservative counterrevolution, given its starring role among the era's most reviled villains? In what ways did it challenge, or attempt to challenge, the ascendancy of such a dystopian neoliberal vision parading as the new reality? And in what ways did the university actually perpetuate the anti-intellectualism of the era, in both old and new forms—among the latter, the illusion of a raceless society?

According to Hofstadter, anyone who engages anti-intellectualism as a force in American life must somehow come to terms with one of the most enduring paradoxes of our national experience: "our persistent, intense and sometimes touching faith in the efficacy of popular education" and our equally impassioned refusal to fund it properly.[33] A host of problems have issued from this signal neglect—dilapidated school buildings, inadequate facilities, outmoded technologies, underpaid teachers, overcrowded classrooms are, of course, among the most obvious. And he says, "something else," among which he lists "the cult of athleticism, marching bands . . . ethnic ghetto schools, de-intellectualized curricula. . . . "[34] To be sure, the consequences of such fiscal choices alone render an utterly illiterate and anti-intellectual citizenry more and more likely—and render it less and less of a perceived problem.

The disinclination to lend necessary financial support notwithstanding, Hofstadter nonetheless insists on the pervasiveness and sincerity of the American faith in education. But it is an education of a particular kind, which is a significant part of the problem. He finds that "the belief in mass education was not founded primarily upon a passion for the development of the mind, or upon pride in learning and culture for their own sakes, but rather on the supposed political and economic benefits of education."[35] Americans exhibit an almost religious faith in education, but its implementation should be all business. In the words of the famed historian and educator Henry Steele Commager, it should "be practical and pay dividends," a disposition Hofstadter readily identifies as anti-intellectual.[36] As the era of social spending drew to a close and government responsibility for the general welfare of its citizenry was reduced to the single, driving neoliberal imperative to cut taxes and increase security, popular support and already-meager financial assistance for education at all levels declined precipitously. And the consequence, in terms of the capacity of young people to develop a wide range of critical, civic, cultural, professional literacies, has been nothing less than catastrophic.

Yet conservatives have another tale to tell about education, particularly higher education, and declining rates of literacy in the post–civil rights era. This narrative does not feature the persistent problem of equal access or the spiraling tuition rates that have resulted from steep declines in federal and state funding as major sources of the problem. In fact, for conservatives and neoliberals alike these have all along been part of the solution, as their agendas have favored consistently the privatization of public schools and the corporatization of higher education. Rather, the Right and even some liberals offer a racially inflected explanation for educational decline, which for them has been best exemplified by the weakening or reform of traditional curricular requirements—the horrific result of a threefold invasion: of students of color and young radicals on college campuses, of new "politicized" fields of intellectual inquiry and knowledge production, of new multicultural curricula squeezing out "traditional" fare. Figures like Alan Bloom, whose *Closing of the American Mind* provided one of the most influential screeds against the university and the 1960s more generally, dismissed as insipid and lazy the very struggles that made the academy, among other institutions, more accountable for the highly traditional knowledges and social relations it has tended to reproduce in the interests of corporate, military, and state power—including its role in the racial definition, management and containment of populations.

In fact, Bloom argues that civil rights struggles—or what he dismisses as the "excesses" of black power—merely provided white students, infected by a contagion of laziness, with an alibi for failing to come to classes and turn in assignments:

It [the civil rights activism of northern college students] consisted mostly in going off to marches and demonstrations that were vacationlike, usually during the school term, with the confident expectation that they would not be penalized by their professors for missing assignments while they were off doing important deeds, in places where they had never been and to which they would never return, and where, therefore, they did not have to pay any price for their stand, as did those who had to stay and live there. . . . The last significant student participation in the civil rights movement was in the march on Washington in 1964. After that, Black Power came to the fore, the system of segregation in the South was dismantled, and white students had nothing more to contribute other than to egg on Black Power excesses. . . . [37]

Given the author's rant against the wholesale dumbing-down of generations of American youth, it is rather surprising to witness such an astonishing departure from the protocols of scholarship as well as empirical fact and evidence in the construction of his argument. In Bloom's engagement with a raced population, a Sartrean evasion and passionate emotion have taken over, as he makes clear in his decision to characterize civil rights demonstrations in the South as "vacationlike"—a vulgar diminishment of a very dangerous struggle for racial justice given vivid account in daily newspapers throughout the era. Moreover, he doesn't even bother to get his dates right; the March on Washington occurred in 1963, a year prior to that cited here. Of course, it would be a grave mistake to assume that the rational capacities of conservatives alone suffer as a consequence of racial engagement. Here we would do well to recall Hofstadter's warning that even great minds fall prey to anti-intellectual moments as we turn to our next example. In her otherwise-commanding analysis of politics and violence, Hannah Arendt's unwavering commitment to critical judgment and moral indignation in the face of violent repression, as well as her penchant for facts and evidence, seems impaired when her gaze comes to rest on black youth unrest in the 1960s:

In America, the student movement has been seriously radicalized wherever police and police brutality intervened in essentially nonviolent demonstrations: occupations of administration buildings, sit-ins, et cetera. Serious violence entered the scene only with the appearance of the Black Panther movement on the campuses. Negro students, the majority of them admitted without academic qualification, regarded and organized themselves as an interest group. . . . Their interest was to lower academic standards. They were more cautious than the white rebels, but it was clear from the beginning (even before the incidents at Cornell University or City College in New York) that violence with them was not a matter of theory and rhetoric. . . . [I]t seems that the academic establishment, in its curious tendency to yield more to Negro demands, even if they are clearly silly and outrageous, than to the disinterested and highly moral claims of the white rebels, also thinks in these terms and feels more comfortable when confronted with the interests plus violence than when it is a matter of nonviolent "participatory democracy."[38]

In Arendt's characterization of the student protests of the 1960s, black students are depicted as "violent," "without academic qualification," singularly focused on "lowering academic standards" when not shaking down the academic establishment with "silly and outrageous" demands, whereas their white rebel counterparts occupy "disinterested" ground and advance "highly moral claims." It is interesting to note that the formula in Arendt's narrative is nearly the reverse of Bloom's—"highly moral" white students clearly fare better in the former, whereas in the latter they are castigated as insincere, opportunistic, and lazy. Both depictions of student struggles, however, invoke a racist logic that equates the presence of black students on university campuses with direct threat or indirect contagion. For our purposes, however, the falseness of either position isn't really the point; rather, it is choice of terms, the breakdown in critical disposition toward fact and evidence that betrays the emotion, the passion, driving the racial fantasy. Tragically, such evasive or emotive attitudes are more often the norm than the exception in the academy some forty years later. Susan Jacoby notes that universities capitulated to student demands not because they were intimidated or persuaded by their arguments, but because the accommodation and ghettoization of new areas of inquiry, new fields of study, and new faculty hired to teach them were the most expedient and easiest thing to do. "One of the dirty little secrets of many white liberals on college campuses for the past thirty years," Jacoby writes, "has been that they share Bloom's contempt for multiculturalism but do not openly voice their disdain."[39] Indeed, the changes that civil rights struggles helped to bring to college campuses have led to a situation of resentment, even rage, on the part of some intellectuals whose conceptual worlds have become increasingly divorced from new social realities. Characterizing the persistent indifference to the rules of evidence and reason as a "war on thinking" in contemporary universities, Lewis Gordon explains in his recent book, *Disciplinary Decadence*: "Reality is not always what we want it to be. For some of us, the response is narcissistic rage, where we attempt to force reality to cough up a version of the self that we prefer, a version of reality that is more palatable."[40]

Jacoby's argument that Bloom's disdain for multiculturalism is more widely felt than expressed is surely correct. Rather than deride education-related policy discussions about black access to post-secondary institutions, the demand for curricular reform that reflects subaltern histories and knowledges, or ongoing financial support for newly established programs or departments organized around such fields of inquiry, critics deploy the rhetoric of race neutrality against those who seek to "politicize" education or appeal to the virtue of colorblindness over and against anti-racist policy. Indeed, when questions of racially inscribed injustices occur of late, they are often from white students who claim to be victims of "reverse racism" or abusive "diversity" requirements, or biased professors who refuse to engage "all points of view" (as if they were of equal merit) and approach political questions in the classroom without a sense of "balance." Consequentially speaking, such strategies capitulate to a kind of historical amnesia that is a defining feature of contemporary colorblind commitments—precisely enabling the willful evasion of social reality that renders whites not perpetrators but victims of racist exclusion. Confronting this problem of evidence, Gordon writes: "Particularly egregious is the continued tendency, or perhaps willful effort to misrepresent the realities of black folk," as is the case in situations of "presumed symmetry."[41] Charges of "reverse racism" by critics of affirmative action who assume that blacks have an unfair advantage over whites when it comes to access to the nation's best schools are widespread, yet they blatantly contradict empirical data. "Such accusations assume that blacks control the conditions of their economic and social mobility on a par with whites," Gordon writes, yet the fact "that, for instance, there hasn't been any study demonstrating that blacks have moved out of neighborhoods to more expensive or distant ones because too many whites have moved in pretty much contradicts such a claim."⁴² That the majority of black American youths in the post–civil rights era continue to live in low-income neighborhoods and have access only to severely underfunded, generally resegregated and often failing schools is an issue never confronted. To the degree that they successfully deny or deflect, in spite of the evidence, institutional responsibility for, or willingness to redress, historical and ongoing racial exclusion as well as the university's role in the perpetuation of racist knowledges touted as "official history," "neutral science," or otherwise bestowed with canonical status, those who appeal to "racelessness" should be understood in the same reactionary and aggressively anti-intellectual light. But there are other ways still of subverting pedagogically a robust institutional commitment to anti-racism, thus enabling (a still overwhelmingly white and male) full-time faculty to research and teach as they please, without critical regard for the normative, institutional, and politically consequential assumptions that inevitably inform their scholarly activities.

The recent work of academic celebrity Stanley Fish is a case in point. A Milton scholar and university administrator turned critic-at-large for the *New York Times*, Fish has been engaged in contemporary debates over the purpose and function of the university (particularly the humanities), the university's relation to politics and public life, and the responsibilities of academic intellectuals for the better part of two decades. In 1995, he published *Professional Correctness: Literary Studies and Political Change*, which advanced the cause of disinterested professionalism even as it took its titular cue and dismissive tone from the then-raging right-wing crusade against the scourge of "political correctness" on college campuses. Issuing a ribald critique of the presumptuousness and moralism of literary scholars who seek to end poverty, sexism, or racism through their sensitive and nuanced readings of literary texts, he insisted that English department faculty should remain faithful to their profession and teach students the kind of aesthetically driven analytic skills that define what they most distinctively do—or perish institutionally. Curiously, Fish's intervention on the side of neutrality in what are perceived to be "insular" ivory tower debates invoked and reproduced the neoliberal and colorblinding imperatives that have informed larger national political debates since the early 1980s. Rather than directly challenge the educational value of "multicultural" texts or forms of subaltern critique, which in their best moments unsettle official knowledge and make power visible and accountable, he invoked the economy and issued a pragmatic response to revenue short-falls, particularly in the humanities. After decades of dwindling financial support from state and federal legislatures doubtful of their capacity to boost the GDP, Fish insinuated that the future of English might be at stake if faculty were to fail to produce technically skilled and competent readers and writers—a "disinterested" imperative, he insisted, yet one that nonetheless aligned with the corporate preference for noncritical, compliant, and efficient workers.

The latest edition of this argument, which appeared in 2008 titled *Save the World on Your Own Time*, again mimics the tenor of current right-wing allegations of political indoctrination and the abdication of intellectual responsibility in the university classroom. Advancing the cause of unbiased professionalism through a set of practical and common sense rhetorical appeals, Fish urges his colleagues in the academy to drop the pretense to expanding the civic or moral capacities of students and issues a series of bureaucratic commands upon which he elaborates in chapters under the headings "Do Your Job," "Don't Try to Do Someone Else's Job," and "Don't Let Anyone Else Do Your Job." Such imperatives are calculated to appease those constituencies who subscribe to the conservative Bush-era complaint, echoed through the media and on the floor of Congress, that taxpayers are tired of paying absurd tuitions in order for their sons and daughters to be aggressively won over, in the name of "education," to the radical, even communistic, political views and values of their professors, which they themselves do not support.[43] As such, Fish participates in that most striking feature of contemporary intellectual culture, what Gordon calls the "war on evidence." For Gordon, "where truth collapses into commonness, then critical thinking isn't necessary, which makes the work of accessing evidence unnecessary."[44] Beneath the advance of oversimplified or "evidence-like claims," which demand no thought because their final appeal is to the appearance of things, he argues, are "nihilistic forces," and even "decadent ones"—a point to which I will return.[45] Though Fish repudiates the call for a student academic bill of rights or "intellectual balance" promoted by David Horowitz and his supporters, he nonetheless advances a most "balanced" account of the ways in which both the Right and the Left have transgressed that most sacred of academic missions: an impartial search for truth, which cannot or should not be instrumentalized, let alone sacrificed on the altar of this or that political cause. A curiously evenhanded gesture, given his insistence that balance is "not an academic value," and one in any case rendered disingenuous and unpersuasive, as his account fails to acknowledge on the "right" side of the transgressions ledger the millions of dollars in funding each year given by drug companies and a myriad of other corporations, as well as by government agencies like the Department of Defense, in the relentless drive to commodify, patent, instrumentalize, even weaponize knowledge in the interests of corporate profit or national security. This, as he overstates the prevalence of left-wing politicization.[46] Anticipating challenges to his insistence on university inutility, he offers a dismissive and smug reply:

If universities must distance themselves from any entity that has been accused of being ethically challenged there will be a very long list of people, companies, and industries they will have to renounce as business partners: brokerage firms, pharmaceutical firms, online-gambling companies, oil companies, automobile manufacturers, real-estate developers, cosmetic companies, fast-food restaurants, Hewlett-Packard, Microsoft, Wal-Mart, Target, Martha Stewart, Richard Grasso, and George Steinbrenner. And if you're going to spurn companies involved with Sudan, what about North Korea, Iran, Syria, China, Colombia, the Dominican Republic, Venezuela, Argentina, Russia, Israel, and (in the eyes of many left-leaning academics) the United States? These lists are hardly exhaustive and growing daily. Taking only from the pure will prove to be an expensive proposition (even Walt Disney won't survive the cut) and time consuming too, as the university becomes an extension of Human Rights Watch.[47]

Apparently, the effort to make wise and informed ethical decisions about university funding sources is an impractical waste of time—and far too costly. "It is a question finally of what business we are in," Fish asserts, "and we are in the education business, not the democracy business."[48] Even more disturbing, he adds: "Democracy, we must remember, is a political not an educational project"—a declaration to which I will return in the Conclusion.[49] Of the first proposition, I would like to make a few observations. Perhaps most obvious is his subscription to a neoliberal assumption—education is a business—which is no mere metaphor when taken up in the context of his larger argument. Corporate logic so thoroughly dominates American society—and increasingly its universities—as to negate any felt need to legitimate itself with reference to values outside its own domain. It is for this reason, in fact, that Hofstadter locates business "in the vanguard of anti-intellectualism in our culture"; as the "most powerful and pervasive interest in American life" it shapes common sense, which as Gramsci once argued is inevitably unreflective sense.[50] As Hofstadter reminds us, university education has been valued historically (and currently, as Fish makes clear) not for its democratic imperative to educate citizens, or for its capacities for cultural and intellectual enrichment, but for its capacity to enhance our standard of living, measured of course in predictably narrow economic terms.

Adopting such a pragmatic position, Fish evades the inherent dissonance between an intellectual pursuit and a bottom-line pursuit. Not only are they are motivated by quite different values, but the imperative of profitability can radically deform academic research. And conversely, critical thought can and should pose a challenge to fixed centers of financial or political power, given their awesome potential for abuse. While it is true that in our current context of dwindling public financial support for education the purity of such positions is inevitably qualified by conditions of mutual dependence, their differences need not lead to an incessant and unproductive antagonism; productive partnerships, carefully selected and judiciously negotiated, can emerge. But Fish fails to concede even this, throwing all caution to the wind. He thus finds himself in an ironic and unreasonable situation. On the one hand, academics who engage in pedagogical practices informed by a democratically inspired commitment to rigorous thought that is both power sensitive and ethically responsible violate professional standards and are anathema to the scholarly search for truth. But on the other, academics whose research is financially dependent on corporate money and defense contracts constitute neither a politically consequential circumstance nor a danger to disinterested truth-seeking. But apparently, this latter concern isn't even worth exploring as a "useless" intellectual exercise.

Even if we decide to bracket the problem of state power and financial influence in Fish's argument, we run into more difficulty. In differentiating "professional" and "political" activity, Fish makes a distinction between "analyzing" ethical issues and "deciding" them, declaring "only the first is appropriate to the academic activity."[51] Curiously, the rigid set of oppositions he constructs between approved academic activities—descriptive analysis and unfettered search for truth—on the one hand and those that violate academic protocol—prescriptive analysis and interventionism—on the other is one that he himself has challenged and effectively dissolved in his earlier work.[52] In *Is There a Text in This Class?* (1980), he advanced the proposition that recognition of "the truth" inevitably reflects a perspective (as opposed to something more objective or transcendent) and an act of interpretation (as opposed to a mere discovery). Through a series of sophisticated literary analyses, he demonstrated that putatively neutral efforts to describe a text's meaning betray not only a non-neutral point of view, but a tacit acknowledgment of a broader institutional context, a set of normative assumptions, procedures, and traditions of interpretation to be affirmed or rejected, transformed or destroyed. But this is not what he argues by 2008. Is this a capitulation to popular disdain for university professors to generate sales, or a form of "impassioned" Sartrean self-evasion and self-contradiction? At present, Fish asserts that truth and interpretation, thought and action, university and non-university are opposed and easily separable activities or sites. In advancing a narrowly technical ideal of academic competence, Fish denies what he had previously acknowledged, what Derrida calls "the politico-institutional structures that constitute and regulate our practice, our competences, our performances."[53] In this instance, Fish commits himself to an anti-intellectual position. Fish willfully suspends the pedagogical conditions that would make such structures visible to students, that would require students (and teachers) to *think* about their own practices in the broader context of their institutional and political effectivity, and that would enable them to assume, in good measure, moral and political responsibility for their responses to them. To the contrary, Fish denies the very possibility of assuming such responsibility in the context of the university:

Teachers can, by virtue of their training and expertise, present complex materials in ways that make them accessible to novices. Teachers can also put students in possession of the analytical tools employed by up-to-date researchers in the field. But teachers cannot, except for a serendipity that by definition cannot be counted on, fashion moral character, or inculcate respect for others, or produce citizens of a certain temper. Or, rather, they cannot do these things unless they abandon responsibilities that belong to them by contract in order to take up responsibilities that belong properly to others.[54]

Fish does not deny that political issues do arise in the course of classroom conversation, but he insists that they not be further "politicized" as such, but rather "academicized," or detached *"from the context of its real world urgency, where there is a vote to be taken or an agenda to be embraced, and insert it into a context of academic urgency, where there is an account to be offered or an analysis to be performed."*[55] But what is one to make of the insistence that academic activity should be separated from "real world urgency" *as a matter of principle* in the current moment of ecological, economic, social, and political crises—crises the next generation of youth is condemned to inherit? The position advanced here is that university educators have no obligation to help students negotiate the demand for critical and creative response such crises inevitably entail—moreover, they violate a professional code if they do so. President Obama, who issued a national call to service, would surely be disappointed. A report published by the British Academy in September 2008 titled "Punching Our Weight: The Humanities and Social Sciences in Public Policy Making" provides an interesting counter-position. The report issues a call for researchers in these highlighted areas to serve in the public interest by addressing in their work the various social and economic challenges posed by globalization, which include generating innovative and comprehensive measurements of human well-being, overcoming barriers to cross-cultural communications, improving the effectiveness of public programs, and providing historical perspectives on contemporary policy problems. But Fish's support of university inutility rejects the viability of university research and pedagogy attempting to "improve" anything from early childhood education, to green design in city planning, to immigration reform, to peaceful mediation of civil wars. Fish's call here is not for censorship, or for balance, but for an "academic" discussion in precisely that typically pejorative sense of being unactionable or inconsequential—at least for the over 15 million students who enter post-secondary education. He elaborates his position in revealing detail:

this is not to say that academic work touches on none of the issues central to politics, ethics, civics, and economics; it is just when those issues arise in an academic context, they should be discussed in academic terms; that is, they should be objects of analysis, comparison, historical placement, etc.; the arguments put forward in relation to them should be dissected and assessed as arguments and not as preliminaries to action on the part of those doing the assessment. The action one takes (or should take) at the conclusion of an academic discussion is the action of rendering an academic verdict as in "that argument makes sense," "there is a hole in the reasoning here," "the author does (or does not) realize her intention," "in this debate, X has the better of Y," "the case is still not proven." . . . The judgment of whether a policy is the right one for the country is not appropriate in the classroom, where you are (or should be) more interested in the structure and history of the ideas than in recommending them (or dis-recommending them) to your students . . . dissecting them [ideas] is what you are supposed to do if you are paid to be an academic. . . . Recommending them is what you do when you are a parent, or a political activist, or an op-ed columnist, all things you may be when the school day ends, but not things you should be on the university's or state's dime.[56]

For Fish, the pedagogical encounter, like the pursuit of education itself, is or should be morally and politically neutral. He has attempted to "adiaphorize" such activities, to invoke Zygmunt Bauman's useful term. Adiaphorization, Bauman explains, renders "certain actions, or certain objects of action, morally neutral or irrelevant—exempt from the category of the phenomena suitable for moral evaluation."[57] The effect of adiaphorization is achieved, Bauman asserts, by "excluding some categories of people from the realm of moral subjects," in this case teachers and students, or through "covering up the link between partial action and the ultimate effect of coordinated moves," for our purposes, denying the inevitable effect that confrontation with the social world—through literature or history or some other medium—has on our understanding of our place and role within it, or "through enthroning procedural discipline . . . in the role of the all-overriding criterion of moral performance," in this case, Fish's insistence that professional focus remains locked on literary formalism and the rules of grammar.[58] For Bauman, adiaphorization enables a particular form of postmodern violence; it is "the principle tool for severing moral guilt from acts of participation in cruelty."[59] Though the context in which he initially explores the concept is Nazi Germany, he sees the possibilities for the ready appropriation of such a strategy in our contemporary neoliberal world order.

Fish himself offers an example of how such "neutral" thinking under university auspices enables acts of unspeakable cruelty in a recent opinion piece for the *New York Times* entitled "Psychology and Torture," which explored the American Psychological Association's decision to reverse a longstanding policy by voting to ban its members from participating in interrogations in various U.S. detention centers worldwide, including Guantanamo Bay. Posing the question of why psychologists came to this decision relatively late, in comparison to their colleagues in the American Medical Association or the American Psychiatric Association, he notes that psychology "is not exclusively a healing profession."[60] In other words, "their product is not mental health, but knowledge; their skills are not diagnostic, but analytic—what makes someone do something—and it is an open question as to whether there are limits, aside from the limits of legality, to the uses to which these skills might be put."[61] Thus when he speaks to academics about academic responsibility, about what is appropriate to debate within the hallowed halls of academe, he says that knowledge should not be leveraged in the interests of specific worldly social or political effects; when speaking as an op-ed columnist, he claims that the ethical dimensions of psychologists' assistance in the procurement of "willing cooperation" on the part of detainees are "an open question"—just, apparently, not for those in training in the academy. Just as neoliberal economic policy and the raceless racisms are driven by a privatizing imperative, so too Fish renders critical thought itself a privatized activity—thinking that ventures beyond the formal, technical expertise of the scholar should apparently be ceded to parental authority or significantly, given his new job with the *Times*, that of the op-ed columnist. The question of a credential or stated expertise, let alone the differences between academic and journalistic standards, is here irrelevant. Even on questions of torture, professional detachment, like personal belief, is removed from the inventory of items available for public analysis and debate. Of the relationship between adiaphorization, privatization, and contemporary forms of violence, Bauman argues:

The characteristically postmodern stocks of violence are "privatized"—dispersed, diffuse and unfocused. . . . They are also "capillary" penetrating the most minute cells of the social tissue. Their ubiquitous presence has a double, ambivalent effect of exhilarating experience of ultimate emancipation . . . on the one hand, and gnawing fear of a totally deregulated and uncontrollable Hobbesian world on the other.[62]

In the absence of rigorous public dialogue, deliberation, and debate, the contemporary "carnival of cruelty" that Bauman describes has rendered the tenuous survival of vast populations of the world's mostly racial poor a form of entertainment, as it recast citizens in the mode of myriad individual, disconnected, and "neutral" spectators—active only to the degree that they might applaud or hiss, but never giving thought to intervention on behalf of those forced to live the nightmare.

Though Fish commences his 2008 book lampooning what for him are the ludicrous claims of university mission statements, which typically invoke democratic principle and civic commitments, he acknowledges that his position is a minority view. He cites rather exuberantly a great many who have challenged his views specifically. Among them is Mark D. Gearen, president of Hobart and William Smith Colleges, who argues that Fish's insistence that teachers "do their jobs" "'belies a rich history and deep tradition of civic responsibility within American Higher Education,' a tradition he adds, that is 'articulated nearly universally in the mission statements of colleges and universities across the country.'"[63] Against the 900 college and university executive officers that Gearen cites who concur with the university's responsibility to "to influence the democratic knowledge, dispositions, and habits of the heart that graduates carry with them into the public sphere. . . . " Fish insists that in this debate, his side is stacked with "worthies like Aristotle, Kant, Cardinal Newman, Max Weber, Learned Hand, Harry Kalven, John Hope Franklin and Jacques Derrida."[64] Although we find among those listed here a dedication to university autonomy, even a few advocates of the highly traditional conception of "useless knowledge," their positions are considerably more complex and nuanced than Fish allows. Again, as we've seen with Bloom and Arendt, the scholarly capacity—and professional commitment—to faithfully recapitulate the positions of others as we advance our own is suddenly impaired. That philosophers of the critical tradition from Kant and Schelling to Nietzsche and even Heidegger were adamantly opposed to the reduction of academic responsibility to professional education is well known—with a history I engage in the next chapter. But I would like to pause over this invocation of Derrida, as few contemporary thinkers have engaged the question of the university, and university responsibility, with greater care and devotion.

Far from supporting Fish's agenda, Derrida has called for the assumption of a new "responsibility of thinking" which specifically refutes the professionalization that Fish advocates. In his *Eyes of the University*, Derrida explicitly states:

The new responsibility of the "thinking" of which we are speaking cannot fail to be accompanied, at least, by a movement of suspicion, even of rejection with respect to the professionalization of the university in these two senses, and especially in the first, which regulates university life according to the supply and demand of the marketplace and according to a purely technical ideal of competence. To this extent at least, such "thinking" can, at a minimum, result in reproducing a highly traditional politics of knowledge. And the effects can be those that belong to a social hierarchy in the exercise of techno-political power.[65]

Warning against the "traditional politics of knowledge" that Fish advocates, Derrida does, however, contemplate the risk involved in the decision "to think" that this new order of responsibility demands. Thinking is a far more capacious activity for Derrida than for Fish (who actually argues that English faculty should devote much their time in the classroom to grammar lessons); it involves "the principle of reason and what is beyond the principle of reason"—an ethics, a politics, for example. Because of this, he declares that the decision to think is "always risky, it always risks the worst."[66] And he invokes in considerable detail the lengthy and sordid history of the European and North American university's complicity with military abuses, including abetting torture, as well as its compromised position, its subjection to the "technologies of informationalization" in relation to the corporate sector upon which it increasingly relies.[67] Yet he insists that efforts to "eliminate this risk through an institutional program is quite simply to erect a barricade against a future. *The decision of thinking cannot be an intra-institutional event, an academic moment.*"[68] Against Fish's analytic insistence on the viability of isolating the university from "real world urgency," of reducing thought to an insular academic exercise, Derrida asserts the radical openness of the university, muddies the distinction between what is inside and outside the university, and claims, moreover, that such "an illusion of closure" "would make the university available to any sort of interest, or else render it perfectly useless."[69] Of course, a "perfectly useless" university is what Fish is after. But Derrida rejects this possibility and concludes provocatively: "Beware of ends; but what would a university be without ends?"[70]

Further, Derrida situates himself in that camp that would be read as "threat" by the likes of Stanley Fish—and subject to his "nihilistic" abuse:

But the approach I am advocating here is often felt by certain guardians of the "humanities" or of the positive sciences as a threat. It is interpreted as such by those who most often have never sought to understand the history and the system of norms specific to their own institution, the deontology of their own profession. They do not wish to know how their discipline has been constituted, particularly in its modern professional form, since the beginning of the nineteenth century and under the watchful vigilance of the principle of reason. *For the principle of reason can have obscurantist and nihilist effects. They can be seen more or less everywhere . . . among those who believe they are defending philosophy, literature, and the humanities against the new modes of questioning that are also a new relation to language and tradition, a new affirmation, and new ways of taking responsibility.*"[71]

We find this nihilism "lurking," Derrida says, "when on occasion great professors . . . lose all sense of proportion and control . . . they forget the principles that they claim to defend in their work and suddenly begin to heap insults . . . on the subject of texts that they have obviously never opened. . . . "[72] Now let us consider the following commentary by Fish. He invokes Derrida as a "worthy" authority when it constitutes a politically expedient counter to Gearen and dismisses him when it doesn't—yet in the same breath Fish depicts *those who challenge his views* as disingenuous. Categorically rejecting those who argue that "what currently counts as knowledge should always be suspect because it will typically reflect the interests and preferences of those in power," Fish insists that such a position is merely "standard vulgar postmodernism of the kind that one gets by reading a page or two of some French theorist, and what is interesting about its appearance in these debates is that those who mouth it don't believe it for a minute; it's just a matter of political tactics."[73] Yet again, he advances "evidence-like" claims that discourage thought. It's rather dicey to assume no one "believes" such arguments even as they mouth them, but Fish can surely count himself among those who resist Derrida's pedagogical insistence on the contextually bound nature of meaning, or the "politico-institutional" structures that inevitably mediate our hermeneutic practices and competencies—unless it can advance his own political strategy.

But Fish's nihilism takes other forms as well. In a review of a former student's new book, *The Last Professors: The Corporate University and the Fate of the Humanities*, Fish ponders whether the conception of the university the book advocates, "an enterprise characterized by determined inutility," has a chance in today's fiscal climate. The book's author answers a resounding no. Fish comments:

What is happening in traditional universities where the ethos of the liberal arts is still given lip service is the forthright policy of for-profit universities, which make no pretense of valuing what used to be called "higher learning." John Sperling, founder of the group that gave us Phoenix University, is refreshingly blunt: "Coming here is not a rite of passage. We are not trying to develop value systems or for that 'expand their minds' nonsense." The for-profit university is the logical end of a shift from a model of education centered in an individual professor who delivers insight and inspiration to a model that begins and ends with the imperative to deliver the information and skills necessary to gain employment.[74]

With curious equanimity Fish appears to accept the arrival of the for-profit university; neither here nor in his book does he offer any legitimating discourse for the university's more righteous pursuit of "determined inutility." Perhaps that would be too utilitarian. Instead he offers his readership the very nihilism that Derrida anticipates: "People sometimes believe that they were born too late or too early. After reading Donoghue's book I feel that I have timed it just right, for it seems that I have had a career that would not have been available to me had I entered the world 50 years later. Just lucky, I guess."[75] Readers anticipating a rousing defense of humanistic inquiry will be sorely disappointed. Fish's sole recourse, unsurprisingly, is to the kind of utterly privatized response to which neoliberal commitments inevitably lead—and to which his recent work has consistently pointed, sacrificing his own "professional" integrity and intellectual capacities along the way.

In my analysis of Fish's influential body of work, I have attempted to show the ways in which some academics have, in "disinterested" pursuit of the truth, embraced forms of anti-intellectualism that serve to render critical thought, moral evaluation, and democratic engagement a transgression of professional values and a danger to university life. The upshot is an endorsement of pedagogical practices that deny teachers and students alike the opportunity, the time, the space, and the critical skills to re-evaluate the human consequences of living in this neoliberalized and "raceless" new world order. His subscription to professional neutrality, as well as his conception of the university as an institution of "determined inutility," while it may not overtly champion a neoliberal agenda or colorblind sensibilities, tacitly endorses its depoliticizing, dehistoricizing, privatizing, and efficiency-oriented imperatives. As I argued in the Introduction to this book, calls for "specialized" and "non-political" academic research and instruction presume the legitimacy of colorblinding social and political analysis and investment; such commitments are co-constitutive and mutually endorsing. Fish remains ever the champion of neutrality, even as his books consistently mimic the logic of right-wing critiques of the university as a site of liberal multicultural indoctrination.

Perhaps these entwined allegiances explain why Fish breaks with his emphatic insistence on the virtues of professional disavowal to endorse his former colleague's book, *The Trouble with Diversity*, by Walter Benn Michaels, the author of the (in)famous call to literary pragmatism in his "Against Theory," with Stephen Knapp. Unlike Fish, Michaels suggests that academics have a responsibility to engage students on pressing political questions, in particular issues relating to economic inequality. But like Fish, he criticizes what he views as a disingenuous, even dangerous, dimension of left-wing hegemony on university campuses. More specifically, he insists that the academic infatuation with racial identity and cultural difference has come at the cost of critical attention—he would insist *any* attention—to pervasive and widening economic disparities in contemporary American life. Invoking the desire for a world without race, a quintessential expression of colorblind aspiration, Michaels laments the assertion of the famed sociologists Michael Omi and Howard Winant, who argue that "race . . . will always be at the center of the American experience."[76] In obvious disagreement with this observation, Michaels poses the question, rhetorically, of why academicians are "so eager to keep race at the center of the American experience"—apparently believing that the role that race continues to play in American life is less a function of past and present racial configurations than an act of (stubborn) volition on the part of misguided liberals.[77] Continuing this line of argument, he asks: "Why does racial difference remain so important to us when the racism it was used to justify is so widely condemned and when the basic idea about race that gave it power—the idea that there are fundamental physical or cultural differences between people that line up with our division of them into black, white, et cetera—has been discredited."[78] Thus he imagines a world in which racism in general, as opposed to one particular kind of racial definition, management, and accompanying modes of racist expression, not only has been formally dismantled but also has lost its politically persuasive power. Though a pervasive belief in the post–civil rights era, such assumptions foreclose the possibility of a new racism, one that camouflages itself in the pretense to colorblindness or race transcendence—and explains persistent racially predicated differences in income, jobs, education, medical care, and life expectancy in terms of individual character flaws or personal failings, rather than as a consequence of structured exclusions that have outlived formal desegregation.

What are the effects of such appeals to racelessness—not only politically and socially, but intellectually? David Goldberg suggests there are at least three. First, the commitment to colorblindness translates into a "relative silencing of public analysis or serious discussion of everyday racisms" that nonetheless persist in contemporary societies, a symbolically violent "repression of racial reference." In other words, invoking race—or what has been popularly condemned as "playing the race card"—implies that racial reference is not only an inappropriate rhetorical ploy but an entirely irrelevant social category. Forms of race consciousness—whether from white neo-Nazi groups or from black political organizations—are not only equated but disqualified as extremist in equal measure. Second, such silencing makes more or less impossible the ability "to connect historical configurations with contemporary racial formations," to understand present inequalities as the (dis)accumulative legacy of hundreds of years of exploitation and exclusion. Finally, the invocation of racelessness serves to displace "the tensions of contemporary racially charge relations to the relative invisibility of private spheres, seemingly out of reach of public policy intervention."[79] Racism is "privatized," as Michaels also argues, but not in the nuanced way that Goldberg here suggests. Mainstream definitions of racism have reduced the concept to an individual, or private, pathology to be sure, but Goldberg is also arguing that the structural coordinates that reproduce everyday racism have been privatized and deregulated according to a specifically neoliberal logic. In other words, the state's official role in defining, managing, and containing raced populations has been transferred to the private sector, thus enabling the rapid market-based resegregation of the body politic in ways perceived to be beyond state intervention.

It is important nonetheless to point out that Goldberg has, like Michaels, also criticized the politically deleterious effects of what he calls the "cultural turn" in race theory and its romance with racial identities and their various hybridities—which for him have translated into a palpable indifference to historically transforming rac*isms*. Michaels, however, collapses the important distinctions among various modes of response to the myopia of so much race talk in the university, a distinction that Goldberg makes between the contemporary *anti-racialism* to which Michaels subscribes—in other words, the insistent call for the "end of race" as a relevant social category, to expunge it from contemporary political vocabularies—with the more robust challenge of *anti-racism*, which insists on neither colorblind transcendence nor liberal celebrations of diversity or tolerance, but on policies that end racism.[80]

But more than this concession to the colorblind fallacy, Michaels dismisses the entire project of anti-racism as false, claiming that we've been duped by a relentless focus on race and racism into perpetuating actual class structures and the inequalities to which they give rise. As a result of our obsession with cultural differences over and against class differences, our capacities to think, our conceptual apparatuses, have been polluted. We think of class in cultural terms—as an identity category that begs "respect." As a result class inequality stands, but we've managed to get rid of "classism." Michaels explains the duplicity at work as follows:

And, not content with pretending that our real problem is cultural difference rather than economic difference, we have also started to treat economic difference as if it were cultural difference. So now we're urged to be more respectful of poor people and to stop thinking of them as victims, since to treat them as victims is condescending—it denies them their "agency." And if we can stop thinking of the poor as people who have too little money and start thinking of them instead as people who have too little respect, then it's our attitude toward the poor, not their poverty, that becomes the problem to be solved, and we can focus our efforts of reform not on getting rid of classes but on getting rid of what we like to call "classism." . . . the trick is to think of inequality as a consequence of our prejudices rather than as a consequence of our social system and thus to turn the project of creating a more egalitarian society into the project of getting people . . . to stop being racist, sexist, classist, homophobes.[81]

In Michaels's account, anti-racist scholarship and pedagogy, reduced to the celebration of diversity, amount to an exercise in tolerance, learning to respect others—even as the very term suggests that what one is prompted to "tolerate" is precisely unworthy of said respect.[82] Delimiting the scope of what he misidentifies as "anti-racist" discourse to such dubious injunctions produces its own displacements—of questions of history and power in the perpetuation of racist exclusions. Second, these allegedly "anti-racist" commitments, in effect, amount to a kind of ideological mystification that actually reproduces and perpetuates class inequality. Michaels argues that "antiracism plays an essentially conservative role in American politics today and . . . universities—as something like the diversity avant-garde— play an equally conservative role" pandering to such benighted interests.[83] Third, Michaels's bemoaning of the appearance of students of color on college campuses among others responsible for reproducing this identitarian agenda strangely recalls that logic of contamination which both Bloom and Arendt ascribe to students of color in different ways. Although Michaels is right to point out the inattention given to pressing political issues like ever-widening income inequality, he ruthlessly pits an investment in economic justice against an investment in racial justice. In so doing, he denies the pedagogical possibility of exploring with students the very ways in which neoliberal and colorblinding imperatives have over the last four decades *worked together* to dismantle the social state, impoverish—in inclusively multiracial and multiethnic fashion—vast segments of the American public, and criminalize the poor, and in particular the racial poor. Contrary to what I have been arguing throughout this chapter, Michaels denies the profound impact of the Southern strategy on the ascendancy and consolidation of conservative interests since the late 1960s—and thus denies, even in the face of Atwater's very public admission to the contrary that racism has a role to play in advancing neoliberal policies. But he also rejects, in keeping with the colorblind commitment to historical amnesia, and what I have been calling a racially predicated dimension of American anti-intellectualism, that a critical understanding of the past matters. He argues that our "current near obsession with the importance of history is profoundly misplaced. *Like the idea of diversity itself,* history functions at best as a kind of distraction from present injustices and at worst as a way of perpetuating them."[84] Not only is Michaels against "theory," but also history, the politics of difference, and a textured analysis of the discursive apparatus of race, leaving one to wonder what grounds the very condition for critical and capacious thought in his classroom. Consider his commentary on those who "blame racism" in the context of the utterly ineffectual governmental response to the victims of Hurricane Katrina:

> The Republican party policies that left the poor behind were not racist, and the economic inequality in American society has grown under Democratic presidents as well as Republicans. This doesn't mean, of course, that racism didn't play a role in New Orleans. It just means that in a society without any racial discrimination, there would still have been poor people who couldn't find their way out of New Orleans. Whereas in a society without poor people (even a racist society without poor people), there wouldn't have been.[85]

Michaels admits that racism may have played a role in New Orleans, but only if those affected were also poor. But what does this formulation leave out? Given the ways in which neoliberal policy has negatively impacted nearly all Americans, but punished people of color in particular—as was its intention, Atwater reminds us, accounting for no small part of its popularity among disgruntled whites—I can't fathom what Michaels means when he says governmental policies were not racist. Given neoliberalism's production of a racial poor and new market-driven forms of resegregation, I don't know the point of invoking the fantasy of "a racist society without poor people," which remains by definition a society premised on the ruthless and dehumanizing exclusion of racially defined populations. In any case, it is a fantasy that utterly contradicts and evades the realities of our present moment.

Michaels is hardly alone in his insistence that the "cultural turn" in the academy has meant catastrophe for progressives who want to move forward on the "real issue" of economic justice and the eradication of poverty, as I have argued elsewhere.[86] And Fish has many supporters in his efforts to restore professionalism and "inutility" to an allegedly overly politicized, even radicalized university classroom. However, I have attempted to show that the pedagogical commitments that Michaels and Fish advocate serve to limit the kind of capacious intellectual engagement with the social world that students should be encouraged, at every turn, to participate in. Moreover, wittingly or unwittingly, each of them participates in advancing the illusion of a colorblind and race-transcendent society that requires one neither to act in the interests of racial justice nor to even contemplate its absence—this, despite of the dire consequences such indifference has had and will continue to have on democratic public life.

On the Necessity of Racial Reckoning: Toward a Democratic Agenda That Is Inevitably an Educational Agenda

The defeat of McCain-Palin in 2008 signaled for many not only the end of the Bush era, but also the apparent decline of the Southern strategy, which successive reactionary administrations, Republican and Democrat alike, had put effectively to use in the interests of reversing the near-universal support the social state once enjoyed, as well as many of the advances of the civil rights era. Even America's "first black president," Bill Clinton, stooped so low, as I've argued elsewhere.[87] Though without question, the same anti-government and anti-tax sloganeering reappeared in the grassroots mobilizations of the far right after the election, along with overtly racist imagery and invective, the very demographics of those Southern states are rapidly changing and diversifying, rendering dubious the utility of the Southern strategy in national political affairs. The new administration, in contrast, aspires to a politics that is not only above race, but above politics as well, where politics is understood to mean the vulgar manipulation of and gratuitous pandering to the crass self-interests and fears of an electorate in order to incite particular beliefs and actions. However, questions remain about whether the presumption that Obama's presidency commences an officially "post-racial" and "post-partisan" period of American politics will continue to hold true, providing yet another kind of dubious departure from reality and reason. To be sure the George W. Bush administration, if unsurpassed in the degree of its commitment to anti-intellectualism, was certainly not alone in its willingness to deceive and manipulate everyday "folks." Over the past century, there have been political leaders—Franklin Roosevelt, John Kennedy, and Bill Clinton— who successfully tempered their intelligence, invoked a colloquial idiom, claimed an affinity for common values and tastes (Bill and his Big Mac attacks) and survived. Others who were less adept—Adlai Stevenson, Al Gore, John Kerry—simply perished, as their opponents effectively labeled them as too cerebral, too elite, if not also effete, for effective leadership. While it is true that on the campaign trail, Obama exemplified thoughtfulness and circumspection and spoke with eloquence and dignity, he also proved adept at staying connected with the everyday, playing hoops with his mates from high school the morning of the election, assuaging the fears of children who faced a daunting move with the promise of a puppy.

In the service of heightening such "exuberant identification" (as Judith Butler describes it) with Obama's leadership, a few items are missing from the presidential agenda altogether, and their absence weighs heavily against soaring hopes for genuine democratic renewal. Successive bailouts for financials and other industries have proven unhelpful for everyday citizens—and particularly citizens of color—facing alarming levels of unemployment, impoverishment, and home foreclosure. Yet Obama has chosen to abet the nation's collective refusal to discuss race and, more emphatically, racial injustice—his one speech on the subject notwithstanding. In so doing, has he not capitulated to what his attorney general, Eric Holder, once called a "nation of cowards"? I think he has, though I would not reduce such willful collective myopia to a form of cowardice alone (craven as it may be at times). Rather, such evasion takes shape under what Arendt once described as a kind of normalized "thoughtlessness," to characterize social and institutional conditions that make thinking a deeply spurious affair, improbable if not quite impossible. I have argued throughout this chapter that the commitment to colorblindness cannot be reduced to an individual—or collective—fear or pathology, but that it signals a systemic, institutionally encouraged war on evidence, reason, and social reality. This is a war fought, to be sure, in the highly rationalized interests of resources, wealth, and power, but it also a war waged with absolutist, religious-like faith in social homogeneity raised like a barricade against the scourge of a world with Others.

In spite of the fashionable refusal to speak of race, evidence of ongoing structural racism continues to accumulate in all aspects of social life: income, rates of employment, and access to quality education, housing, medical care. These figures have only become more alarming as black Americans suffer disproportionately in job losses, home losses, and unemployment associated with the global economic crisis.[88] But nothing so harks back to the bad old days of racial apartheid, nothing is quite so obscene, as the shockingly disproportionate numbers of young black men and women currently in the criminal justice system. By 2008, David Goldberg notes that

. . . roughly a third of African-American men have suffered through the criminal justice system in one way or another, leaving them at the margins of civil society and largely without a voice. African-American youth under 18 tried as adults are ten times more likely than white youth convicted of similar crimes to receive life sentences without the possibility of parole (in California it is 22 times more likely). Recent reports indicate that police more and more are arresting children, overwhelmingly black, as young as 6 years old on felony charges—charges that include handcuffs, fingerprints, mugshots and criminal files—for such childish acts as a tantrum at school or riding a bike on the sidewalk.[89]

The race to incarcerate that commenced in the late 1960s has since broken up families, where parental rights weren't dissolved altogether, and increased poverty and unemployment as it denied ex-felons the right to public housing, food stamps, veterans' benefits, and in most instances voting rights, leading to more crime and more poverty in already poor communities. The vast—and still widening—gulf between the perception of a post-racist world and the hard realities too many Americans of color face leaves many concerned not only about the future of black politics and anti-racist agendas more generally, but also about the health of a democracy that ignores the costs of such shocking transgressions against its very ideals and values.

Given the dire straits most Americans and Americans of color in particular face, what is perhaps most worrying to progressives is that Obama's campaign and his transition to the presidency—entirely in keeping with the tactics of political campaigning and politics itself in the last half century, in spite of its pledge of change—did eventually succumb to what Paul Gilroy describes (after Walter Benjamin) as the ongoing "aestheticization and theatricalization" of politics. In *Against Race* (2001), Gilroy warned that "many of the technological and aesthetic patterns of political communication established by the fascist movements" of the mid-twentieth century have "passed straightforwardly over into the mainstream of political life in democratic polities."[90] He writes in eerily prescient terms:

Though the glamorous interplay of leader and led remains a constant source of dramatic tension and libidinal pleasure, the strategies of political advertising for which the work of Leni Riefenstahl provided an extraordinary initial template have been considerably refined during the last sixty years and live on in contemporary advertising. The body, personality, and family of the leader are not the only foci in this influential model. The theatrical and political event, the party rally in which ordinary viewers can both discover and dissolve themselves in the rapturous, ecstatic unity of the many, is another fixed point.[91]

American political campaigns are no exception. As Chris Hedges argues, contemporary audiences learned long ago how to "speak in the comforting epistemology of images."[92] Just as racist imagery and violent exclusions were central to the formation of national unity in fascist Europe, so too did they play a central role in galvanizing the resentments of white voters in the United States for the past several decades. Ironically race would appear to perform another "magical" vindicating moment in the present as Obama's victory is perceived to put paid to America's vicious racial history.

The central ingredients at work in the 2008 Democratic campaign are sadly hard to misrecognize: the romantic emphasis on aesthetics, glamour, personality, body, and family of Barack Obama are too much in evidence. As a rule, political campaigning over the last half-century has tended to trade frank and specific discussion of the hard realities that confronted us, and possible policy responses to these problems, with "cheap slogans and reassuring personal narratives."[93] Rather than exercise citizens' capacities for critical reflection and moral judgment, campaigns have become "experiential." "They are designed," Hedges insists, "to ignite pseudo-religious feelings of euphoria, empowerment and collective salvation."[94] My point here is less that Obama has been singularly committed to manipulating the electorate in such calculated fashion, but rather to take the measure of the degree to which politics, the civic literacies it presupposes and the public spaces for dialogue and debate that it requires, have atrophied, particularly in the last forty years of fundamentalist—and deeply anti-intellectual—conservative rule. Obama has inherited an electorate that has been profoundly mis-educated in the practices of democratic public life, and, rather than indulging those weaknesses further with yet other fantasies of post-partisanship or post-racism, the new administration, pushed by intellectuals and educators in and out of the university in various spheres of public life, must take up the challenge of renewing civic values, responsibilities, and participation.

Progressives who nonetheless want to see coming to fruition in the

Obama's presidency a resounding victory for democratic futures must share Judith Butler's concern over the "nearly messianic expectation" invested in the man, in the personality. She cautions:

In the place of an impossible promise, we need a series of concrete actions that can begin to reverse the terrible abrogation of justice committed by the Bush regime; anything less will lead to a dramatic and consequential disillusionment. The question is what measure of dis-illusion is necessary in order to retrieve a critical politics, and what more dramatic form of dis-illusionment will return us to the intense political cynicism of the last years. Some relief from illusion is necessary, so that we might remember that politics is less about the person and the impossible and beautiful promise he represents than it is about concrete changes in policy that might begin, over time, and with difficulty, [to] bring about conditions of greater justice."[95]

In a few pre-inaugural speeches, Obama made an appeal to "the better angels of our nature," invoking Abraham Lincoln's eloquent phrase, but he would have been wiser to call forth our more secular, civic capacities given the monumental challenges ahead of us. For Chris Hedges the traditional tools that enable democratic public life to flourish are utterly useless "in a world that lacks the capacity to use them." He insists that

the core values of our open society, the ability to think for oneself, to draw independent conclusions, to express dissent when judgment and common sense indicate something is wrong, to be self-critical, to challenge authority, to understand historical fact, to separate truth from lies, to advocate for change and to acknowledge that there are other views, different ways of being, that are morally and socially acceptable, are dying.[96]

Hedges is uncompromising in his assignment of blame: "The multiple failures that beset the country," he argues, "from our mismanaged economy to our shredding Constitutional rights to our lack of universal health care to our imperial debacles in the Middle East, can be laid at the door of institutions that produce and sustain our educated elite."[97] Transformed into "glorified vocational schools for corporations," liberal arts education, with its broadly humanistic vision and its emphasis on volunteerism and public service, has been systemically dismantled for decades. Universities now produce "expert professionals" trained to focus on "narrow, specialized knowledge independent of social ideas or conceptions of the common good."[98] "The flight from the humanities," he concludes, has become a flight from conscience. It has created an elite class of experts who seldom look beyond their tasks and disciplines to put what they do in a wider, social context. And by absenting themselves from the moral and social questions raised by the humanities, they have opted to serve a corporate structure that has destroyed the culture around them.

Our elites—the ones in Congress, the ones on Wall Street, and the ones being produced at prestigious universities and business schools—do not have the capacity to fix our financial mess. Indeed, they will only make it worse. They have no concept, thanks to the educations they have received, of how to replace a failed system with a new one. They are petty, timid, and uncreative bureaucrats superbly trained to carry out systems management. They see only piecemeal solutions that will satisfy the corporate structure. Their entire focus is numbers, profit and personal advancement. They lack a moral and intellectual core.[99]

Yet at no other time have we been more in need of a critically engaged, creative, and thoughtful citizenry who can face with courage and conviction the challenges—political, economic, ecological, spiritual—that we face both nationally and internationally. Obama is a product of this elite system and will not push against its interests, unless compelled by an informed and active citizenry. "Obama used hundreds of millions of dollars in campaign funds to appeal to and manipulate this illiteracy and irrationalism to his advantage," observes Hedges.[100] And indeed the electorate was invited to focus increasingly on the person of this potential leader—his eloquence, his gravity, his unfailing cool, even his jump shot—and a compelling personal narrative that simultaneously invoked the triumphalism of America's beloved immigration mythology and offered a redemptive conclusion to its most egregious racial sins. However, Hedges warns that "these forces will prove to be his most deadly nemesis once they collide with the awful reality that awaits us."[101]

I suspect Hedges is largely correct in his assessment. Yet we can not accept that our capacity to think, our educational system, and with it American democracy itself, have reached a terminal stage. And it is because I reject these premises that I argue strongly for academics, administrators, teachers, intellectuals, and others to assume their responsibilities as educators who play a vital role in molding citizens who can actively and critically participate in democratic public life. Hedges is undoubtedly right about one thing. The electorate is fast headed on that collision course with the reality that the Bush administration repudiated and that it apparently managed to repress for so long. As Obama himself acknowledged in his Inauguration Day speech, few presidents have taken the oath of office under conditions quite so devastating. Perhaps for this reason, ultimately, he has been compared to former presidents Abraham Lincoln, also a one-term senator from Illinois who confronted a nation ravaged by civil war; Franklin Delano Roosevelt, who led America through the Great Depression and Second World War; and John Fitzgerald Kennedy, the civil rights-era commander in chief who inspired America with his youthful idealism and his sense of hope. But it is also for this reason that I've gone even further back in American history and invoked the legacy of Thomas Jefferson, who also served in the county's highest office in turbulent times, who like Obama would lead the nation through the convulsions of revolutionary change. Jefferson witnessed a political revolution in France and then in the United States, and was able, as a result of those who fought and died for their country, for its ideals of life, liberty, and equality, to ascend to the position of president of a new nation divided in its search for the way forward. Moreover, he was to serve while Western nations were experiencing yet another, equally profound revolution in economic development; he was a plantation owner and adherent of an agrarian way of life that was about to give way to new forces of industrialization, which would transform the country in ways quite unknown and unimaginable. And there was the fact of slavery, America's original sin, about which he wrote most eloquently and ambivalently.

In order to meet all of these political, economic, and spiritual challenges, the nation's third president understood all too well the necessity of an educated citizenry. Having survived his own bitter and contentious political campaign, Jefferson had witnessed first-hand the nefarious and—as we have seen—cataclysmic danger that anti-intellectual, populist demagoguery poses for a democratic nation. Surely it was this complex set of conditions and experiences that inspired his radical educational thought, for it was Jefferson who was one of the first to put forth a multi-tiered plan for free and universal public education as the primary means of safeguarding a young and fragile democratic nation. And it is this legacy that seems to me to offer the most important lessons for the Obama administration, and for those anxious to serve the country in its current state of multiple crises. For Jefferson, education was the primary means of producing the kind of critically informed and active citizenry necessary to both nurture and sustain a vibrant public sphere; he believed that democracy was the highest form of political organization for any nation because it provided the conditions for its citizens to grow both intellectually and morally through the exercise of these faculties. Consider this passage from Jefferson's moving preamble to the 1776 "Bill for the More General Diffusion of Knowledge," which bears the hallmark of his views on the relationship between education and public life:

Whereas . . . certain forms of government are better calculated than others to protect individuals in the free exercise of their natural rights . . . experience hath shewn, that even under the best forms, those entrusted with power have . . . perverted it into tyranny; and it is believed that *the most effectual means of preventing this would be, to illuminate, as far as practicable, the minds of the people at large;* And whereas it is generally true that people will be happiest whose laws are best, and are best administered, and that laws will be wisely formed, and honestly administered, in proportion as those who form and administer them are wise and honest.[102]

Unlike Stanley Fish and others who insist that democracy is not an educational project, Jefferson made education central to his philosophical thought and political commitments; it proved the best means for both preserving the natural rights of citizens from all forms of tyranny and a means for enabling wise and honest self-government. Jefferson conceived of education as a preeminently political issue—and politics as a preeminently educational concern.

As Obama confronts the challenges of the wars he has inherited, an economy experiencing a shift as profound as the industrial revolution which displaced agrarianism as a way of life, the moral stain of a vast carceral empire at home and war abroad, as well as a citizenry riven by the divisive and demagogic rhetoric of four decades of conservative counterrevolution, the legacy of Jefferson, and his insistence on the preeminence of education, may well provide the way forward—and, too, a warning. I have attempted to argue that a (raceless) racist logic has shaped each element of these knotted crises—the "civilizational" war on terror as well as the nation's willingness to transform the welfare state into a neoliberal warfare state—and the ease with which it criminalized the social ills that issued from that pervasive and repressive shift. In fact, as early as 2001, ACLU director Graham Boyd noted that the United States was

incarcerating African-American men at a rate approximately four times the rate of incarceration of black men in South Africa under apartheid. Worse still, we have managed to replicate—at least on a statistical level—the shame of chattel slavery in this country: The number of black men in prison . . . has already equaled the number of men enslaved in 1820. . . . [And] if current trends continue, only 15 years remain before the United States incarcerates as many African-American men as were forced into chattel bondage at slavery's peak, in 1860.[103]

Following Boyd's prediction, the ranks of the incarcerated have swollen from 2 million to 2.3 million in the ensuing eight years. We have moved from a time in which black Americans were legally defined as property, to one in which they have been granted 3/5 humanity. From sub-humanity, they rose to the ranks of second-class citizens, and once a full schedule of rights had been achieved equally "before the law," those rights and entitlements were dismantled along with the social state, which held the promise of their provision. In the fantasy world where "there is no such thing as society," there are now only dysfunctional men, women, and their families locked up or locked out of the American Dream. Still marked by the original sin of slavery, which we have not entirely repudiated, we now find ourselves in an era ominously reminiscent of that biblical season of plague, only this time it is not divine power striking down the first-born children of Pharaoh's kingdom because he refused to grant full freedom to all people, but rather the sovereign power of the state seizing every third son born black. Or perhaps we should push even further back in locating an apt metaphor for the present to ancient Babylon, to the building of that colossal tower of Babel, which eventually wrought divine destruction, condemning humanity to endless confused chatter and conflict. Whatever path of destruction Jefferson envisioned for a nation that refused to take heed of its own moral recklessness and injustice, we would do well to heed his warning. In his *Notes on the State of Virginia*, he wrote: "Indeed I tremble for my country when I reflect that God is just: that his justice cannot sleep for ever."[104] Averting catastrophe—the organizing theme of the second half of this book—will require a most arduous task for the nation's citizenry: a critical and consistent commitment to think and reflect, to act as citizens who are worthy of a democracy.

Section II

THEORIZING RACE, STATE, AND VIOLENCE:
THE PEDAGOGICAL IMPERATIVE

CHAPTER FOUR

Generation Kill: Nietzschean
Meditations on the University,
Youth, War, and Guns

Here our philosophy must begin not with wonder but with horror. . . .

—FRIEDRICH NIETZSCHE

If, as a result of the shocking upheavals that have marked our en-
try into the new millennium, the nature and purpose of higher education
has been the subject of heated debate, so too has the question of security.
Over the last decade, on university campuses across the United States the
obsession with security has come to assume varied meanings and multiple
forms. Yet most of these have little to do with creating conditions for safe
and peaceful coexistence among students or nations. In the aftermath of
the terrorist attacks of September 11, 2001, the U.S. Department of Defense poured billions of dollars into universities' defense-related technological research and development, becoming higher education's third
largest provider of federal funds; university presidents partnered with the
Federal Bureau of Investigation in a joint task force to fight the growing
global threat posed by ideological "extremists"; and new degree programs
and courses in homeland security emerged, while existing curricular of-
ferings, from Middle East area studies to peace studies, came under fire
for harboring alleged pro-terrorist sympathizers.[1] And again in the after-

math of the Virginia Tech massacre of April 16, 2007, the issue of campus security assumed top priority. The day after the shootings, a student movement was formed called Students for Concealed Carry on Campus (SCCC) whose mission is to secure students' right to self-defense by granting them the right to carry concealed weapons on campus. One year later the movement boasted over 22,000 members on 500 campuses nationwide, numbers bolstered by a subsequent shooting rampage at Northern Illinois University in February of 2008. By the spring of 2008 twelve states were considering legislation to grant college students the same gun ownership rights as every other citizen. In each instance of domestic tragedy, the politics of "prevention" assumed aggressive and bellicose militaristic form.

In an interview conducted shortly after 9/11, Jacques Derrida characterized the new security protocol as symptomatic of an ongoing "autoimmunity" logic; drawing on an epidemiological parallel, he elaborated on "that strange behavior where a living being, in quasi-*suicidal* fashion, 'itself' works to destroy its own protection, to immunize itself *against* its 'own' immunity."[2] "What is put at risk by this *terrifying* autoimmunitary logic," he gravely insisted, "is nothing less than the existence of the world."[3] Since then, I've wondered about the troubling figure of societal suicide. How is it possible that a free and democratic society, precisely in the act of securing itself, or claiming to secure itself, could quicken its own demise? Where does the suicidal urge come from—is it a function of a deep, abiding illness in the collective psyche or a fleeting impulse linked to traumatic loss, or some imagined heroism? Is this really the future we face and, if so, how do we determine our degree of risk? Do we invoke the same assessment scale that is used for individual suicides? Gender, for example, is a factor; males are at greater risk, but how does one determine the gender of a society—by its masculinist inclination? Evidence of depression is another sign. Does one look to dips in the stock market or consumer confidence indices? An increase in sales of anti-depressant medications? How about a rise in recent suicide attempts? Derrida describes the Cold War as a "first moment," a "first autoimmunity." Was there recent significant trauma or loss? Without question. Was capacity for rational thinking lost? So it would seem. Was there little or no social support? Would loss of global support work here? As one goes down such a list, the signs don't look promising. Derrida suggests that what makes the impending threat so terrifying is precisely that it comes from "the to-come, from the fu-ture."[4] Thus it occurred to me that such a society, compelled to fight to the death, according to this autoimmunitary logic, to fight, in other words, its own future and risk its own existence, could do no better than to arm all of its children.

This chapter examines this strange security obsession and the often-militarized response it garners on university campuses. It is strange even for the times, I would insist, because we tend to imagine the university to be the very institution devoted to "light and truth," where the capacity for thinking is never suspended. "As far as I know," Derrida notes, "no-body has ever founded a university against reason."[5] We want to believe that the university's unflinching pursuit of truth through reason is freely conducted, never rendered subordinate to the dictates of external powers, whether the government, the military, or corporate interests. We believe, further, that the university's commitment to reason and knowledge guar-antees its role as an institution for order and peace, one never on the side of coercion, violence, or war. And we would imagine that if such pressure is exerted in so sanctified a space, in the name of security or patriotism, for example, a countervailing insistence on the priority of its freedom would surely triumph. What would the stamp of university approval mean, after all, if its free pursuit of knowledge and truth could be so compromised? And because of these unswerving commitments, it would prove an in-defatigable guardian against the deadly autoimmunitary logics Derrida describes and would ensure, through its primary role in the critical educa-tion of young people, a peaceful and just future for democratic society.

But it is not clear that this is at all the case, or ever was the case. Michel Foucault has provocatively argued against this sanitized idea in *"Society Must Be Defended"*:

It is an idea that is probably bound up with the whole Western organization of knowledge, namely, the idea that knowledge and truth cannot not belong to the register of order and peace, that knowledge and truth can never be found on the side of violence, disorder, and war. . . . the important thing . . . about this idea that knowledge and truth cannot belong to war, and can only belong to order and peace, is that the modern State has now reimplanted it in what we might call the eighteenth century's "disciplinarization" of knowledges.[6]

In order to give much-needed historical depth to what are all-too-frequently presentist analyses of the challenges that the university has long confronted and continues to confront in relation to truth, knowledge, violence, and war, I look to one of modernity's most influential philosophers, Friedrich Nietzsche, and his early lectures, *On the Future of Our Educational Institutions,* which, unlike subsequent treatments of similar themes, grants singular attention to the question of youth. It is an unmatched theoretical contribution in this regard, and we may find it necessary, in light of his analysis of the university's alleged freedoms, and its commitment to youth and its futurity, to reevaluate and complicate the institution's "peaceful" pursuit of truth and knowledge as part of its broader educational mission. I will argue that there is, in fact, a deepening crisis of thought in the university, and so a crisis of academic freedom, which has tremendous implications not only for the future of the institution, but also for the sustainability of democratic futures more generally.

In January of 1872, the young Nietzsche gave a series of five public lectures titled "On the Future of Our Educational Institutions" to a large and distinguished audience in the Museum of the University of Basel, Switzerland. Declaring himself "too foreign" and "too little firmly rooted in local conditions," he demurred on his ability to provide an astute, even credible, assessment of the specificities of the Swiss context; he was even less interested in offering grand, universal claims about education, or as he put it, "prophesying out of the whole vast horizon of civilized people of today."[7] The lectures, rather, were designed more specifically "to divine the future" of Germany's formal educational apparatus "out of the viscera of the present"[8]—critically examining each phase of the system from elementary education, or *Volksshule,* to the trade school, or *Realshule,* to the Gymnasium, and then to the University. Given such a proviso, one might wonder why his audience would be inclined to indulge a speaker who offered neither local nor general—and thus seemingly unactionable—insight on educational matters. The rationale Nietzsche proposed, quite strikingly, was none other than that, given the city's "disproportionately grandiose" efforts to advance the education of its citizenry, those assembled before him had already proven themselves worthy of his counsel. Nietzsche claimed to avail himself of the pleasures afforded one in spiritual commune with congregants of superior wisdom "who have reflected on education and questions of education."[9] "Only before such listeners will I," he continued, "with the greatness of the task and the shortness of the time, be able to make myself understood—if they, namely, instantly guess what could only be suggested, complete, what must be concealed, if they generally only need to be reminded, not to be instructed."[10] It was a provocation cleverly dispatched in the guise of lavish praise. Forewarned of the lecturer's willful indirection and ambiguity—a tactic in the pitched battle against his contemporaries' obsession with the "self-evident," their utilitarian enthusiasms, and their ready confusion of instruction for education—listeners would indeed have to work to achieve a measure of clarity and insight. In the preface to the book he planned for the lectures, Nietzsche called forth a "calm reader" and a cunning one—a reader who "has still not unlearned how to think while he reads; [who] still understands how to read the secret between the lines. . . . He who is calm and unconcerned enough to be able to set out together on a distant way with the author whose goal will first be shown in full clarity to a much later generation."[11] No practical advice or prescriptions would be forthcoming, nothing to titillate the empirically inclined or, in his phrase, "the friends of tables."

For our purposes here, we shall reflect primarily on his rather ominous meditations concerning German higher education; for him, the fate of the university—its futurity or its conceptual, if not quite institutional, collapse—was inextricably caught between the pretension to and the actual conditions of university autonomy and academic freedom. In doing so, we should heed his own cautious refusal to engage in abstract generalizations or fatuous instrumentalities in advance of academic interests, as well as his insistence that we take up the opportunity to think through, carefully and capaciously, the difficulty of education. Unlike Nietzsche, however, we assume an audience deeply conflicted over what constitutes the role of higher education, its freedoms and its responsibilities, in our present post-9/11 moment. As we shall see, at perhaps no other time have such themes, foundational for a democratic society, given way to greater social dissension and challenge.

Nietzsche's circumscribed approach to the topic at hand was not his only cause for concern in the forthcoming public address. Not only was he "too foreign," Nietzsche anticipated that he might also be perceived as "too young" to speak to such grand imperatives. He was but twenty-seven

years old at the time of this extraordinary honor, and relative to his colleagues in attendance at the lectures had little experience in the university,
having accepted a chair in classical philology at Basel at the tender age of
twenty-four. But perhaps this was time enough for so committed a thinker
to discern the limits of academic life, or more precisely where academic
life and the philosophical life parted company and, like a dissimulating
and disillusioned marital couple, became bitter and openly antagonistic.
What began as an ambivalent relationship, a marriage of convenience entered in haste and naivety, would eventually end in divorce before the
decade's close. Well over a century prior to Bill Readings's (1995) influential eulogy for the late twentieth-century North American academy, Nietzsche castigated new generations of scholars who wandered self-satisfied
"among [the] ruins" of the German university, citing both external and
internal institutional conditions that encouraged cowardice, conformity,
and subservience—habits of mind that ran counter to the production of
Thought.[12] Heralded as a sacrosanct establishment singularly devoted to
the pursuit of truth through the practice of right reason, the university
from Nietzsche's perspective proved a far more worldly and compromised,
if not corrupt, enterprise. Not only was its alleged autonomy imperiled
by state power and the dictates of political economy, the institution itself
nurtured intolerance for dissident argumentation, a violation of principle
Nietzsche experienced, in fact, first hand. The lecture series coincided
with the publication of his first book, *The Birth of Tragedy,* which was
greeted with enthusiastic praise by intellectuals like the composer Richard
Wagner. However, his peers in the academy, including one scholar four
years his junior, who would eventually become Germany's leading philol-
ogist, as well as his own teacher and mentor, Friedrich Ritschl, maligned
the text. Generally less well known in the context of his oeuvre, the young
Nietzsche's engagement with the institutional dimensions of education—
and indeed the tragic condition of learning itself[13]—would nonetheless
prove influential for the twentieth century's most prominent intellectuals, including Michel Foucault and Jacques Derrida, who were concerned
not only with the dual encroachment of the state and the economy on
university independence but also with modes of scholarly subjection lived
nevertheless as academic freedom.

In evaluating the contents of Nietzsche's charges against the university and the scholars it produces, we must account simultaneously for their strangely unorthodox and elliptical form, which may or may not bear on his efforts rhetorically to finesse the question of his youth. Intentionality is inevitably a fictional crusade, but perhaps never more so than in a text like Nietzsche's, in which it is impossible decisively to distinguish the philosopher's "own" view from that of the persona he adopts in the lectures. In prudence, however, we must take further pains to attend to the complexity of the artifice through which Nietzsche delivered the 1872 lectures and be particularly wary of easy ascription of inclination, belief, or commitment to its author. To be sure, the judgment on the university is unequivocally harsh; the lectures have been referred to more precisely as Nietzsche's "anti-education manifesto" and the lectures do speak to the very impossibility of thought in the academy; yet at the same time they invoke the absolute necessity of educational institutions, albeit regenerated and renewed.[14] They are condemnatory, to be sure, but their verdict is also curiously heterogeneous and generative, reminding us of their *performed* nature, their attempt to *dramatize* the questions they also explore. Some critics have suggested that it is because of Nietzsche's age and inexperience that the lectures employ such a bizarre, distancing narrative structure and rhetorical style. And indeed, in the opening remarks of his first lecture, Nietzsche acknowledges the limitations of one "ever so young" in confronting the seriousness of the themes at hand—though the acknowledgment also speaks to his obvious rhetorical skill and classical training in thus assuming a *topos* of modesty. Yet he quickly recovers the moment by further asserting that his audience must not discount the possibility that—as a much younger man—"he had *heard* something right about the disquieting future of our educational institutions," which he would proceed to recount for them in good measure.[15] Thus Nietzsche positions himself before his listeners as an "ear-witness" to a dialogue on this important topic between two wise and worthy men, who produce in turn an elaborately interwoven and devastating critique of formal education upon which he is both fortunate enough and bold enough to eavesdrop. The text holds out the promise that what has hitherto been overlooked in the university will be richly compensated by what is overheard. The contrivance enables the narrator to remove himself from what he is about to repeat, and thus avoid responsibility in some measure for the contentious, even outrageous, assertions that will issue from his lips. Yet at the same time, folding himself in the text in this way, Nietzsche implicates himself in the problematic he describes. The framing mechanism that distances also draws its audience in, doubtless to the very edge of their seats, in heightened anticipation of learning about that which brought them to the lecture, and yet, so scandalous, was not meant for them to hear.

Thus begins the first lecture and the strange narrative transport back to an idyllic time when Nietzsche recasts himself as a much younger, care-free student taking a year off to spend in the university city of Bonn with a close friend of similar age. Nietzsche recalls a late summer day spent along the Rhine with his comrade, given over in equal measure to pistol shoot-ing (about which, he remarks, they were quite passionate) and to solemn, philosophical reflection marking the anniversary of the friends' efforts to organize a small circle devoted to cultural production and critique. The scene of Platonic Romance does not remain so enchanted for long, as the two young men are abruptly interrupted in the process of loading and fir-ing their weapons by an enraged old man and his companion, who seize each of them violently by the arm. Having misread their target practice as a duel, the "gray old man" addresses them thus: "Here there will not be dueling! It is least permitted to you, you studying youths! Away with the pistols! Let it rest, be reconciled, shake hands! How can this be? These would be the salt of the earth, the intelligence of the future, the seed of our hopes—and these cannot for once make themselves free from the crazy catechism of honor and its principle of the justice of the fist?"[16] The two pistol shooters correct the old man's misimpression in curt and disrespect-ful tones. They have their own perspectives on dueling and have no use for his commentary, thus they continue to discharge their weapons and further enrage both the old man and his protégé. The old man, full of hatred and helplessness, looks to his companion: "What should we do? These young men are ruining me through their explosions."[17] Taking the cue, the younger man castigates the two gun-toting menaces, charging them thus: "You should of course know that your exploding pleasures are in the present case a true assassination attempt against philosophy. Observe this honorable man—he is in a position to ask you not to shoot here."[18] Ironically, the youths, once they holster their weapons, feel equally threatened in *their* capacity to philosophize by the philosopher's presence.

A more mature Nietzsche recalls his anguish: "A grim feeling came over us. What is any philosophy, we thought, when it hinders being by oneself and enjoying oneself alone with a friend, when it holds us down from becoming philosophers ourselves."[19] The "gray old man" laughs outright at their concern: "How is this? You feared that a philosopher would hinder you from philosophizing? Such a thing may no doubt be found: and you have still not experienced it? Have you no experiences at the university?"[20] The older Nietzsche confides to his audience, tellingly, if not a little mischievously, "We even still had at that time the harmless belief that anyone who possessed the office and title of philosopher at the university was also a philosopher: we were quite without experiences and badly instructed."[21] A series of oppositions is quickly established between youth and maturity, between a kind of frenetic, violent, and thoughtless activity and the calm, pristine silence of reflective consciousness, between a conceptualization of philosophical thought lived as romance and one lived as tragedy. What ensues is a brief fisticuffs over which pair is to remain on the lonely spot of land to which both parties lay special claim for that evening, and the conditions and consequences of their occupying it together.

Given the "vertiginous nesting of identities" in Nietzsche's lectures, much scholarly discourse has not unwisely taken up the perplexing question of the perspective with which the audience should identify.[22] Who are we to assume speaks for Nietzsche: the younger version of himself, the gray philosopher, or his companion, a disillusioned young educator? And which perspective seems trustworthy, if any: a philosopher who is given to false assumptions? Our passionate, pistol-shooting youths? Or are they perhaps all painted with the same ironic brushstrokes? The lectures ultimately were unfinished (seven were forecast) and Nietzsche felt deeply unsatisfied with the results of his labor, deciding against the publication of the series and sharing them instead with close friends. For this reason, Derrida has raised doubts about the very signature of the lectures in his careful reading of them in *Otobiographies*, wisely noting Nietzsche's own eventual rejection of their contents.[23] Not only are we confounded by the purposeful opacity of the narrative, for which we are instructed to "read the secret between the lines," but we remain unsure of the trustworthiness of their perspective—not least of which that of the author himself.

The lectures' opening drama thus provokes several observations and even more questions. To begin, we might note that the encounter between the two young students and the honorable philosopher and his companion may be understood not only as a distancing device, or even a gesture of feigned modesty from the philosopher not generally know for his humility, but also as a crafty rhetorical construction that enables us to think about the university through the specificity of a pedagogical encounter that seemingly, significantly, takes place outside its walls,[24] and this from a variety of perspectives simultaneously: from that of the students, the disillusioned young teacher and scholar, and the mature, indeed "gray," philosopher. The "future" in the lectures' title thus signifies doubly: invoking in the abstract those conditions or counterconditions that will shape the future of higher education, but also foregrounding the question of the young, who are the concrete embodiment of the promise of university—who will not only attend the university but also will eventually teach, administer, and transform the institution—upon which futurity and possibility rest. The young are, as he phrases it, the "intelligence of the future, the seeds of our hopes."[25] Nietzsche's conception of the university to come is informed simultaneously by its corrupt tendencies already in evidence, as the old philosopher and his young protégé bear witness, as well as by the realm of future possibility, in the figure of rowdy students fresh from the Gymnasium. Like all futures, the future of the university is overdetermined, but hardly predetermined, and much will depend on the direction human efforts take. He has offered more than a singular perspective or an isolated moment in the inner workings of the university; he has conveyed with considerable economy a narrowed window on an entire (and entirely flawed) system of education in the very process of reproducing itself.

More profoundly, such a multi-perspectival and multi-layered dissection of formal educational institutions enables him to render more complexly, and by this I mean more multiply and relationally, the very notion of the freedom upon which university futurity rests—a point to which I will return in detail. In brief, let us note here that such freedom for Nietzsche is a quite infrequent occurrence. A universal right only in crude abstraction, freedom as depicted in the above scene and throughout the lectures is in fact a privilege unequally distributed among the men. To be free presupposes a condition of dependence from which one has escaped—in fact, it requires such social division.[26] Thus, freedom is better understood as a relation, one that marks the asymmetry of social condition and implies a social difference, a distinction determined by power within the specificity of a given context (doubly marked in the encounter by the weight of institutional authority mediated by another force, the threat of violence). As a privilege bestowed by those in power, freedom insofar as it circulates in the university does so by the grace of state powers external to it, as the rest of the lectures make tragically visible, thus challenging any pretense to university autonomy. More strikingly still, it is not at all clear what the achievement of freedom in some relative sense affords one—certainly no guarantee of being heard, let alone understood or effectual in the manner one desires. Insofar as we are encouraged to attribute something approximating independence of thought to our gray philosopher, we find him isolated and ill-tempered, forced to witness in horror "the pedagogical impoverishment of the spirit of our times" yet unable to redirect the main currents of contemporary culture that render philosophical reflection an irrelevant if not impossible endeavor—both inside and outside of the university.[27] The students who rebuff the philosopher's insights about dueling may well, as the saying goes, "think and do what they like," but here too we are asked to probe deeper: are they in fact the true source and master of their own (rather herd-like) thoughts and actions? Given the repeated challenges to intentional, independent action, what then is his audience to make of the freedom offered in the catch-phrase "academic freedom," which Nietzsche says signals more precisely a form of enslavement: the "rough and reckless" freedom enjoyed by the "helpless barbarian," the "slave of the day."[28] Though we would do well to query the logic of cultural "degeneration" that informs Nietzsche's characterization of this pretense to intellectual independence, we shall find cause to explore the degree to which "academic freedom" may actually signal the erosion of liberty (or what Arendt would later refer to as "public freedom") and the simultaneous retreat into the private world of individual self-assertion.

But there is yet another mystery placed before us—one I would insist is most urgent and yet strangely neglected. Less remarked upon in the scholarly assessment of the lectures is not only the rather disconcerting figure of the trigger-happy, gun-toting youths who are central characters in the drama. In our post-Virginia Tech, post-Columbine era, in a time of permanent warfare when youth are variously seduced, cajoled, and conscripted to one side or the other of a global war on terror, this is surely a haunting image. Equally disturbing, given the presumptive focus on the peaceful, sanctified halls of higher education, is the pervasive language of war—of battles, enemies, war cries, soldiers, military service, and most unsettling, of national, even civilizational, defense against "degeneration" in the interests of "purifying" the German spirit—in the unfolding narrative of education's futurity. What are we to make of the incessant rhetorical stockpiling of war imagery in the text—of its proximity to the philosopher and the project of the university? What role could an institution premised on the principles of truth and reason—and through these the achievement of peace and justice that is taken to be the very foundation of civilization itself—possibly play in coercion and combat? How are war and violence tied to the production of knowledge and culture vouchsafed by the university? Nietzsche more than hints that modernity's well-rehearsed commitment to reason, law, order, culture, civility, freedom, and justice depends not on the abeyance of war and violence, but on their strategic usage in its interests—and the university's role therein. The observation offered by Nietzsche is less a critique of violence than a naturalistic description of the human inclination toward bellicosity and war. In a direct challenge to Hegel's generous assessment of the state and its ties to education, the gray philosopher argues at length:

For what does one know finally of the difficulty of the task of governing human beings, i.e., to preserve upright law, order, quiet, and peace among many millions of a species in which the great majority are boundlessly egoistic, unjust, unfair, dishonest, envious, wicked, and thereby very limited and queer in the head, and thereby continually to protect the little which the state itself acquires as a possession against greedy neighbors and malicious robbers? Such a hard pressed state grasps after any ally: and indeed one such offers itself in pompous turns of phrase, if he designates it, the state, for example, as this Hegel did, as the "absolutely complete ethical organism" and presents as the task of education for each to find out the place and position where he can be of most useful service to the state—who will take it as a wonder, when the state without further ado falls upon the neck of such an ally offering itself and now even with its deep barbaric voice and full of conviction calls to it: "Yes! You are education! You are culture!"[29]

Nietzsche's philosopher captures in vivid terms not only the rough contours of the "alliance" between the state and its educational apparatus, but also the consequences for allies who "freely" transgress its boundaries: "The state without further ado falls upon the neck of such an ally," he warns. Further, he suggestively proposes that the project of education itself—its commitment to cultural enrichment, to cultivation, and to civilization—thus subordinated to state interests and allegiance (characterized no less as the preservation of law and order) actually creates rather than diminishes, let alone destroys, the very conditions for violence. To be sure, the significance of Nietzsche's theoretical contribution is in exposing the violence of normative liberal institutions, even as later generations of left intellectuals will struggle with, and ultimately reject, the naturalistic inclinations of his political conservatism. As one of the preeminent theorists of modernity, Zygmunt Bauman, explains:

Modernity legitimizes itself as a "civilizing process"—as an ongoing process of making the coarse gentle, the cruel benign, the uncouth refined. Like most legitimations, however, this one is more an advertising copy than an account of reality. At any rate, it hides as much as it reveals. And what it hides is that only through the coercion they perpetuate can the agencies of modernity keep out of bounds the coercion they swore to annihilate; that one person's civilizing process is another person's forceful incapacitation. The civilizing process is not about the uprooting, but about the *redistribution* of violence.[30]

In barbarous lands, the rules of civility do not apply, as colonial history painfully attests. But coercion and force can find approval even within modernity's well-ordered and civil spaces, Bauman elaborates, provided they are *rationally deployed*: "In the land of civility, no coercion (ideally) comes by surprise and from unexpected quarters; it can be rationally calculated, become the 'known necessity' which one can even, following Hegel, celebrate as freedom."[31] In this instance, "civilized violence," or "violence rendered civil" through the "standardizing of forced restrictions or impositions" on those targeted either within or outside of society, is a function of instrumental rationality and the reifications it inevitably produces, rather than a naturalistic or transcendent principle.[32] Have we not seen how the university, thus allied (strategically? coercively?), may serve as the institution par excellence for the provision of the rational calculus, the instrumentalities, the technologies, and the ideological legitimation for the violence executed by the state and its agencies—in Nazi Germany, in the French suppression of Algerian resistance, or, to take a most recent example, in the Pentagon's Minerva Project, which enlists intellectuals in the fight against "Islamic" terrorism? Not only this, but as a further service, it would seem capable of transforming the threat of violence, typically prompting much fear and anxiety, into a welcome kind of security, one "celebrate[d] as freedom" no less. Indeed, as David Theo Goldberg astutely notes, "civility and civil society have been emphasized in moments where the technologies of destruction and degradation are rife," serving as not only a "counter-force to" such conditions but also as an "ideological marker" contrasting the civilized with those denied such status or even its possibility.[33] "Civil wars," he adds, "in states deeming themselves sophisticated, modern and civilized *assume the form of culture wars*" and as we have seen over the past three decades, the university remains a key battleground.[34] But how exactly are we to understand the boundaries of the civilized or the freedoms they secure in this sense?

In raising such questions, Nietzsche's lectures unsettle the core assumptions upon which the modern philosophy of education is founded, as established by Kant, Rousseau, Hegel, Humboldt, and others associated with the liberal humanist university. Indeed, if, as David L. Clark has recently suggested in an illuminating study of eighteenth-century philosophy and war, Kant and the German Idealists have stood accused of extricating themselves from the violence of history "by absorbing its contingent destructiveness into a drama of thought, and by sublating revolutionary war into the mere conflict of the faculties," we shall see that subsequent generations of philosophers, first Nietzsche, then Foucault and Derrida, remain committed to returning the university and its knowledge-producing and disseminating functions to the theater of war.[35] In 1976, just over one hundred years after Nietzsche's lectures at Basel, in fact, Michel Foucault would deliver a lecture at the Collège de France that undertook to examine the relationship between historical knowledge and the practice of war, the disciplinarization of knowledge and the appearance of what he called the "Napoleonic university"—a university newly committed to a particular selection, disciplinarization, and homogenization of knowledges. Declaring that "knowledge is never anything more than a weapon of war," he advanced these Nietzschean themes, revealing the violence that shadows the Western organization of knowledge and its faith in the progress of reason:

the genealogy of knowledge must first . . . outwit the problematic of the Enlightenment. It has to outwit what was at the time described (and was still described in the nineteenth and twentieth centuries) as the progress of enlightenment, the struggle of knowledge against ignorance, of reason against chimeras, of experience against prejudices, of reason against error, and so on. All this has been described as, or symbolized by, light gradually dispelling darkness, and it is this, I think, that we have to get rid of [on the contrary] when we look at the eighteenth century—we have to see, not this relationship between day and night, knowledge and ignorance, but an immense and multiple battle between knowledges in the plural—knowledges that are in conflict because of their very morphology, because they are in the possession of enemies, and because they have intrinsic power effects.[36]

We may find it necessary, at the end of our investigations, to modify Foucault's language, probing what seems like the inevitable weaponization of knowledge production and circulation—as he himself would later abandon efforts to theorize power in such explicitly antagonistic terms, preferring instead an agonistic definition.[37] In our present moment, literally defined by a permanent war against terror, the seduction of what Foucault called the *Nietzschean hypothesis*—that power relations necessarily involve the hostile engagement of forces—cannot be overestimated. At the same time we must be careful to distinguish analytically between a theory of history that elevates violence to a transcendent force in grand, homogenizing sweep and one that is non-naturalist and contingent, that renders struggle in multiple antagonistic and agonistic forms. In the context of the university, the challenge of assessing the appropriate "end" of education—its purpose and our responsibilities toward that "end"—only grows more difficult, as the unabashed commitment to utilitarian, "end-oriented" research becomes increasingly fused with military research that threatens the "end" of humanity. As Derrida pointedly observed:

Today, in the end-orientation of research . . . it is already impossible to distinguish between these two ends. It is impossible, for example, to distinguish programs that one would like to consider "worthy," even technically profitable for humanity, from others that would be destructive. This is not new; but never before has so-called basic scientific research been so deeply committed to ends that are at the same time military ends. The very essence of the military, the limits of military technology and even the limits of the accountability of its programs are no longer definable.[38]

We turn now to explore, first, the relationship between the university and its reputed commitments to the reasoned and autonomous advance of education and culture on the one hand and, on the other, the very complexity of the notion of freedom in its modern edition, which, as we shall see, is firmly rooted in "universalistic" notions of individualism and market economy—which are nonetheless reserved for white Westerners—a freedom vouchsafed through reliance on coercion, force, and violence in its "civilizing" endeavors. And, second, most crucially, we will consider what these might prophesy for youth, for a future of alternative possibilities. Yet at the same time, we must take up the challenge of imagining an exercise of power beyond the relentless culmination of violence, one that entails the possibility of freedom in resistance.

It is when they eventually put away their pistols and settle into a reflective mood that the two rowdy students catch precious bits of dialogue between the old philosopher and his companion. After a verbal lashing by his mentor, the latter is heard defending himself before the philosopher for having abandoned a teaching post. Eager to vindicate his decision, he describes at length the transformation of cultural and educational agendas according to the dictates of "the beloved national economic dogmas of the present," which made his horrified flight essential:

Here we have utility as the goal and the purpose of education, still more exactly acquisition, the highest possible winning of great amounts of money. From out of this direction education would roughly be defined as the insight, with which one keeps oneself "up to date," with which one is familiar with all ways in which money can most easily be made, with which one masters all means through which the traffic between human beings and peoples goes. The authentic task of education according to that would be to form . . . to the highest degree possible "courante" human beings, in the manner in that one calls a coin "courante."[39]

The disillusioned young companion thus underscores the deeply troubled alliance between education and the national economy, an alliance that instrumentalizes education and commodifies knowledge such that it can be sold, traded, franchised, patented, and consumed. Such charges will come as no surprise to those acquainted with the educational signature of our neoliberalized present moment. In this context, a more accelerated version of the one characterized above, scholarly achievement for academics and their pupils alike is evaluated in terms of one's demonstrated superiority as a revenue-generating entity—or the promise of becoming one upon entering the labor market. As Bill Readings bemoaned in *The University in Ruins*, the professor is no longer the hero of the grand narrative of university education, but rather the financially savvy administrator. Even the responsibility of conducting research is secondary to writing grants, applying for scholarships, or finding other means of hustling agencies for funding. But we shall not belabor the point. A formidable and comprehensive literature already exists and continues to grow as critics across the ideological spectrum voice their alarm, and for this reason we will not rehearse the arguments against the reduction of the university mission to one of "growing" the national economy, to borrow the unhappy phrase of one former U.S. president, or indeed the corporate "restructuring" of the university itself.[40]

Significant for our purposes is the consequence of such dramatic transformations, long in their historical unfolding, for thought itself. On this point, the philosopher's disillusioned young companion bristles: "Any education is hateful here that makes solitary, that sticks goals above money and acquisition, that wastes much time."[41] Educational tendencies that transgress the prevailing morality are consequently condemned as "higher egoism" or "immoral . . . educational Epicureanism."[42] What is desired above all else is a "speedy education," in order to quickly become "a money-earning being and indeed such a thorough education in order to be able to become a *very much* money-earning being."[43] For professors and students alike, the watchword is haste, and no more so than in the present era, principally defined by speed. Academics in today's universities confront the same demands for heightened productivity that have come to define the conditions of labor more generally—in the form of teaching more and larger classes, writing grants, serving on administrative committees, filling out activity reports, attending lengthy meetings, responding to e-mail, refereeing journal articles, writing recommendations, and so on. As the disillusioned young educator of Nietzsche's narrative well noted, such frenetic, non-stop activity is hardly conducive to the production of scholarly research or effective pedagogy. And conditions only deteriorate as one descends the university hierarchy—for assistant professors trying to make tenure, for the swelling ranks of adjuncts, and most devastatingly for students, the majority of whom, like no generation before, juggle schoolwork and job(s), yet still face near-insurmountable debt as a result of skyrocketing tuition, reduced financial aid, and dismantled social services.

In his most recent reflections on education, significantly titled "Hurried Life, or Liquid-Modern Challenges to Education," Zygmunt Bauman draws on a metaphorics strikingly similar to Nietzsche's characterization of the "up to date" human products of the "courante" system of education. The contemporary educational mandate, Bauman argues, is to "keep ahead of the style pack." Responsive to the transition from Nietzsche's society of producers to the new "liquid modern" society of consumers, Bauman traces the contours of a new herd mentality: "*Being* ahead is the sole trustworthy recipe for the style pack's acceptance, while *staying* ahead is the only way to make sure the supply of respect is comfortably ample and continuous."[44] The educational imperative that follows from the desire in consumers to stay ahead may be summarized in the commitment to "a life of *rapid learning—and swift forgetting.*"[45] Not to be confused with the ancient Greek commitment to "life-long learning," the contemporary educational imperative does not speak the language of development or maturation; it does not invoke time-consuming commitments to thinking, planning, or acting in the long term, based on the slow, careful accumulation of knowledge, tested and retested, and where found wanting, improved. It neither learns from the lessons of history nor anticipates, let alone prepares for, future needs. The reason to hurry, he argues, "is not to acquire and collect as much as possible, but to discard and replace as much as one can."[46] Thinking, under this mandate, only gets in the way. The lessons of yesterday, after all, will not help one pull out in front of the style pack today, anymore than yesterday's fashion. Knowledge, like all commodities, now has a "use-by" date.

What kind of being does such an educational system produce—what future does it augur not only for education, but for public life more generally? Less and less likely, as Nietzsche predicted, is one who dares to think. James Miller, biographer of Michel Foucault, noted that the idea of leading a philosophical life is quite likely today to be dismissed as "misguided, immodest and self-aggrandizing."[47]As Readings observed in *The University in Ruins*, the question now posed to the university is not "how to turn the institution into a haven for thought but how to think in an institution whose development tends to make thought more and more difficult, less and less necessary."[48] Of course, Nietzsche recognized in his opening comments that the philosopher's competence ends where the future begins. His parable of the pedagogical encounter in the woods provided the vehicle for disclosing the connections and consequences of human conduct and choice in matters educational and the possible futures to which these point—for students of both the Gymnasium and the University, which is where Nietzsche focuses his sympathetic and yet uncompromisingly critical gaze in the second half of the lectures. The future of our educational institutions, he urges, will be a function of how young people negotiate the often contradictory and counterproductive modes of scholarly subjection that are championed as an achievement of individual self-assertion and self-creation, the apogee of academic freedom.

Before exploring Nietzsche's analysis of how students fare in such compromised institutions, I would like to argue that the deepening crisis of thought—and the crisis of academic freedom—to which Nietzsche and generations of intellectuals have come to refer is part of a broader reduction, or privatization, of the very concept of freedom as it circulates throughout the modern period, which has been intimately tied to aggressive individualism on the one hand and to the market economy and the glittering world of consumption on the other. This conception of freedom, it cannot be overemphasized, remained, throughout much of the modern era, a privilege even in its pretense to universal application, excluding non-whites, women, and white men who were not also property owners. As we shall see, it is toward these twin features of modern freedom that formal educational institutions arc, much to the peril of democratic public life and to themselves, as institutions devoted to the education of citizens necessary to sustain and advance public interests. The modern conceptual commitment to what Arendt called variously "public freedom" or liberty, as captured in the pledge for "liberty and justice for all," came nevertheless to be realized, or lived, as autonomous individualism. Freedom in this sense precisely translates into a freedom *from* social dependence and social responsibility. The conception of freedom as the ability to govern oneself, an ideal that inflamed many revolutionary movements and ushered the West into modernity, was, rather abruptly, traded in for the dream of being "left alone" by government. Even as constitutional governments were being formed in the eighteenth century, the question of whether the end of government was to be prosperity or freedom remained a deeply unsettled issue. (And thus the end of education, as we shall see, remains equally ambivalent.) Arendt's attentive reading of one of the founding documents of the French Revolution, Maximilien Robespierre's "Principles of Revolutionary Governments," reveals an extraordinary equivocation and ambivalence about the role of government and the kind of freedom it was bound to honor and protect. She writes:

He started by defining the aim of constitutional government as the preservation of the republic which revolutionary government had founded for the purpose of establishing public freedom. Yet, no sooner had he defined the chief aim of constitutional government as the "preservation of public freedom" than he turned about, as it were, and corrected himself: "Under constitutional rule it is almost enough to protect individuals against the abuses of public power." With this second sentence, power is still public and in the hands of government, but the individual has become powerless and must be protected against it. *Freedom, on the other hand, has shifted places; it resides no longer in the public realm but in the private life of the citizens and so must be defended against the public and its power.*[49]

Freedom remains a value to be protected, but it is now a freedom dispatched to the realm of private life. Citing a similar tendency in the American context, she concludes that the "fatal passion for riches," that particular pursuit of happiness, tended to extinguish the very impulse toward political and moral duty such that revolutionary notions of "*public* happiness and *political* freedom" disappeared altogether from the American scene.[50] Ironically, it was the unleashing of consumer desires and market freedoms from communal obligation and authority that would thus come to serve as a palliative or compensation for the loss of public freedom and community autonomy. Of course, the trade-off came at catastrophic cost. In the contest between the self-assertive, sovereign individual and the imperatives of capital, the former inevitably loses, as the acquisitive, imperialistic inclination of markets necessarily induces a progressive erosion of liberty, a corruption of politics, and a deeper retreat into private life. With the loss of communal self-rule and social obligation, the clash of all those individual "free" wills is mediated of necessity by new modes of regulation, coercion, and force. This pitched competition, however, should not be understood as merely the interplay of similarly free agents; some establish the norms of the social order that the others will be compelled to obey. "Hence the duality of modern individuality," Bauman notes, "on the one hand, it is the natural inalienable appurtenance of every human being; on the other hand, however, it is something to be created, trained, legislated upon and enforced by authorities" entrusted to maintain the social order.[51] Not all individuals, as we have already noted, are found equally amenable to such refining and civilizing efforts. The modern conception of civility is more than just casually inflected with racial (as well as class and gendered) significance, and the forms of domination to which it gives legitimacy shape the entire social order, its "regimes of privileges and immunities" to invoke Achille Mbembe's memorable phrase.[52] For those who fall outside the ever-thickening walls of civil society, training in the art of autonomous individualism is less an option than is strict containment of perceived anti-social or uncivil inclinations. Without the threat of force, the dream of perpetual peace proves illusive in a context in which acquisitive, self-interested individuals are pitted against one another in the market game of winner-take-all. Thus the question of security quickly comes to the fore— in the interests of both acquiring guarantees of safety and nurturing the resentment that comes from the constraints such guarantees inevitably imply.[53]

Our specific challenge is to understand how these tensions play out in the context of the university and its commitment to academic freedom, which for Nietzsche proves a similarly reductive and privatized freedom, associated with the protocols of self-assertion and acquisition. How do young people—students in the pre-university and university phases of their educational careers—negotiate the promise of autonomous individualism and at the same time the relentless imposition of norm and order in the interests of cultivating character and civility? Is it the possibility of renegade thought that renders thinking so perilous an endeavor, to be all but officially expunged from the corridors of education? As we think through this question, we must also consider which condition, in truth, creates more potential violence—the relentless instrumentalization of thought or its very absence? In place of the arduous and protracted journey to intellectual autonomy, that elusive dream of enlightenment, we have already seen how the incursions of the political economy and the imperatives of a "speedy education" have undermined the conditions for, as well as the necessity of, thought and reflection. In later lectures, Nietzsche explains—or rather reveals—"what he has heard" about the consequences for thought when students are seduced by the cult of individualism. The gray philosopher warns his companion that this most treacherous abuse of students begins in the Gymnasium. There, student preparation for university culminates in the so-called "German work," in essence, an "appeal to the individual," which takes the form of a series of assignments devoted to "personal shaping," which he characterizes as a theme that is "in and for itself unpedagogical, through which the student is prevailed upon to give a description of his own life, of his own development."[54] For the philosopher, the result of the German work proves disastrous as "probably most all students, without their guilt, have to suffer their lives from this too-early-demanded work of the personality, from this unripe generation of thoughts." Not only do most students "suffer their lives" for this early invitation to self-indulgence and excess, but its success portends the ruination of the future literary establishment: "and now often the whole later literary action of a human being appears as the sad result of that pedagogical original sin against the spirit."[55]

In thinking through the possible futures of education, we may well consider this moment of "pedagogical original sin" as well as its connection to what the philosopher refers to as the production of the "guilty innocent" in relation to those students who eventually enter the university system. When they are juxtaposed in this fashion, we notice at once a recurrent characterization of youthful innocence and exuberance that makes all the more painful the unfolding narrative about their trust and participation in an educational system that mitigates the possibility for critical thought and reflective action, renouncing its very mission. Herein lies the birth of tragedy in education. On the one hand, we witness a violence done to youth, in all their audacious naiveté and vulnerability, that is represented as and indeed experienced by young people as intellectual independence, about which they understand nothing and against which they are all but helpless to resist. On the other, we also see their growing complicity with, and participation in, the forms of violence to which thoughtlessness eventually gives way, which they neither recognize nor oppose.

Though it is a form of coercion experienced as individual choice and self-creation, Nietzsche's gray philosopher recognizes that students enjoy the German work, describing how "the staggering feeling of the required independence clothes these products with a first and foremost, but never returning, captivating magic."[56] Yet the results are nothing short of ruinous for the young person's intellectual growth and maturation:

All audacities of nature are called forth out of their depths, all vanities, held back by no more powerful barrier, are allowed for the first time to assume a literary form: the young human being feels himself from now on as one who has become ready, as a being capable, indeed required, to speak, to converse. Those themes obligate him to deliver his vote on poets' works or to press together historical persons in the form of a character portrait or independently to present serious ethical problems, or even, with a turned around light, to illuminate his own becoming and to deliver a critical report on himself: in short, a whole world of the most reflective tasks spreads itself out before the surprised, up-till-now almost unconscious, young human being and is abandoned to his decision.[57]

The acquisition of premature independence and self-reliance virtually guarantees that students will never achieve the maturity necessary for self-reflective, critical intellectual thought. Their students thus abandoned to the development of "free personality," teachers default on their principal obligation: to teach them how to think and live in a society of other human beings, which requires the capacity for judgment, the awareness of self-limitation, the recognition of interests, and the confidence required for decision making. The aggrandizing injunction to self-narrate hardly guarantees such insight. "To think, really to think," as the postcolonial phenomenologist Lewis Gordon eloquently argues, "is to engage the frightening evidence of our own conceptual limitations and to realize, in such limits, the magnitude of all that transcends us."[58] Nietzsche, of course, was less concerned with the ways in which the performance of "free personality," like acquisitive individualism, bodes poorly for future awareness of self-limitation or for recognition of communal obligation and authority than with the ways such indulgences derailed potential genius. More chillingly still is the philosopher's observation that what feels like independent assertion to the student only provides fodder for the most conventional forms of regulation and censorship. How do teachers respond to these "first original achievements"? They do so primarily by redressing "all excesses of form and thought, that is to everything that in this age is characteristic and individual."[59] The ironic result of which is this: this first burst of "authentic independence"—compelled yet also eager to express itself "all too early in time . . . in awkwardness, in sharpness, and grotesque features, thus precisely the individuality"—is exactly what is excised, "reproved and rejected by the teacher in favor of an unoriginal average respectability."[60] The consequence for youth is neither intellectual growth nor political agency, but "self-complacency," unripened intellectual production driven by haste and vanity, as well as "unfermented and characterless" expression inevitably supportive of the established order.[61]

In the university, we witness similarly privative and insular scholarly pursuits, in addition to more sophisticated betrayals of thought with the ascendancy of scientism, historicism, and positivistic pretensions to moral neutrality. Of the penchant for historicism, Nietzsche's gray philosopher moans: "To suppress and cripple it, to divert or to starve it, to that end all those youths of 'modern times,' already resting in the lab of the 'self-evident,' eagerly exert themselves: and the favorite means is to paralyze that natural philosophic drive through historical culture."[62] In the place of deep philosophical reflection of "eternal" problems, students in philosophy seminars are asked to ponder insular questions of the most conforming and socially irrelevant academic type: "what this or that philosopher has thought or not, whether this or that writing can justly be ascribed to him, or whether this or that kind of reading deserves priority." With this "neutral dealing of philosophy," the gray old man insists, *philosophy itself is banished from the university.*"[63]

As a result, "our academic 'independents,'" Nietzsche's philosopher notes with irony, are forced to live without philosophy and art—the pillars of ancient Greek *paideia*—because of the present-day university's indifference to "such dead educational inclinations," and for this reason they are unfit and unprepared for the intellectual demands of the university. He calls them, for this reason, the "guilty innocent," who surely are not responsible for creating such conditions, yet accommodate themselves to them, participate in them, vacillating moodily between the same exultant illusion of academic freedom as their counterparts of the Gymnasium and a crushing self-doubt and helplessness:

You must understand the secret language that this guilty innocent uses before himself: then you would also learn to understand the inner essence of that independence that likes to be worn externally for show. None of the noble, well-equipped youths remained distant from that restless, tiresome, confounding, enervating educational necessity: for that time, in which he is apparently the single free man in a clerks' and servants' reality, he pays for that grandiose illusion of freedom through ever-renewing torments and doubts. He feels that he cannot lead himself, he cannot help himself: then he dives poor in hopes into the daily world and into daily work: the most trivial activity envelops him. . . . Suddenly he again rouses himself: he still feels the power, not waned, that enabled him to hold himself aloft. Pride and noble resolution form and grow in him. It terrifies him to sink so early into the narrow, petty moderation of a specialty.[64]

Over time the student suffers under the weight of early educational indulgences that invite self-satisfied self-narration over and against intensive and systemic study of classic thought, as was Nietzsche's predilection. Eventually, the guilty innocent confronts in agony and acute embarrassment all that he doesn't know. The student's attempt to rouse himself from his own narrowness, he notes, is "in vain." Thus we learn how the patience for, and the eventual investment in, the "trivial activity" and the "petty moderation" of specialization already in evidence in the pedagogy of the philosophy seminar begin to take hold. But even this tragic turn in intellectual interest doesn't hold for long: the guilty innocents come to pay dearly for their grandiose illusion of freedom as they run in full flight from thought itself. Nietzsche's philosopher continues the tragic parable:

In an empty and disconsolate mood he sees his plans go up in smoke: his condition is abominable and undignified: he alternates between overexcited activity and melancholic enervation. Then he is tired, lazy, fearful of work, terrified in the face of everything great and hating himself. He dissects his capacities and thinks he is looking into a hollow or chaotically filled space. Then again he plunges from the heights of the dreamed self-importance into ironic skepticism. . . . He now seeks his consolation in hasty, incessant activity in order to hide from himself under it.[65]

Moving between "overexcited activity" and "melancholic enervation," between "self-importance" and "ironic skepticism," this self-hating creature hides from himself in "hasty, incessant activity," which in further irony is precisely what the university (necessarily complacent, we recall, in its relation to the state) encourages and rewards. Just as the teacher of the Gymnasium works to replace the initial sparks of authentic individuality with the mediocrity of respectable convention, Nietzsche's philosopher insinuates the presence of the State in the most mundane of pedagogical encounters in the university: The teacher speaks what he wants to listening students who hear what they want, a "double independence" praised "with high glee as 'academic freedom.'"[66] Only, the gray old man insists, "behind both groups at a discreet distance stands the state, with a certain taut overseer's mien, in order to remind from time to time that it is the purpose, the goal, the be-all-and-end-all of this strange speaking-and-listening procedure."[67] Thus he reveals how the state's proclaimed commitment to mass education, as evidenced by its surplus of educational institutions and teachers, is merely cover for its "hidden feud" with the very spirit of education.[68]

To be sure, there can be little disagreement with the troubling characterization of education reduced to a means of economic advance that carefully brackets all non-instrumental questions of social concern, or reduced to a stage for forms of self-aggrandizing individualism that avoid the imposition of a dialogic encounter with others (in the form of other histories, critical traditions, archives)—all of which serve capitalist interests well, but undermine the viability of democratic societies committed to the Arendtian notion of "public happiness and individual freedom." But the philosopher's concern appears not to lie with the interests of communal self-rule and participatory democracy. Rather, his purpose has been to reveal how far German education has fallen from the Platonic ideal of an "empire of the intellect," and how the state, arming its citizenry with the pretension of an education, renders them slaves: "Because the genuine German spirit is hated, because one fears the aristocratic nature of true education, because one wants to drive the great individuals thereby into self-imposed exile," he argues, "so that one may plant and nurture pretensions to education in the many, because one seeks to run away from the narrow and hard discipline of great leaders, so that one may persuade the mass it will find the way even by itself—under the guiding star of the state!"[69] Most disturbing is the solace Nietzsche's philosopher finds in ultranationalist and pugilistic sentiment: "though the state thus fights [the German spirit] is nonetheless brave: it will thoroughly save itself in fighting into a purer period" and it will be "noble" and "victorious."[70] Whether this is a straightforward resolution or deeply ironic, of course, we don't know.

Such solace anticipates, in the end, the old philosopher's counsel to the specific suffering of youths who have been thus abandoned to their own devices. The young Nietzsche and his companion may yet find an appropriate use for their weapons. "Think of the fate of the *Burschenschaft*," the old philosopher insists, "a tragically serious and singularly instructive attempt to disperse that filmy mist [condensed over the university] and to open up the view for the future in the direction of the high cloud-walking German spirit."[71] The *Burschenschaft* was a violent, revolutionary student movement that grew out of the Wars of Liberation against Napoleon.[72] But the philosopher nonetheless describes the actions of the youth in vividly heroic terms: "In the war the youth had carried home the unexpected worthiest of prizes of battle, the freedom of the fatherland."[73] Chillingly, we note, these revolutionary youth eventually brought the war to the university, where they witnessed in terror "the un-German barbarism, artfully hidden among eruditions of all kinds" among their peers who there had been "abandoned to a repulsive youthful giddiness."[74] And it is through the glories of battle that youth finally become self-consciously aware of their collective betrayal and achieve intellectual acuity and insight:

the student foresaw in what depths a true educational institution must be rooted: namely in an inner renewal and excitation of the purest moral powers. And this should be retold forever of the students to their fame. On the slaughtering field he may have learned what he could learn least of all in the sphere of "academic freedom': that one needs great leaders, and that all education begins with obedience. . . . Now he learned to understand Tacitus, now he grasped Kant's categorical imperative.[75]

The violence of a thoroughly instrumentalized education based on acquisition and pedagogically induced self-aggrandizement produces beings who live in a world where others are either recast as reified objects or made to disappear altogether. The clash of interests thus eventually begets the revolutionary violence of students in open revolt against the state and its decadent institutions. And this comes to characterize the true lesson of academic freedom. But what Nietzsche's philosopher has described is hardly a revolution for independence as the eighteenth century has defined it for us, but rather the reseating of an aristocracy, founded on the "purest moral powers" (an absolutism ironically encouraging its own kind of anti-intellectualism), which simultaneously destroys the possibility of a viable democratic polity, and the necessity for thought in the interests of substantive democratic and liberatory self-rule.

Let us ponder this distinction a bit more. Interestingly, Zygmunt Bauman, in his recent essay on education already cited above, like Nietzsche takes the measure of the vast distance between the learning and memorizing injunctions of the ancient Greek notion of *paideia* and the contemporary university system in which teachers and students alike are obliged, as we may recall, to undertake an endless task of fast learning and forgetting. Whether thought is sacrificed in the name of instrumental rationalities or increased economic efficiency and speed, the upshot is tragic, not from the perspective of Nietzschean intellectual aristocracy, but rather because of a democratic society's inability to learn from its history and make the painstaking effort to confront and redress its transgressions in the pursuit of public freedom and more just and sustainable futures. For Bauman, as for Nietzsche, the consequences of this pedagogical betrayal of successive generations of students are the same—only violence and destruction. Thus we might add another twist to Carl von Clausewitz's obsessively quoted insistence that "war is a continuation of politics by other means" by claiming that in the absence of the conditions for thought that enable politics, war is a continuation of the project of education by other means.[76] Nor should we be surprised that in Bauman's meditation on contemporary education, the specter of armed youth and death-dealing weapons and the language of war quickly come to the fore of his exposition, as they did in Nietzsche's. In Bauman's extended metaphor, teachers of the modern era served as the "launchers of ballistic missiles," instructing students, now morphed into weapons of mass destruction, to stay on their predetermined course for maximal momentum. Ballistic missiles were ideal for positional warfare, when targets were stationary or inert and missiles were the only elements of the battle in motion. Once targets become mobile, once they become invisible to the gunner, as is now the case in our allegedly advanced "liquid modern era," ballistic missiles become useless or nearly so. The solution is educational, as Nietzsche would say, and doubly so: a smart, or "intelligent missile." A smart missile, Bauman explains, is

a missile that can change its direction in full flight, depending on changing circumstances, one that can spot immediately the target's movements, learn from them whatever can be learned about the target's current direction and speed—and extrapolate from the gathered information the spot in which their trajectories may cross. Such smart missiles cannot suspend, let alone finish the gathering and processing of information as it travels— its target may never stop moving and changing its direction and speed, so that plotting the place of encounter needs to be constantly updated and corrected.[77]

Accordingly, the students-as-smart-missiles learn as they go, requiring the conditions of instruction to change accordingly. In the instantaneous transmission and reception of targeted information, the negation of the necessary space and time for focused and judicious thought and reflection inevitably results, Bauman asserts, in the negation of the very conditions for politics. The resultant destruction, now reconceived as the apparent end of education, achieves greater efficiency and impact:

So what [smart missile students] need to be initially supplied with is the *ability* to learn, and learn fast. This is obvious. What is less visible, however, though no less crucial than the skill of quick learning, is the ability to instantly *forget* what has been learned before. . . . They should not overly cherish the information they acquired a moment earlier and on no account should they develop a habit of behaving in a way that the information suggested. All information they acquire ages rapidly and, instead of providing reliable guidance, may lead astray, if it not promptly dismissed—erased from memory. What the "brains" of the smart missiles must never forget is that the knowledge they acquire is eminently *disposable*, good only until further notice and of only temporary usefulness, and that the warrant of success is not to overlook the moment when that acquired knowledge is of no more use and needs to be thrown away, forgotten, and replaced.[78]

Bauman's metaphor serves well to underscore the breadth and scope of the violence of such evolved "educational" imperatives, as it simultaneously underscores the ways in which precarity of the world young people inhabit multiplies daily. Yet, they have been afforded neither the educational resources nor the guidance of their elders, which might help them imagine a future that is other than apocalyptic. As a consequence of our devastatingly misguided priorities and our negligence, we have, in short, produced smart bombs and explosive children.

As much as we may resist generalizing from the particularities of contemporary gun-toting youth such as Seung-Hui Cho or Steven Kazmierczak, or the thousands of youth transformed into ticking human time-bombs for one side or another of a permanent global war of terror, there is, as Nietzsche would say, something "instructive" in remembering them as a tragic index of the insufferable conditions that most contemporary young people face and the possible futures to which they point. Whatever ambivalence we feel about the conclusion of Nietzsche's bizarre lectures—indeed, he well shared our ambivalence—he was correct in his prescient observation (which, recall, he insisted would become clear only to future generations) that our educational institutions, in their capitulation to business, to military, to state interests, have utterly abandoned their responsibilities to youth and to the future.

In 1987, the conservative critic and self-described intellectual descendant of Nietzsche, Allan Bloom, penned his (in)famous diatribe against the university, *The Closing of the American Mind.* An instant national bestseller when it appeared, it has achieved in the ensuing years the status of a much-venerated classic, shaping for over two decades common-sense conceptions about the university and about young people. In the book's conclusion, Bloom bemoaned that "the university now offers no distinctive visage to the young person. . . . There is no vision, nor is there a set of competing visions, of what an educated man is. The question has disappeared, for to pose it would be a threat to the peace."[79] Bloom's diagnosis, however, is flawed in both of its principal observations. First, the university rarely has a coherent *vision of the young person* to whom it should offer a conception of "the educated man." Bloom's book is in no small way responsible for this absence, given the brilliant success and pervasive influence of his grotesque characterization of the younger generations as illiterate, inarticulate, in the throes of Dionysian frenzy, and utterly unworthy and incapable of receiving an Enlightened university education. "Picture a thirteen-year-old boy," he famously wrote,

sitting in the living room of his family home doing his math assignment while wearing his Walkman headphones or watching MTV. He enjoys the liberties hard won over centuries by the alliance of philosophic genius and political heroism, consecrated by the blood of martyrs; he is provided with comfort and leisure by the most productive economy ever known to mankind; science has penetrated the secrets of nature in order to provide him with the marvelous, lifelike electronic sound and image reproduction he is enjoying. And in what does progress culminate? A pubescent child whose body throbs with orgasmic rhythms; whose feelings are made articulate in hymns to the joys of onanism or the killing of parents; whose ambition is to win fame and wealth in imitating the drag-queen who makes the music. In short, life is made into a nonstop, commercially prepackaged masturbatory fantasy.[80]

Youth in this context are transformed into dangerous parasites feeding off the "genius" and "heroism" "hard won over centuries"—hardly, as Nietzsche described, to his credit, the very "seeds of our hopes" and our future.

Even progressive thinkers engaged in the ongoing struggle over academic freedom in the generalized assault on the university, as Henry Giroux has long pointed out, seldom reference youth—what it means to prepare them for the future, to enable them to evaluate different futures, what their needs are in these interests, and what the university's responsibility is in relation to student needs.[81] When student academic freedom is occasionally invoked by the Right it is typically a ruse, as in the singular perversion of David Horowitz, whose principal aim is precisely to "protect" students from thought, to abolish thought from the university altogether in the interests of turning it into what is ironically called a "think tank." Yet a commitment to the university as a place to think "without condition," as Derrida would say, if not in absolute freedom, and to the future of the university predicated on Thought, must begin with engaging students and those conditions in and outside the academy that routinely undermine their critical capacities and, with this, their political agency.

However we choose to characterize youth, whatever undesirable features we assign to them, are more precisely a function of the world they have inherited, as shaped by adult decision—a world marred by extreme uncertainty, instability, volatility, and war. In his comprehensive study of recent school shootings, Douglas Kellner aptly notes that today's youth, unlike previous generations, face even more anxiety-producing and dangerous threats as a result of terrorism, war, ecological destruction, and ever-worsening political and economic realities. Their realities—myriad and diverse to be sure—are shaped in the main by the dissolution of the family, downward mobility, staggering unemployment, particularly for youth of color, growing abuse and domestic conflict, drug and alcohol abuse, poor education and dilapidated schools, and escalating criminalization and imprisonment.[82] Such lived realities not only shape student access to education, but they impose, for those who manage the tuition, the crushing constraints of time, as the majority of youth must juggle one or more jobs as well as the demands their studies impose. Even upon entering the classroom, today's students must also negotiate the changing conditions of university education that inevitably mediate their academic motivations and performance, from growing class sizes and diminishing teaching resources—including such essentials as up-to-date computing and digital technologies—to increasing inaccessibility of faculty, who face multiple new responsibilities and time demands of their own. But for this indiscretion, faculty are largely let off the hook, not because it is largely out of their hands, but rather because the debt students almost inevitably accrue sends them searching for skills training, leaving neither time for, nor interest in, higher learning.

Second, the pervasive "peace" on university campuses to which Bloom refers is proving more and more chimerical, if it ever existed, as its mission, its research agendas, and its pedagogical imperatives shift more and more to military interests. As our historical reading of Nietzsche makes evident, and the last three decades have made unbearably obvious, universities have been inundated with war talk. Bloom himself proved a most stalwart warrior in what became known on campuses across the country as "the culture wars." As Donald Lazere brilliantly exposes on the occasion of the twentieth anniversary of *The Closing of the American Mind*, beneath Bloom's discourse of truth and light and peace is an avowed Straussian eager for battle and the destruction of enemies. But this logic of antagonism was never limited to the culture wars. As Derrida observed, the creep of militarization throughout the university has redefined "the entire field of information," not just disciplines associated with the technosciences, but all aspects of academic research:

At the service of war, of national and international security, research programs have to encompass the entire field of information, the stockpiling of knowledge, the workings and thus also the essence of language and of all semiotic systems, translation, coding and decoding, the play of presence and absence, hermeneutics, semantics, structural and generative linguistics, pragmatics, rhetoric. I am accumulating all these disciplines in a haphazard way, on purpose, but I will end with literature, poetry and the arts, and fiction in general: the theory that has these disciplines as its objects can be just as useful in ideological warfare as it is in experimentation with variables in all-too-familiar perversions of the referential function.[83]

The consequences of advancing militarization for humanistic inquiry are already well known, as the expertise of intellectuals who specialize in the languages and cultures of Islam, for example, are tapped by officials in the Pentagon and Department of Defense for the honing and perfecting of tactics and methods of torture.[84] Under such obscene conditions, the university response "to the call of the principle of reason . . . to render reason," as Derrida describes, now serves the interests of "extraordinary rendition." To paraphrase Arendt, it is enough, apparently, to know how to assemble and advance new technologies of war, how to break the enemy by whatever means necessary, we no longer need to be able to talk about them, or question them—much less be required to think about the consequences of the recourse to violence and the inevitably violent response it garners.

Unless we confront such challenges, the logic of permanent war will surely continue to increase global fear, insecurity, and volatility, as well as the generalized anxiety, nihilism, and suffering of youth. For Kellner, the myriad difficulties youth face erupt in violence—particular male violence—as a result of the escalating militarism, jingoistic patriotism, and extremist gun culture that are the definitive legacy of right-wing policies (supported in the main by both Democrats and Republicans) of the last three decades. The danger, against the backdrop of the nation's lengthy history of civic violence, is to perceive such shifts as normative, natural, and inevitable-or, worse still, to imagine that such a tragic state of affairs is not our concern.[85] Surely our youth deserve a future better than the apocalyptic one now on order.

CHAPTER FIVE

Critique of Racial Violence: The Theologico-Political Reflections of Lewis R. Gordon

To read what was never written.

—WALTER BENJAMIN

In our globalized, neoliberalized, post-9/11 world, the threat of violence multiplies daily, as do the sources, rationales, types of violence; the justifications for violence; and the threat of international and domestic terrorism. State violence, insurrectionary violence against the state. Racial violence, the violence of racial erasure. Justification, counter-justification. Sophisticated, crude. Religious, ideological. Legal, illegal. If there is a way to break the chain of global violence, I don't imagine the solutions to be bureaucratic, or technical, or privatized, or militarized, or profit-driven. It is a tragedy then that those universities organized primarily, if not exclusively, in these interests will have very little to offer us in a time of our greatest need. For I do think productive and nonviolent modes of response are in the realm of the educative, but one that draws, as I hope to demonstrate in this chapter, on complex histories, philosophies, theological, literary, and artistic traditions, globally entwined and regionally elaborated, that require the most careful, creative, compassionate, and self-critical interpretive and analytic capacities intellectuals in and out of the academy can call forth.

In 2004, Hent de Vries, director of the Amsterdam School of Cultural Analysis at the University of Amsterdam, and Lawrence E. Sullivan, director of the Center for the Study of World Religions at the Divinity School of Harvard University, organized an international conference to discuss and debate the contemporary resurgence of religion and its consequences for both the concept of the political (i.e., notions of sovereignty, democracy, the public sphere) and politics itself (i.e., its juridical, administrative, and policy-oriented aspect and institutional arrangement). The bulk of these presentations eventually made their way to publication in revised and expanded form in 2006 in an anthology titled *Political Theologies: Public Religions in a Post-Secular World*, a roughly 800–page volume remarkable as much for its considerable length as for the density and richness of its contributions to so timely a topic. What prompted this intense scholarly attention to questions of the theologico-political by dozens of intellectuals of outstanding international reputation—among them, Jürgen Habermas, Chantal Mouffe, Judith Butler, Jean-Luc Nancy, Claude Lefort, Ernesto Laclau, Wendy Brown, Talal Asad, Samuel Weber, even Pope Benedict XVI—is what appears to be a starkly ironic consequence of neoliberal globalization: in short, the pervasive ascendancy and force of "public religions" in an era marked by the presumptive triumph of Enlightenment secularization. The global spread or imposition, as is often the case in underdeveloped countries, of particular forms of political and economic life—of parliamentary or representative modes of democratic governance and capitalist entrepreneurship and mass marketization—has in turn produced widespread resistance by social and cultural movements whose discontent is often expressed in *theological-political* terms, which, the editors carefully note, may or may not make them necessarily *religious*.

While productive responses to this apparent paradox prove frustratingly provisional when not entirely elusive, difficult questions, the editors warn, are legion: How does one talk about the religious? Does modern sovereignty in fact derive all its power from secularized theological sources, as some conservative jurists have asserted, or are various religious traditions merely epiphenomenal effects of larger social and economic processes, as Marx and others have argued? Just how universal is the rigid division between the public sphere of politics and the private realm of individual morality and belief systems generally informed by various religious traditions, taken to be among the defining—though increasingly contested—features of modern democratic states? How successful is the insistent reassertion of said separation between church and state, and the presumptive neutrality of the latter, in countering forms of dissent, even violence, that claim to be religiously inspired? Is another language required? What impact do theologically justified acts of terrorism have on the authority and power of religious traditions—as sources of moral suasion and inspiration as well as social cohesion and identity? Conversely, how does legal violence in the form of police action and war reflect upon the moral limits of the modern liberal state? And what kinds of pressures—accommodating or undermining—do the world's religions exert on those political institutions, economic relations, and cultural configurations associated with neoliberal globalization?[1] The manifold and complex challenges of such a formidable set of interrelated inquiries, the editors astutely conclude, require a collective effort informed by richly interdisciplinary perspectives and varied methodological approaches, from the historical, cultural, and sociological to the ontological and metaphysical.

When the international collaboration was first discussed in 1997–98, according to its chief architects, "political theology" was a term "seldom heard in wider academic debate, beyond historical references to the writings of Ernst Kantorowicz, Carl Schmitt, and 'theologies of liberation.'"[2] Mainstream scholarly indifference abruptly ended in the years following September 11, 2001, as questions about the relationship between religion and violence, politics and force, legally sanctioned war and acts of terror, and what are, in essence, "morally good and morally evil ways of killing" in the new global world order became more insistent, if no less opaque, contradictory, and often crudely ideological.[3] Intellectual exercises in distinguishing between just war and terrorism based on levels of cruelty inflicted or even the threat posed to entire ways of life have foundered on a review of historical evidence that favors neither, revealing that it is quite often the alleged "civilizational status" of the actors involved that proves decisive in the designation of legality and thus legitimacy. "What is really at stake is not a clash of civilizations (a conflict between two incompatible sets of values) but the fight of civilization against the uncivilized," asserts Talal Asad, citing the discursive (as well as technological and military) continuities between the contemporary war on terrorism and the "small wars" of an earlier colonial era.[4] Observing the need for a nuanced, scholarly self-reflection often missing in debates on contemporary violence and its scenes of legitimation, Judith Butler suggestively asserts that "a critique of violence is an inquiry into the conditions of violence, but it is also an interrogation of how violence is circumscribed in advance by the questions we pose of it. What is violence, then, such that we can pose this question of it, and do we not need to know how to handle this question before we ask, as we must, what are the legitimate and illegitimate forms of violence?"[5] Liberal modernity's assumption of equivalence between law and justice has proven as troubled as the presumed distance between its structures of legality and its recourse to coercive force and brutality.

To be sure, the relevance of the concept of political theology, if questionable only a decade ago, is now indisputable, not only in terms of how scholars might extend the historical reach and analytic depth of the pressured relation between various faith traditions and structures of governance, but also, and uncomfortably, in terms of the challenges thereby posed to Western modernity's self-understanding in terms of its longstanding commitments to political liberalism, the secular state or laïcité, civility, and tolerance. Even the work of the former Nazi legal scholar Carl Schmitt has enjoyed a pervasive revival, as many of the collected essays attest. Curiously, however, the same academic attention has not been given to the more radically inflected traditions of liberation theology, nor, it seems, for those philosophical engagements with political theology produced by intellectuals hailing from Africa and the Caribbean, part of the geo-political region that constitutes what Enrique Dussel calls "the underside of modernity." For this omission, the editors offer the following rationale:

One should not yield too quickly to the temptation to associate the descriptive-reconstructive (that is to say, the institutional-juridical . . .) and the normative-constructive (that is to say, the political . . .) uses of the concept of the theological-political with the more explicitly confessional (or "appellative") adoption of the term. The last can be found in twentieth-century Catholic and Protestant theologies of revolutionary hope . . . , especially in Latin American and Third World liberation theologies of the 1960s and 1970s.[6]

The decision to privilege analytically a broad philosophical inquiry about the knotted interconnections between the state, politics and the political, and questions of religion and faith over a more narrow investigation of a specific set of religious beliefs and practices, however it names itself, would appear at first glance entirely reasonable and appropriate. Yet the distinction remains troubling to the degree that it reduces the complexity of liberation theologies to the experiential or "confessional," effectively denying not only their deeply political anti-racist, anti-colonialist project but also the philosophical contributions of their third world—and first world—antecedents, adherents, theorists, and critics in advancing scholarly conversations on the theologico-political. The exclusion is all the more puzzling in light of the fact that heretofore much debate over questions of violence involving the relationship between state sovereignty and its modes of imposition and legitimation on the one hand and the rhetorical and tactical strategies of revolutionary challenge on the other has focused on those geopolitical contexts marked by forms of internal racial domination and colonial conquest and the subsequent struggles for civil rights and independence to which these have given rise.[7] If the power and authority of the modern state and its racially configured legal and administrative apparatuses could be said to derive from both secular and sacred sources—so too the modern state can thus be said to create the conditions, vocabularies, and justifications for religiously driven resistances among its racially rendered subject populations. As Asad and others have insisted, colonial histories can hardly be considered irrelevant to the present obsession with political Islam or the widespread panic ignited over the threat of mass movements of displaced and dispossessed black and brown populations to the cultural "integrity" and unity of host communities.

Of what, then, is such an absence a symptom? In what follows, I would like to explore this question as well as advance a series of arguments in which I hope to reveal the costs of such exclusion in the interests of a richer, more complex accounting of the intersections between political theologies, liberal modernity, and the racial state—a conception of the state that recognizes the racially conceived history and the raced exclusions to which it has given rise.[8] I will conclude by exploring the political and ethical implications of the latter, as much for contemporary theory and its critics, as for the nature of the responsibility it implies for socially conscious and committed intellectuals. To focus on and consolidate such a potentially expansive and unwieldy topic, I revisit Walter Benjamin's notoriously difficult essay, "Critique of Violence," which was published in 1921, when the author was but twenty-nine years old. It was an early essay, to be sure, but one which, for reasons I will soon elaborate, has attracted the considered attention of generations of intellectuals, including Carl Schmitt, Hannah Arendt, Jürgen Habermas, Jacques Derrida, Giorgio Agamben, and Judith Butler, to name but a few. I hope to assuage the reader's potential impatience with yet another commentary by taking some of the difficulties posed by "Critique of Violence" in an altogether different direction, through a careful juxtaposition of these with the theologico-political reflections of Lewis R. Gordon, a philosopher and social theorist who was born seventy years after Benjamin, in 1962, in Kingston, Jamaica, and emigrated to the United States in his teens.

Like his predecessor, Gordon is Jewish—a designation used here to underscore the religious tradition from which some of the conceptual and analytic tools of both men are drawn—and is also committed, in a similarly unorthodox way, to aspects of Marxist critique as well as to the sustained contemplation of the tragic dimensions of human existence. Gordon also situates himself firmly in the tradition of Africana philosophy, not simply by virtue of his origin or identity, but rather by virtue of his ongoing commitment to the socio-historical experiences and theologico-political and philosophical traditions reflective of the lived realities of black populations to which he consistently returns. My task here is thus not simply to advance a new reading of Benjamin's essay by drawing on the considerable insight of Gordon's body of work; it is, rather, to pursue what might be learned from a dialogic relation between two critical thinkers, two young men, born in different centuries and different socio-historical and cultural contexts, who faced the problem of maturity—of confronting what it means to think and act responsibly in an adult world beset by violence and injustice arising from state racism, acute political crises, and a culture of decadence—a world which demanded of each of them, as a Jew and a black respectively, to justify his existence.[9] In contexts of institutionally inspired and sanctioned inhumanity, what does responsibility require? We will begin such an inquiry with Gordon's subtle reinterpretation of the Kantian project of Enlightenment from his 1995 *Bad Faith and Anti-Black Racism* (the bulk of which was written in 1992, when the author was a thirty-year-old graduate student at Yale):

racism involves a form of moral laziness in the face of institutions that encourage such laziness. In this sense the racist is sometimes regarded as an "unenlightened" individual. Kant, to his credit, writes that *"Enlightenment is man's emergence from self-incurred immaturity."* He adds, "Laziness and cowardice are the reasons why such a large portion of men . . . gladly remain immature for life. . . . It is so convenient to be immature!" Kant's conception of "self-incurred immaturity" is similar to Sartre's conception of bad faith—self-incurred unfreedom. Observe Sartre's description of the anti-Semite in *Anti-Semite and Jew* as "a man who is afraid. Not of the Jews, to be sure but of himself, of his own consciousness, of his liberty, of his instincts, of his responsibilities, of solitariness, of change, of society, and the world—of everything except the Jews. He is a coward who does not want to admit his cowardice to himself." . . . Both Kant and Sartre are urging humanity to grow up.[10]

Whereas Gordon underscores the relationship between racism and "self-incurred immaturity," he rejects, as we shall see, a major tenet of Kantian self-regarding reason, of understanding that fails to acknowledge a world with Others.

The term "Critique," or *Kritik* in Benjamin's original title, derives etymologically from *krinein* ("to separate"), appropriately signaling the author's efforts to establish a more refined and broader understanding of the concept of violence through a careful classificatory system of its different derivations and modes. Like Klee's anarchic *Angelus Novus*, a destructive force which shattered the false presumption of history's progressive unfolding, Benjamin hoped to unleash a similarly revolutionary force in "Critique of Violence" that would "radically rupture the eternal cycle of violence and counterviolence constituting human history."[11] The essay thus commences with a bold rejection of conventional thought on the question of violence, its adjudication through the discourse of law, and its calculus of means and ends. In recognition of the ways in which state-sanctioned violence, or in his parlance "legal violence," seeks inevitably to ground itself in just, even humanitarian ends, he sought a standpoint outside of positive legal philosophy, in what he calls "divine violence." Legal violence consists of either law-instating or law-preserving violence. The former emerges with the very inception of the polity when law is made, while the latter ensures that the law will exert a binding force on the populations it governs. Further, he argues, lawmaking violence is the product of "mythical violence," such that it derives from "fate"; it has, in other words, no justification other than or outside itself. The law precisely establishes the terms of its own justification and deliberation, which is part of what is inferred by the violence of its founding act. Reflecting upon the unchecked and coercive force of the law in its dual manifestation, he asserts: "law nevertheless appears . . . in so ambiguous a moral light that the question poses itself whether there are no other than violent means for regulating conflicting human interests."[12] Divine violence poses at least a partial answer to his query insofar as Benjamin imagines it as a kind of violence waged against the coercive force of the law that is itself fundamentally noncoercive and nonviolent. "If mythical violence is lawmaking, divine violence is law-destroying," Benjamin argues, and "if the former sets boundaries, the latter boundlessly destroys them; if mythical violence brings at once guilt and retribution, divine power only expiates; if the former threatens, the latter strikes; if the former is bloody, the latter is lethal without spilling blood."[13]

Before addressing the question of what the author means by a kind of nonviolent or "bloodless" violence, I should like to remind the reader that it is Benjamin's "anti-liberal" challenge to the rule of law and the legitimacy of its monopoly on violence, his collapsing, in fact, of any meaningful distinction between legal authority and violence, and his championing of an anarchic, law-destroying violence that has run him afoul of a great many contemporary political theorists eager to distance themselves from what they perceived to be his revolutionary conservatism. That he engages the work of Carl Schmitt, though not uncritically, seems to have sealed his fate in this regard for many. Habermas, for example, charges that Benjamin's essay on violence, like the work of Schmitt upon which it draws, champions "the violent destruction of the normative as such."[14] Openly critical of the "messianico-Marxism" that runs through "Critique of Violence," the subject of his own 1992 essay, "The Force of the Law," Derrida similarly repudiates Benjamin's theme of destruction and its disturbing affinities with fascism's assault on the rule of law and its zest for annihilation. "When one thinks of the gas chambers and the cremation ovens," he writes, "this allusion to an extermination that would be expiatory because bloodless must cause one to shudder. One is terrified at the idea of an interpretation that would make of the holocaust an expiation and an indecipherable signature of a just and violent anger of God."[15] Embracing the ethics of deconstruction over Benjaminian "destruction," he explicitly values that force over which his antagonist openly worries—an ideal of justice that is never approximated by positive or transcendent law.

More recently, Judith Butler has occasioned a distinctly different, more sympathetic reading that locates in Benjamin not only a critique of legal violence but also the basis for a theory of responsibility that has at its core an ongoing struggle with nonviolence.[16] In contrast to the charges of incipient fascism in Benjamin's criticism of the rule of law and failures of parliamentary democracy wielded by Habermas, Derrida, and others, she poses another possibility: "it follows equally that if the law that binds its subjects is itself part of a fascist legal apparatus, then it would appear that such an apparatus is precisely the kind of law whose binding force should be opposed and resisted until the apparatus fails."[17] Yet, even in light of this reading, Benjamin's assessment of the rule of law affords her some ambivalence. She concedes: "Benjamin's critique of law, however, remains nonspecific, so that a general opposition to the binding, even coercive character of law seems less savory once we consider the rise of fascism, as well as the flouting of both constitutional and international law that characterizes U.S. foreign policy in its practices of war, torture, and illegal detention."[18]

Although Butler's last point is well taken, I would like to dwell a bit longer on her prior acknowledgment of the possibility of a legal structure that serves to legitimate a brutalizing system of injustice—a responsibility largely displaced by the critical rush to judgment—and, in doing so, revisit the nature of Benjamin's alleged "anti-liberalism" to determine what it is about the traditions of political modernity itself that compelled Benjamin to level so provocative a critique. What accounts for such passionate accusations of endemic violence? What constitutes the underside of its "progressive" historical unfolding, to invoke yet another of the liberal shibboleths he has characteristically questioned? I would like to propose here that any effort to theorize the entwined interconnections among sovereign power, legal authority, violence, and religion must begin with a conceptualization of the modern nation-state as *racially ordered and determined*. To be clear: the designation is not limited to the Nazi state, which Benjamin himself witnessed coming into being—or the apartheid state. In describing modern states in general as always already *racial states*, I draw specifically on the work of David Theo Goldberg, who insists that race marks and orders the emergence, development, and transformations (conceptually, philosophically, materially) of the modern nation-state— from what Enrique Dussel calls the "first modernity," from the "voyages of discovery" (which Goldberg notes also bears racial significance), and the debates between Las Casas and Sepulveda over Indian enslavement in the Americas, through the second "planetary modernity"; equally, he insists, it does so from the seventeenth century and Enlightenment deliberations over the constitutions of colonial and liberal states, European and U.S. slavery and its eventual disestablishment, "national character," and citizenship criteria expressed in covert racial terms when not guided by the overt fantasy of racial purity, to the current post-apartheid moment, enveloped as it is in legal decisions around colorblindness, immigration debates, the emergence of "fortress Europe," and the American "prison industrial complex."[19]

The assertion that modern states are racial states, as we'll see, weighs significantly on the prevailing conception of modern liberalism, "modernity's definitive doctrine of self and society, morality and politics," to the degree that its vaunted commitments to universalism, equality, freedom, tolerance, progress, and the force of right reason are racially conceived and predicated.[20] Groundbreaking in yet another sense, Goldberg's work also counters dominant presumptions of the state as an autonomous sphere or its opposite, a conceptualization granting it mere epiphenomenal status, serving more or less the dictates of the economy or capitalist modes of production. Modern states, *necessarily* racial states, Goldberg argues, operate according to their own logics:

The state has the power by definition to assert itself or to control those (things) within the state . . . [and] the power to exclude from state protection. . . . For central to the sorts of racial constitution that have centrally defined modernity is the power to exclude and by extension include in racially ordered terms, to dominate through the power to categorize differentially and hierarchically, to set aside by setting apart. . . . [These are] processes aided integrally by . . . the law and policy-making, by bureaucratic apparatuses and governmental technologies like census categories, by invented histories and traditions, ceremonies and cultural imaginings.[21]

Modern state power has been traditionally defined by its monopoly on force. What Goldberg draws attention to here, in ways that resonate with Benjamin's critique of sovereign power, is the state's efforts to monopolize the power to *categorize and interpret* legality and illegality, personhood and property, citizen and noncitizen, friend and enemy—a process through which it acquires its own justification. The state determines who is human and who is property, who will be protected under the mantel of citizenship and who might be stripped of the rights it purports to guarantee, who will be a resident and who will remain alien, who will be declared friend and ally and who will be rendered a threat to national security, a plague to be exterminated, or an enemy combatant to be imprisoned and tortured. Like Benjamin, Goldberg understands, through careful review of the historical record, the lawmaking and law-preserving functions of the modern state as deeply exclusionary of racially conceived difference and, in material consequence, as unquestionably violent. So, too, its founding, or law-instating, moment. The social contract tradition—one such "invented tradition" enabling state power—offers Goldberg a key *metaphor*, not an accurate historical accounting, for engaging state origin, constitution, and legitimation as a form of legal violence. The very notion of a "contract" and the guarantees upon which it is founded—individual rights, property—underscore a "presumption of voluntarism" that "completely denies the constitution of power and its effects" within certain groups, legitimating the racial and gendered exclusion and exploitation it thus renders invisible.[22] It is the implication of this conceptualization of modern racial states and all that issues from this basic revision of state theory that are sacrificed with the exclusion of the theologico-political and philosophical contributions of those theorists who speak from "modernity's underside," contributions I hope now to elaborate.

What does it mean, to take seriously the question of race, or its corollary, "the Jewish question," in Benjamin's early twentieth-century European context, in the consideration of state power and the conditions that mark the legitimate and illegitimate uses of violence? Let us consider, in this regard, another narrative that engages implicitly and advances conceptually Benjamin's discussion of legal violence and divine violence, drawing, like Benjamin's enigmatic essay, on both mythical and historical example. I turn now to Gordon's 1999 essay "Frederick Douglass as an

Existentialist," a provocative reading of Douglass's second autobiography, *My Bondage, My Freedom*, as part of what I am calling Gordon's extended critique of racial violence.

For Gordon, forms of state-sponsored racial violence—from the centuries-old institution of slavery in the southern United States to the more heterogeneous contemporary commitments to racial management internally, in the form of mass criminalization and incarceration, and externally, in the form of neocolonial imposition—pose a problem in both political and theological terms. Extending the philosophical insights of his predecessors, from the nineteenth-century scholarship of Edward Blyden to the twentieth-century contributions of Frantz Fanon, Gordon underscores the degree to which various forms of exploitation share a common stake in some form of biblical justification, which in many ways prefigures the languages of response and resistance. Neocolonial regimes, he writes, face "the classical *theodicean* problem of legitimacy that has plagued many a previous imperial order: How can it legitimate its conquest without depending on conquest itself as its source of legitimation?"[23] Like Benjamin, Gordon explores the possibilities of a revolutionary challenge to legal violence and its modes of justification through the violence of critique. Challenging Schmitt's logic of exception, Benjamin wrote, and Gordon would agree, that "the tradition of the oppressed teaches us that the 'state of emergency' in which we live is not the exception but the rule" and that our task is "to attain to a conception of history that is in keeping with this insight . . . to bring about a real state of emergency . . . in the struggle against Fascism."[24] In a chapter titled "Tragic Intellectuals," Gordon poses the responsibility of the intellectual to address the assumed legitimacy of systemic injustice in strikingly similar terms: "The intellectual also faces the question of producing intellectual work that properly dramatizes the articulation of that need [for structural change]" thus "setting the stage" for undoing conditions of "unjust justice" paradoxically by "formulating a just justice in a system that offers no alternative but a just injustice."[25] Just as Benjamin's critique of legal violence poses a challenge to the traditions of both positive law and Schmittian natural law, to the degree that it contests the sovereign's monopoly on decision (i.e., producing its own counterhistory, declaring its own state of emergency), so too Gordon frames Frederick Douglass's struggle as one against "legal positivism" and "the problem of obeying the U.S. Constitution."[26] Douglass opposes the singular authority of this legal code by asserting that it is "an interpretable document" and thus underscoring the critically hermeneutic nature of democratic struggle.[27] But from where does the possibility emerge of thinking against or beyond, and by doing so destroying, the binding force of the law?

As we have seen, Benjamin invokes the concept of divine violence, which provides a critical perspective beyond the law, thus initiating the destruction of its coercive force. Lewis Gordon's response to this question, I argue, bears an uncanny resemblance. Gordon probes the question of human freedom in the context of the classic conflict between the nineteenth-century political theorist and philosopher of existence, Frederick Douglass, and the slave master once assigned to "break" him, Edward Covey—a scene central to all three of the former slave's autobiographies—specifically concerned to decipher "how Douglass *reads* this important event in his life."[28] The famed fight with Covey raises a number of concerns for Gordon that carry anthropological, philosophical, and theologico-political import, but most fundamentally he is struck by Douglass's contemplation of what it means to be a human being, which leads him to resist the slave-breaker. The biological fact of human being notwithstanding, he focuses on its normative, existential dimensions: "one *becomes* a human being," he argues.[29] To explain the significance of Douglass's decision to challenge Covey, Gordon turns to the well-known Hebrew analogy: the story of Adam and Eve from the book of Genesis. There, he argues, Yahweh's injunction not to eat the fruit from the tree of knowledge serves "a unique identity forming role."[30] Prior to Yahweh's command, Adam and Eve lived in a world without self-realization, but the prohibition introduced a new consciousness in which the possibility of disobeying or obeying Yahweh emerges, ironically constituting, in either instance, a consciousness beyond Yahweh. In Gordon's interpretation, the "fall," as it were, initiated by Adam and Eve's decision to act of their own accord, actually preceded the eating of the fruit. Whatever their choice, in deciding to obey or disobey the divine commandment, they faced the question of their responsibility. Thus Gordon poses the relation between Genesis and slavery in this way: "It is the negative instantiation of [Adam and Eve's] freedom, which here is, ironically, their humanity. Their humanity is the moment of maturation in which they realize, out of their lived experience, the responsibility of constituting, at least morally, who they are. For the slave, this moment is manifested in the distinction between the institution of slavery and the lived reality of being a slave."[31] If the institution of slavery defines the slave as property, as part of the master's estate, and thus an object or thing without consciousness, without interiority, the very act of reflection by the slave on his own condition initiates a rupture with the entire system. He experiences himself as having a point of view, a consciousness, an inside. A powerful correlate to Douglass's realization is, for Gordon, located in Frantz Fanon's efforts to articulate the "Lived-Experience of the Black" under conditions of colonialism in *Black Skin, White Masks*, a reality which also involves living with what he called "epidermal schematization," the "conscious realization of denied insides, a reductionism premised on surfaces."[32] There is an obvious repetition of the Old Testament injunction against knowledge and the slave owners' theo-political injunction against literacy, which was not lost on the slaves themselves. Gordon explains that the uniquely dehumanizing project of U.S. slavery was such that the attainment of literacy, of self-knowledge and self-mastery, initiated a distinctly humanizing possibility. He unpacks the analogy further:

The historical reality was that slave owners imposed their relation to slaves with a hubristic analogy of being on a par with Yahweh made flesh in the form of a white Christ. The obvious difference, however, is the interpretation of Genesis 2 as *a loving act of indirection* on Yahweh's part by his pointing to knowledge in the negative in order to achieve the positive consequence of human consciousness and freedom. However loving U.S. slave owners claimed to have been, the bottom line was that the injunction against literacy was for another purpose. Yahweh loves humanity and poses an injunction that initiates the humanizing process. Conversely, the slave owners' relation to the slaves is misanthropic: he attempts, at all cost, to deny their humanity.[33]

We see in the institutionalization of slavery not merely the secularization of divine law in modern juridical and legal state apparatuses, but the ruthless appropriation and reinterpretation of their meanings in the interests of dehumanizing practices of coercion and control. Gordon characterizes the slaves' recognition of Yahweh as benevolent and loving rather than punitive and vengeful as both a rejection of this secular dispensation and a strategic and syncretic adoption of Christian faith placing great emphasis on the Hebrew Bible, which effectively constitutes for him a "re-Semiticizing," even a re-coloring ("Palestinizing") of Christianity.[34] Thus, like Benjamin, Gordon invokes a different Jewish tradition of understanding divine commandment, one that separates the imperative that the law articulates from the question of its enforceability, thereby creating the conditions for the human confrontation with responsibility.

Consider the above depiction of Yahweh's "loving act of indirection," enabling the humanizing process by virtue of Adam and Eve's confrontation with ethical choice, or the slaves' resistance to the masters' theopolitical injunction, in light of Benjamin's God and the ethical space opened by divine commandment. Judith Butler's highly nuanced reading of the "Critique" posits that "over and against the idea of a coercive and guilt-inducing law, Benjamin invokes the commandment as mandating only that an individual struggle with the ethical edict communicated by the imperative. This is an imperative that does *not* dictate, but *leaves open* the modes of its applicability, the possibilities of its interpretation, including the conditions under which it may be refused."[35] Yahweh, according to Gordon, is not misanthropic. So too in Benjamin's "Critique," the Jewish God associated with the commandment is precisely opposed to coercion and guilt, in contrast to the guilt-inducing consequences of lawmaking and law-preserving violence, an exemplification of which he offers in the allusion to the myth of Niobe. According to the legend, Niobe incurs the wrath of the gods and is turned to stone. Butler explains the analogy as follows: Just as law "petrifies the subject, arresting life in the moment of guilt," so too Niobe, though she lives, is "paralyzed within that living: she becomes permanently guilty, and the guilt turns into rock the subject who bears it."[36] Niobe's hubris inflames the gods, who initiate punishment, thus producing the subject bound by law—a subject permanently guilty and thus subject to apparently infinite retribution. That Niobe is left to conclude that she is the sole source of her own suffering is a further extension of that violence.[37]

By the conclusion of "Critique of Violence," Benjamin resolves that the destruction of all legal violence remains the sole ethical option and thus remains obligatory. Divine violence, let us recall, is "bloodless" violence wielded against the coercive force of mythical, lawmaking violence that imposes permanent guilt and infinite retribution on its subjects. Before turning to a comparative analysis of the question of legal violence and response in Gordon, I want to underscore here again that it is Benjamin's condemnation of the law in general that has caused significant unease among subsequent generations of critics all too familiar, alas, with the destructive force of European fascism's contempt for the rule of law. I argue, however, that the parallel is too hastily drawn, or is, rather, erroneously drawn to the degree that fascist rule, far from being "lawless" actually appeals to "higher" sources of the law. Such was the conclusion drawn by Hannah Arendt's magnificent study, *The Origins of Totalitarianism,* which warrants a lengthy quotation:

> It is the monstrous, yet seemingly unanswerable claim of totalitarian rule that, far from being "lawless," it goes to the sources of authority from which positive laws receive their ultimate legitimation, . . . that far from wielding its power in the interest of one man, it is quite prepared to sacrifice everybody's vital immediate interests to the execution of what it assumes to be the *law of History* or the *law of Nature. . . .* The discrepancy between law and justice could never be bridged because the standards of right and wrong into which positive law translates its own authority . . . are *necessarily general* and must be valid for countless and predictable cases, so that each concrete individual case with its unrepeatable set of circumstances somehow escapes it. . . . The law of Nature or the law of History, if properly executed, is expected to produce mankind as its end product; and this expectation lies behind *the claim to global rule* of all totalitarian governments.[38]

Arendt's wording here is of paramount importance to an understanding not simply of fascism's legal expression, but of modern racial state formation more generally. Arendt denies that the suspension of law is at work in totalitarian states and alludes instead to "the discrepancy between law and justice" at work in the fascist legal apparatus. This distance is, moreover, the singular, intolerable condition of totalitarian states, rather than a characteristic feature of modern states in general—a Benjaminian presumption she disavows in her famed "On Violence." Yet, as David Goldberg persuasively argues, it is precisely the increasing centrality of the law and its proliferation with the rise of modern states which deflects critical attention away from the abuses of state authority and power and serves to quiet resistance.[39] Displacing the kind of order once achieved through religious determination, the dual appeals to the law of Nature and the law of History have not only provided the basis for state legitimation but also defined the rule of law in modern racial states. In the face of rapidly expanding and diversifying populations, increasing anonymity and alienation, Goldberg asserts, modern law offered a kind of "abstracted connectivity" between "fabricated similarities" the law itself helped to fashion through its own modes of classification, thus achieving a "national fantasy of homogeneity."[40] The uniform imposition of such legal abstraction—and so the seeming impartiality and neutrality—generates an inherently alienating and dehumanizing effect. For those excluded from state-imposed logics of similitude, the consequences prove particularly severe as racially marked subjects are rendered recognizable "only as strangers or criminals."[41] Goldberg distinguishes between different regimes of race according to their modes of racial definition and legal justification—naturalist regimes impose order on raced populations by using law to effect and legitimate brute force, rendering it more benign and palatable. Natural law is invoked to mark the difference between modern civilized states and uncivilized ones frozen in a state of nature. Historicist regimes, in contrast, invoke the constitutionalism of the law, "ruling racially through law, shaping race in terms of legality."[42] Lawlessness, as defined by the latter context, results in the failure to live up to one's historically delimited and delineated potential. The exceptionalism of particular racial states—Nazi German, the antebellum southern United States, apartheid South Africa—is thus not a function of the racial definition of the state, its modes of racial management, or its racially mandated violence, which is widespread across modern nation-states. What makes these states exceptional is, Goldberg argues, the extremity and unmitigated nature of the violence wielded in the name of race.[43] The violence endemic to such states may reveal less an anomaly than a moment of crisis signaled by the shift from one mode of racial governance to another.[44]

That Benjamin advanced the distinction between legal and divine violence to initiate the destruction of the former finds a compelling historical analogue in Gordon's account of Frederick Douglass's understanding of his situation, and his subsequent decision to take responsibility for it, culminating in a revolutionary challenge to the coercive force of a legalized system of enslavement that not only dehumanizes its victims, but charges them with the guilt of their own suffering, in perpetuity. The gravity of Benjamin's critique is reflected in the lived reality of the violence imposed by the modern racial state, in the context of which to "be" Jewish or black is to be "guilty." Gordon draws numerous parallels between the liberatory project of Douglass and that of the famed analyst of the colonial situation, Franz Fanon, for both commence "with autobiographical reflections that lead to reflections on violence."[45] Elsewhere Gordon cites Fanon's meditation on the unfolding consequences of an imposed Manichean political theology for its victims: "A feeling of inferiority? No, a feeling of nonexistence. Sin is Negro as virtue is white. All those white men in a group, guns in their hands, cannot be wrong. I am guilty. I do not know of what, but I know that I am no good."[46] When Douglass resolves to defend himself against Covey, Gordon reminds us that this "defense" also took on religious resonance, in the form of a charm given to him by an African slave allegedly endowed with the power to protect him from the slave-breaker's impending flogging as well as in the invocation of Christian prayer—though Douglass is familiar with the limits of the latter, as Covey was a devout Christian. For Gordon, the charm and the prayer symbolize Douglass's moment of resolve (as well as a leitmotif of West African and Christian ritual belief in spiritual maturation through physical trial), but the concrete reality of the struggle against Covey is *in the flesh*. He draws critical attention to following passage from Douglass's *My Bondage, My Freedom*:

Whence came the daring spirit necessary to grapple with a man who, eight-and-forty hours before, could, with his slightest word have made me tremble like a leaf in a storm, I do not know; at any rate, *I was resolved to fight*, and what was better still, I was actually hard at it. The fighting madness had come upon me, and I found my strong fingers firmly attached to the throat of my cowardly tormentor; as heedless of the consequences, at the moment as though we stood as equals before the law. The very color of the man was forgotten. I felt as supple as a cat, and was ready for the snakish creature at every turn. Every blow of his was parried, though I dealt no blows in turn. I was strictly on the *defensive*, preventing him from injuring me, rather than trying to injure him. I flung him on the ground several times, when he meant to have hurled me there. I held him so firmly by the throat, that his blood followed my nails. He held me, and I held him.[47]

Douglass's observation that "the very color of the man was forgotten" in the struggle that ensued, Gordon suggests, reveals the vulnerability of the very institution of slavery and with it, the collapse of a skewed, racist perceptual field passing itself off as objective existential reality. The scene, in Benjamin's terms, may be described as violent, but violent in a way that is "bloodless" and "expiating" to the degree that the subject has challenged the very ground of legal violence and is no longer bound to its infinite dispensation of punishment and guilt. It is this imposition of nonbeing and the system of legal injustice that sustains it that Douglass resolves to struggle against unto death. In the context of the racial state, the force of destruction aimed at legal violence is not "destructive of the normative as such," as Habermas and others assert, but rather destructive of those unjust normative arrangements that strike at what Gordon would call the very possibility of becoming human, or what Benjamin terms "the soul of the living." But what does this mean?

Again, the parallels between Benjamin's depiction of the subject of legal violence and the lived experience of anguish and suffering of the nonwhite subjects of racial state violence are striking. Benjamin invokes the legend of Niobe, turned to rock, alive and yet entombed, only able to weep, in order to castigate the production of the subject bound by law "as an eternally mute bearer of guilt."[48] Douglass conveys the state of his own nonbeing—"I was nothing before"—as a consequence of the living death sentence imposed by slavery in similar terms, referring to "the dark and pestiferous tomb of slavery." Douglass's observations about the stakes of his own humanity in his fight with Covey are instructive:

Well, my dear reader, this battle with Mr. Covey . . . was the turning point in my "life as a slave." It rekindled in my breast the smoldering embers of liberty; it brought up my Baltimore dreams, and revived a sense of my own manhood. I was a changed being after that fight. I was nothing before; I WAS A MAN NOW. It recalled to life my crushed self-respect and my self-confidence, and inspired me with a renewed determination to be A FREEMAN. A man, without force, is without the essential dignity of humanity. Human nature is so constituted, that it cannot *honor* a helpless man, although it can *pity* him; and even this it cannot do long, if the signs of power do not arise. . . . After resisting [Covey], I felt as I had never felt before. It was a resurrection from the dark and pestiferous tomb of slavery, to the heaven of comparative freedom. I was no longer a servile coward trembling under the frown of a brother worm of the dust, but my long-cowed spirit was roused to an attitude of manly independence. I had reached the point, at which I was *not afraid to die.* This spirit made me a freeman in fact, while I remained a slave in form. When a slave cannot be flogged he is more than half free. He has a domain as broad as his own manly heart to defend, and he is really "*a power on earth.*"[49]

Gordon draws at least three conclusions from the fight with Covey relevant to our discussion here. First, he proposes that at the heart of Douglass's narrative of transition from "life as a slave," a zone of nonbeing, to that of "a man" of "comparable freedom" lies the question of agency. The descriptor "comparable" registers Douglass's acknowledgment that freedom is never complete and requires not only individual "force"—a condition of one's "humanity," or, in Gordon's reading, "agency"—but also structural change, in this instance the very destruction of the soul-murdering institution of slavery. Gordon's insistence on the contingency of "becoming" human as a function of one's recognition and assumption of ethical responsibility in the form of committed change shares much in common with the conception of responsibility that emerges from Benjamin's "Critique of Violence," always already a critique, if only implicitly, of racial violence in the context of turn-of-the-century Europe and in modernity more generally.

Second, the assumption of responsibility entails what Gordon calls "a contemplation of the metaethical level of morality's relevance in exigent situations" and thus the experience of anguish in "the human capacity not only to judge morality, but also to go beyond it."[50] As we have seen in the case of Walter Benjamin and his critics, the revolutionary willingness to "go beyond" a given moral or legal order is not without its problems. Benjamin would seem to anticipate such appropriately placed concern in following to its logical conclusion the violent challenge to a sovereign authority from the perspectives of its most zealous adherents and detractors. He offers commentary on an exchange he draws from another source: "Their argumentation, exemplified in an extreme case by the revolutionary killing of the oppressor, runs as follows: 'If I do not kill I shall never establish the world dominion of justice. . . .'" In response another party declaims, "'that is the argument of the intelligent terrorist. . . . We, however, profess that higher even than the happiness and justice of existence stands existence itself.'"[51] Benjamin repudiates the facile commitments of both "we" and "they" positions. Benjamin insists:

The proposition that existence stands higher than a just existence is false and ignominious, if existence is to mean nothing other than mere life—and it has this meaning in the argument referred to. It contains a mighty truth, however, if existence, or better, life (words whose ambiguity is readily dispelled, analogously to that of freedom, when they are referred to two distinct spheres), means the irreducible, total condition that is "man"; if the proposition is intended to mean that the nonexistence of man is something more terrible than the (admittedly subordinate) not-yet-attained condition of the just man.[52]

The distinction Benjamin makes between "existence" and "life" is similarly made by Douglass: "I remained with Mr. Covey one year (I cannot say I *lived* with him)."[53] And like Benjamin, Gordon draws from such distinction similar conclusions: that for life to mean anything it must entail the condition of freedom, "a form of being with open possibilities, with self-reflection—in other words, human being."[54] But what of the potential for spilling blood in pursuit of freedom? "The question 'May I kill?' meets its irreducible answer," Benjamin insists, "in the commandment 'Thou shalt not kill.'"[55] But here we must recall that divine commandment lacks the power to enforce; it initiates, rather, an ethical struggle conditioned by the fact of its interpretability. Such possibility is universally granted, for Benjamin, and is precisely not the preserve of a chosen or pure people, a characteristic thematic of fascist rhetoric. Further, I would argue that "going beyond" an official moral and legal order for either Benjamin or Gordon is not akin to the fascist appeal to a form of absolutist authority—the law of Nature or the law of History—the imposition of which excludes the possibility of critical thought, reflection, and interpretation on the part of its subjects. Both resist the temptation to determine in advance the "just" interpretation of divine commandment and so preclude the humanizing activity of contemplation and ethical choice. Yet in advocating a nonviolent or bloodless violence that destroys the institutional legitimation of coercive force that strikes at the very core of humanity, neither theorist can be read as pacifist. Gordon's reading of Douglass's autobiographical accounting of the decision to resist Covey underscores that the former slave's critical reflection and resolve led to struggle *in the flesh*. Though Douglass took a decidedly defensive posture in the fight with Covey, Gordon's position is one that explicitly condemns a facile equation of the potentiality of violent resistance by the oppressed with the forms of violence wielded by the oppressor. In a reading of Fanon's discussion of violence in *Wretched of the Earth*, Gordon asserts that "the colonized people's struggle for liberation would not . . . be treated as equal to the colonizers' violence. For in the accomplishment of the former's struggle is the possibility, fragile though it may be, of a world that is not, by dint of its very structure, violent."[56] At the heart, then, of revolutionary action in the service of humanity is a struggle with nonviolence itself.

Adherence to the divine commandment similarly entails for Benjamin a distinction between "mere life" and what he calls "the soul of the living," a figure he unpacks in an all-too-brief discussion of "educating violence." According to Benjamin, divine power takes two forms: religious tradition and "educating violence," unleashing what we might call the violence of critique:

This divine power is attested not only by religious tradition but is also found in present-day life in a least one sanctioned manifestation. The *educative power*, which in its perfected form stands outside the law, is one of its manifestations. These are defined, therefore, not by miracles directly performed by God, but by the expiating moment in them that strikes without bloodshed and, finally, by the absence of all law-making. To this extent it is justifiable to call this violence, too, annihilating; but it is so only relatively, with regard to goods, right, life and suchlike, never absolutely, with regard to the soul of the living.[57]

Divine violence thus safeguards "the soul of the living." The terrible "nonexistence of man" to which Benjamin refers earlier is the result not of the annihilation of men from earth, but of the soul murder of humanity. Such a necrophilic project emerges—and this is the third and final point—from what Gordon calls "a carefully crafted discipline of unseeing" that projects an absence in the space of human being, reducing one's ontological status to that of property or thing, entombed in perpetual guilt and punishment—the imposition, in essence, of the status of the living dead.[58] Gordon notes the insistent deployment of analogies between Douglass and farm animals within the context of U.S. slave society, a systemic effort to deny the slaves' humanity. He writes:

This denial, properly executed, requires denying the presence of other human beings in such relations. It makes such beings a form of presence that is an absence, paradoxically, an absence of human presence. That being so, such beings fall below the category of Otherness, for an Other is another human being. With a being erased to a realm of property, even linguistic appeals—cries for recognition—are muffled, unheard; waving hands, gestures for acknowledgment, are invisible. It is not that they do not trigger impulses between the eye and the brain; it is that there has been a carefully crafted discipline of unseeing.[59]

The coercive apparatus of legal violence not only seeks to overdetermine and arrest various modes of hermeneutic intervention in the world, but also undermines the subject's very capacity to see what she sees and to think reflectively and act responsibly upon what she sees. The kind of force necessary to disrupt such disciplined inhumanity is what I take Benjamin to mean when he speaks provocatively of "educative power," which, like its divine counterpart, is a force outside the law. It is perhaps for this reason that the violence of the law, according to Benjamin, rampages all the more blindly "*against thinkers*, from whom the state is not protected by law."[60] It is also, conversely, what drives the preoccupation, across Gordon's substantial body of work, with questions about what sustains and disrupts the human activity of *thought, reflection, interpretation, and reading* in confrontation with social reality.

Gordon concludes his reflections on Frederick Douglass, the peculiar situation of the antebellum U.S. slave system, and his existential quest for freedom with a reminder that the ongoing struggle of Others against similar projects of demotion extends across the twentieth century. So, too, it may be said for the twenty-first. In 2007, Lewis Gordon and Jane Anna Gordon penned a deeply reflective, moving mediation on Hurricane Katrina and the nature of catastrophe more generally, titled, significantly, "Reading the Signs: A Philosophical Look at Disaster."[61] Analysis of the earlier Douglass essay and this most recent contribution to theopolitical and philosophical thought offers a uniquely penetrating perspective on the astounding flexibility and durability of the modern state and its capacities to define, manage, and contain those populations it renders racially distinct and increasingly disposable. While a sustained engagement with the latter essay is beyond the scope of the present inquiry, the historical linkages between the heterogeneous forms of violence, and indeed social death, wielded by the racial state against humanity, extending from nineteenth-century enslavement to twenty-first century abandonment cannot be left unacknowledged.

For Jane and Lewis Gordon, natural disasters aren't "naturally disastrous"; rather, disasters result from a failure to read the signs. "Reading the Signs" thus poses the question of what it means to learn from disaster—how to read the warnings—and as well what impediments block such learning, leading inevitably to catastrophe. The anxiety and fear occasioned by the event itself can occlude the signs themselves, such that victims of disaster, unavoidably marked, can be swept up in the continuum of warnings, "swallowed up in the avalanche of ill-fated signs."[62] Victims, in effect, become signs of the disaster that befell them, harbingers of realities we do not want to face, suffering we refuse to see. It is difficult not to recall the media images associated with the black and brown victims of Katrina in New Orleans—trapped on rooftops, without water, food, or medicine, waving for help, and largely ignored by passing helicopters; warehoused in the Superdome while separated from family or watching loved ones die in front of them, demanding assistance before the cameras of stunned reporters; stranded on highways, force to flee on foot, denied entrance to neighboring towns by armed militia who fired upon those who ignored the warning—and not recall Gordon's reflections on nonbeing, "even linguistic appeals—cries for recognition—are muffled, unheard; waving hands, gestures for acknowledgment, are invisible."[63] The victims, again, of a "carefully crafted discipline of unseeing" that is predicated on racial definition and exclusion are here transformed into a kind of monstrosity, which the Gordons understand in relation to the Latin *monere*, "to warn or admonish."[64] Thus, it was the black and brown poor of New Orleans, among all Katrina's victims, who came to function, according Gordon and Gordon, as a form of *divine warning*.

Race in the context of this catastrophe generated two categories of people: the "innocent" by virtue of being white; and the "already guilty" by virtue of being black.[65] The latter's color served as a mark or stain, or, in the Gordons' terminology, a "sign," that mitigated against them properly being seen as victims and transformed them into scapegoats:

that event portrayed white (and therefore innocent) victims of a circumstance that was a function of black (and therefore illicit) presence, for the whites did not collapse into the signifier or continuum of disaster. They became the "we" who faced the "warning," exemplified by the chain of signs from storm to flooding to an overflow of black presence calling for containment. . . . Thus, the constant affirmation of [white] humanity by the media in the midst of disaster was also that of black inhumanity, of the danger of an unbound black population. The stories of illicit behavior, of rape and pillage, were themselves the continuum, the movement of signs, that "we" should shun such populations.[66]

In the official rhetoric of contemporary American theodicy, evil arrives from elsewhere, a dark force outside the (white) community, or from beyond national borders, rather than from the failure to see the suffering of others and assume responsibility for alleviating it. The failure to take appropriate responsibility turns on the desire to blame the victims, to insist on their own responsibility for their plight, rather than confront "the failure of the nation's leadership to develop an adequate political response."[67] After the levees broke in New Orleans, the dominant media flooded the airwaves with their own brand of filth. The Associated Press reported numerous stories of massive looting, murders, rioting, and rapes among low-income black residents of the devastated city, though all were later found to be unsubstantiated.[68] Some evangelicals insisted that the catastrophe was a form of divine punishment against the sinful city. A contributing editor of the *Wall Street Journal* went so far as to advocate a more secular response to the endemic criminality of Katrina victims by openly insisting that looters be shot. The paradoxical moment is also tragic: "in our aversion to addressing disasters as signs and our mythopoetic understanding of them . . . as divine warnings," the Gordons observe, "we actively create monsters and enemies and thereby maintain moments of hysteria, refusing actually to interpret and take responsibility for the kinds of response that may be needed to alleviate human misery."[69]

The injunction against literacy that marked a primary condition of the nineteenth-century slave establishment finds its corollary in a contemporary theologico-political imposition of another kind of illiteracy, which imperils individual and social agency by preempting the possibility of reading and learning from catastrophe. "Remaining in crisis, standing paralyzed, in the face of disaster cannot be the telos of education," the Gordons write.[70] Noting the Latin derivation of "education" from *educare*, "to lead out," they pose, again, the question of "going beyond" the official moral and political order in ways reminiscent of Benjaminian commitment to educative power: "What more fitting a response could there be to what we have been calling the sign-continuum of disaster than to learn how to go beyond it?"[71]

By way of conclusion, I want to consider the implications of Benjamin's and the Gordons's analysis of modernity, violence, critique, religion, and responsibility in terms of their resonance for the present task of intellectuals. What have we learned about the prohibition against reading, the necessity of reading, and the failure to read—the challenges of willed seeing and unseeing, of hearing and not-hearing?

In his thoughtful and provocative introduction to *Political Theologies*, Hent de Vries raises a crucial question: "What has happened to 'religion' in its present and increasingly public manifestation, propelled by global media, economic markets, and foreign policies as much as by resistance to them?"[72] I have argued throughout this chapter that what such a question pre-empts is perhaps of greater significance than what it poses in terms of the kinds of answers we might be able successfully to enlist about the contemporary resurgence of religion. The contextual referents offered here—global media, economy, politics—precisely preclude the force of race in the shifting relevance of the theologico-political. Indeed, in theorizing the complex relationship between race and modernity's secular advance (or retreat), it is possible to talk about the ways in which race itself functions as a political theology, perhaps most visibly in the U.S. southern slave system, in Nazi Germany, or in apartheid South Africa, but pervasively, nonetheless, across modern nation-states. Goldberg explains how race thinking has come to assume such compelling status in liberal modernity's unfolding:

The force of race begins to take hold among Europeans as the social hold of religion shifts in the face of increasing individualization and the emerging power of scientific rationality, epistemological anti-foundationalism, and the ground of moral self-generation. Race assumes increasing social hegemony as monogenism gives way to speculations around polygenesis, differentiated origins, and species proliferation, first, then evolution and eugenicism in the latter half of the nineteenth century. . . . Over time, race comes to generate a secularized theology and a civic religion, underpinned initially by appeals to God's dictum but increasingly resorting to scientific validation.

The political theology of race seeks account for origins, circumscribes rationality, motivates the social fabric and its constitutive forms of exclusion, orders politics and grounds power, liberating cruelty from constraint.[73]

In short, as the hegemonic power of religion recedes, the secularized or civic religion of race assumes greater social authority. But what of the implications of Goldberg's argument in the context of official commitment to neoliberalism's raceless world order? Does this curious logic of racial supercession of the religious work in the opposite direction? When race is no longer speakable in public, does religion once again emerge as a significant force on the social and political world? Goldberg answers in the affirmative. Perhaps this pervasive shift in contemporary racial reference accounts, in part, for the curious incongruity, indeed incoherence, of the juxtaposition, now ubiquitous in the post-9/11 era, between the West and Islam. The strange equation presumed by the comparison of a geopolitical region with a religious tradition makes no sense, unless situated in a context in which both categories function explicitly or implicitly as markers of race. Recalling the critical lexicon of Jane and Lewis Gordon, Talal Asad draws attention, if implicitly, to the knotted relationship between ethnoracial identity and religion and the fear it produces: "Anxiety regarding the real motives of people (especially anxiety in Euro-America about Middle Easterners who are in the process of assimilating Western culture) rests on the polysemy of signs."[74] Rewriting Barthes, he challenges the official conversion of people into signs in the interests of generating suspicion, fear, uncertainty, and terror.

The complex dynamics, the root causes, and the dehumanizing consequences of the seemingly endless cycle of violence and counterviolence are profoundly obscured through the careful deployment of official language and sanctioned hermeneutics that render the coercion and brutality that accompany liberal modernity's commitment to law and order (the flipside of which is the necessary expulsion of the disorder that heterogeneity threatens) invisible and its created enemies exploitable and expendable. Such tendency, moreover, requires self-conscious reflection of the ways in which charges of fascism or terrorism serve to cover over what Asad describes, in more defiant terms, as the West's "culture of war." The intellectual challenge here is not only to engage critically the contemporary relationship among race, religion, state sovereignty, and resistance. It extends as well to intellectuals' relationship to theory and to the very question of responsibility.

Although Gordon has not directly engaged "Critique of Violence," he does challenge aspects of Derrida's critical response to Benjamin's analysis of the intolerable distance between right and justice and his subsequent claims for the significance of deconstructive theory. He writes:

In 1992, Jacques Derrida . . . declared that "the 'sufferance' of deconstruction, what makes it suffer and what makes those it torments suffer, is perhaps the absence of rules, of norms, and definitive criteria that would allow one to distinguish unequivocally between *droit* and justice." Derrida advances textual poststructuralism as a tragic hero. I think Derrida is right, to the extent that deconstruction—through deconstructionists—constantly articulates the failure of narcissistic desire, including the narcissism of univocality and unequivocality in our moral and political systems. The irony here is that . . . this aspect of deconstruction makes it an "unequivocal moral demand." The generosity and genius of Derrida the man suggests that this conclusion may be what he means by deconstruction's tragic status as well. . . . Whether it's *Oedipus the King*, *Things Fall Apart*, or for that matter, *Les damnes de la terre*, *The Black Jacobins*, or Hansberry's *Les Blancs*, a hallmark of actual tragedies and, consequently, actual tragic heroes, is the demand for recompense. Something must be set right.[75]

Though in fairness Derrida would return again and again to the problem of political theology in the years following his famed "Force of the Law," Gordon raises, more centrally, the question of how such theoretical insight has been appropriated by North American scholars of race in ways that not only reject the viability and desirability of a project of liberation, but exempt them from the responsibilities of engaging contemporary social reality. Characteristically indifferent to academic fashion, the critique is as boldly incisive as it is ethically committed:

Although North American deconstructionists suggest that they may not be able to distinguish unequivocally between right and justice, that may be a consequence of realities (or for that matter, unrealities) in which they live. The problem is in the bad-faith presentation of ideological commitment to begin with—signaled by a rightful, and often righteous, avowal against deciding rightness and justice itself. The tragedy of the situation can be realized, however, through the question of ethical ramifications in the face of current, global possibility. Nothing can be said, that is, to a Third and growing Fourth World people's violent response to First World opulence and the ongoing violence unleashed for the sake of its profit and, at times, preservation. The linguistic play of the African intelligentsia on American terrain becomes, then, a question of whose ideology they are protecting. Their attack on liberation that accompanies the indecidability of *droit* and justice is all too obvious here.[76]

Gordon's body of work attests to the pervasiveness of contemporary racist expression, exploitation, and exclusion and modes of legality implicated therein. The challenges for dismantling these now-global apparatuses of legal violence boggle the intellect and indeed require nothing less than a deep commitment of faith. When Gordon was still a young man, he precociously observed that "theorists theorize in a racist world. The degree to which the world is made evident will have an impact on the question of whether the theorist not only sees, but also admits what is seen."[77] And, indeed, whether the theorist commits to read what was never written.

CHAPTER SIX

Beyond the Racial Blindspot:
DuBoisian Visions for a
Reconstructed America

Like Walter Benjamin, to whom we were introduced in previous chapter, W.E.B. Du Bois rejected a basic tenet of liberal modernity: the false presumption of history's linear progression. Witness, rather, to particularly American forms of sociopolitical advance and regression, violence and counterviolence, Du Bois sought to intervene in unfolding worldwide catastrophe through the promise of higher learning. Though it is a volume of Du Bois's vast oeuvre typically overlooked on such issues, *Black Reconstruction in America* (1935) speaks to the central importance of education in the struggle for substantively democratic and just societies. As the crises of turn-of-the-twentieth-century America find too many parallels to the contemporary moment, Du Bois's magisterial study offers an uncompromising and uncanny assessment of rapacious Gilded Age greed enabled by a corrupt and undemocratic mode of governance, a deregulated economy that generated shocking levels of economic disparity, the distraction of an imperial war, and, of course, the vicious and pervasive racist exclusion that marked the era—one that eventually ended in global depression and war. More significant still is his robust endorsement of education as the preeminent means for a people to inch their way back from the brink of social apocalypse—even as that self-same educational system was then under merciless attack. When I read *Black Reconstruction* for the first time a decade ago, the prophetic nature of Du Bois's theory of history, his counternarrative of post-bellum democratic renewal followed by an era of violent retrenchment, the terror revealed in his otherwise graceful, eloquent prose—all were objects of my somewhat abstract appreciation in regard to what appeared to await a nation hell-bent on coursing along a very similar, very troubled path. And now, as the second Gilded Age comes crashing to an end, and the nation some seventy-five years later finds itself once again mired in recession, war, and widespread popular unrest, Du Bois's reflections on the question of education, and higher education in particular, have become all the more critical, all the more urgent.

Indeed by late 2008 Du Bois's prescient observations about the shocking increase in forms of racist exploitation and violence that accompanied that infamous era of excess followed by economic collapse enacted a strange return, were made flesh, and morphed into a horrifying material reality. The collective capacity to feel the full force of the myriad disasters we now face, to understand the reach and extent of the downward spiral of a once-powerful democratic nation, was tempered for the majority by the electoral victory of the nation's first African American president. In the anxiously insistent celebration of the America's newly achieved "post-racial" status—the perceived redemption, even, of its brutal history of slavery and segregation in their state-driven and current market-driven manifestations—there is little recognition of the disastrous consequences of the last four decades of post–civil rights backlash on communities of color. Nor indeed has there been adequate public acknowledgment of the specifically racist dimensions of the financial tsunami that transformed the American landscape almost overnight. As a result of the global financial crisis that commenced in 2008, for example, 40 percent of African Americans "will have experienced unemployment or underemployment in 2010 . . . increasing child poverty from one-third of African-American children to over half."[1] The consequences have proven both tragic and deliberate. In a reversal of the racial redlining practiced for decades, for example, a number of recent lawsuits against the nation's leading banks including Wells Fargo reveal that lenders pushing "toxic" subprime loans consistently targeted minority communities—even those families that would have qualified for lower interest rate loans. In a recent affidavit, a loan officer testified that bank employees frequently referred to these as "'ghetto loans" and their African American beneficiaries were character-ized as "mud people."[2] The consequence of such racist practices has been the decimation of many black and Latino communities, even entire cities, from Detroit to Prince Georges County, Maryland—historically one of the most affluent black communities in the nation. In a further twist to this tale of corruption and cruelty, conservative commentators such as Charles Krauthammer of the *Washington Post*, CNN's Lou Dobbs (before his abrupt departure), Fox News' Neil Cavuto, and editorialists at the *Wall Street Journal* have enraged audiences with the false accusation that it was the federal Community Reinvestment Act of 1977, which banned racist red-lining practices, that forced lenders to make bad loans to Afri-can Americans and other unworthy recipients, which led in turn to global financial collapse—reckless allegations that have been flatly disproven in studies by the Treasury, the Federal Reserve, Harvard's Joint Center for Housing Studies, and others.[3] In this much vaunted, putatively neutral, and "colorblind" era of free market sovereignty we find widespread impov-erishment, unemployment, home foreclosure, particularly for people of color—as well as a groundswell of white resentment inflamed by rapacious anti-intellectual pundits like Rush Limbaugh, Bill O'Reilly, and Glenn Beck recently joined by members of conservative political establishment such as the formerly exiled Newt Gingrich and ever-elusive Dick Cheney, who were carried back to preeminent public visibility in the effluvium. Unwilling to engage the consequences of decades of neoliberal privatiza-tion, deregulation, and dismantling of welfare state provisions, right-wing politicians and pundits hinted darkly of the new president's socialist agenda, as the alleged "government takeover" of banks, auto industries, and healthcare attests. Decrying Obama's alleged inability to keep the country safe from harm, they point to our porous borders, where illegal immigrants take American jobs and terrorists plot the violent destruction of American lives.

Yet for a brief period following his election, Barack Obama's promise of change, hope, collective action, and democratic renewal appeared to check the opposition's abiding faith in a market theology that had already betrayed itself as a most pernicious form of idolatry, at least for thinking citizens forced to live with the mounting pain and devastation it wrought. For their part, conservatives conceded they lost the battle but not the war, as they continued to block the Obama administration's (largely tepid) efforts to respond to the financial crisis (or the ecological crisis, or the healthcare crisis) by invoking the same market logic, veiled in the same reactionary rhetoric that led us to global meltdown in the first instance. But as I've stated repeatedly, this fight cannot be Obama's alone; it is a fight for the very soul of a democracy, and as such requires the critical and creative efforts of an involved and informed citizenry.

With some exceptions, the Obama administration's commitment to education, in sharp contrast to DuBoisian recommendations, hews too closely to the formulas of past conservative presidents in its instrumental-ist perception of the primary purpose of schooling: creating a more com-petent workforce—better in math, better in science—in order to compete once again in a slowly recovering global economy. Appropriating such an economistic vision of the education of citizens—from the very leadership that brought us the present financial crisis and all that issued from it— would appear to be a perilous step backward for a president eager to tread an enlightened path to democratic futures. As Frank Rich of the *New York Times* noted in his assessment of Obama's selection of Lawrence Summers, Harvard's notorious ex-president, as his chief economic officer, "That the highly paid leader of arguably America's most esteemed educational in-stitution . . . would simultaneously freelance as a hedge-fund guy might stand as a symbol of the values of our time." Obama's pick for Education Secretary, Arne Duncan, former CEO of Chicago Public Schools, with a history of privatizing and militarizing public schools can only deepen the shock and disappointment of progressives, to which Rich gave such pointed expression.[4]

The global economic crisis and the election of the nation's first Afri-can American president will influence the future of education at all levels, in anticipated and unanticipated ways. The nature of that change will de-pend on the pressures that students, teachers, administrators, and citizens bring to bear on educational policy—and the degree to which they insist on the connection between a critically informed citizenry and a viable, just democracy. I have argued throughout this book that the university's civic mission is increasingly imperiled by corporatization, militarization, and racial backlash, as access to its resources is increasingly predicated on whiteness and wealth, and the greater public good is more financially and spiritually starved with every advance of militarized force abroad and at home. The present course of the Obama administration, as yet, does not mitigate these concerns. As we emerge from the worst recession since the Great Depression, and are poised to enter into yet another, or "new," New Deal era, I want to explore, in what follows, the pedagogical implications of Du Bois's later work on education, drawing specifically on his writing and speeches from the 1930s and 1940s. His engagement with historic struggles for racial justice and democracy, I argue, has much to teach contemporary progressives in and out of the university attempting to organize against the anti-democratic excesses of a far right that remains deeply influential politically and culturally as well as a federal government still caught in the maw of vested interests. Thus, drawing on Du Bois's insistence that formal education is central to the functioning of a nonrepressive and inclusive polity, I want to reflect on the past antecedents of the present crises in schooling at all levels, which must be taken up within the context of neoliberal social and economic policies as well as the racist backlash against the civil rights gains of the 1960s. Finally, I will explore Du Bois's deeply felt commitment to a future for critical humanistic thought, for linking rigorous scholarship and creative pedagogical engagement to the struggle to secure the very conditions for racial justice and political democracy.

The Scandal of Reconstruction History

Du Bois completed his magnum opus, *Black Reconstruction in America*, in 1935, at the mature age of sixty-eight. A comprehensive volume of more than 700 pages, *Black Reconstruction* offers Du Bois's most fully developed examination of the interconnections between political economy and racial oppression, and between forms of state terrorism wielded against a domestic population in the name of "law and order" and those exported globally, dignified under the rubric of "foreign policy." Not only did Du Bois rewrite the conventional and deeply racist interpretations of Reconstruction as a failed project by the reigning historians of the day, but he revised basic tenets of the philosophy of history held since the Enlightenment. In his account, Reconstruction was an era of unprecedented civil rights victories, as black Americans achieved the rights of full citizenship,

voted in elections, held political office in local, state, and federal government, and established free public education in the South as well as dozens
of black colleges where none had existed before. In short, it was a period of
democratic rebirth in the wake of Civil War when there was hope that the
nation, now unified in freedom, would take its first steps toward the ideals
of its Constitution. But that hope was short lived, as Du Bois recounts; a
swift and pervasive counter-revolutionary response to that period's democratic advance gained national momentum in 1876, with the election of
Rutherford B. Hayes, and culminated in the *Plessy* decision of 1896. The
net result of two decades of reaction was to push black America "back toward slavery." Writing in the midst of the Great Depression, in the midst
of the Jim Crow South (he had returned to Atlanta University after his
resignation from the NAACP), Du Bois rightly challenged the presumptive "forward march" of history.

Indeed, it is ironic that Du Bois witnessed in 1935 depression-era poverty, which crushed Southern blacks, and the collapse of the labor party,
but wrote about the economic crisis of the mid-1890s, the defeat of the
agrarian Populists, and the establishment of Jim Crow. All of which must
have seemed to him to repeat uncannily the Long Depression of the 1870s
and the disciplining of labor by the new industrial capitalists, who easily
manipulated postwar Reconstruction efforts to serve their interests and
just as shamelessly abandoned them when they didn't. How did he make
sense of the complexities of such vertiginous cycles of democratic advance
and decline? Du Bois's answer, in part, was to look to the color line, "the
Blindspot of American political and social development" that crippled the
scholarly search for a truthful and coherent history and "made logical argument almost impossible."[5] Du Bois understood the ill-fated history of
Reconstruction as part and parcel of the ongoing tragedy of American
political life, a tragedy to beggar the Greek, which resides in the nation's
failure to grasp that the "problem of race" involves the very foundations of
American democracy, both political and economic.

Engaging a similar historical circumstance several decades prior to
the Great Depression, Du Bois pondered the capacities of Southern politicians and Northern business leaders (strange bedfellows indeed!) to secure
the unity of interests that otherwise stood worlds apart. *Black Reconstruction* sought to explain, in other words, the loyalty of the white laborer

not to the black laborer, but to a dethroned Southern aristocracy, and to elucidate the eventual obeisance of both to the will of Northern industrialists in the decades following Emancipation. With characteristic grace and insight, he wrote:

Thus by singular coincidence and for a moment, for the few years of an eternal second in a cycle of a thousand years, the orbits of two widely and utterly dissimilar economic systems coincided and the result was a revolution so vast and portentous that few minds ever fully conceived it; for the systems were these: first, that of a democracy which should by universal suffrage establish a dictatorship of the proletariat ending in industrial democracy; and the other, a system by which a little knot of masterful men would so organize capitalism as to bring under their control the natural resources, wealth and industry of a vast and rich country and through that, of the world. For a second, for a pulse of time, these orbits crossed and coincided, but their central suns were a thousand light years apart, even though the blind and ignorant fury of the South and the complacent Philistinism of the North saw them as one.[6]

His substantial and meticulously detailed investigation exposed the uses of racial resentment, inflamed by anti-black ideologies circulating in science, religion, or political theory, to align these vastly opposed "orbits," thus securing the hegemony of powerful business interests as it consolidated white racial rule.

Though his conceptual framework has been dismissed as so much Marxist dogma applied to history, the criticism seems to miss the central contribution of *Black Reconstruction* to contemporary political thought: that in the pursuit of genuine democratization and an equitable distribution of resources, questions of race cannot be meaningfully separated from questions of class. And struggles for freedom and social justice, further, are necessarily global in their effects, if not necessarily in their reach. The untoward abuses of black workers that followed quickly on the heels of their manumission had consequences as well for their white working-class counterparts. To the degree that such unrestricted profiteering enabled American industrialists to advance on global markets, its effects were felt worldwide. In short, the continued allegiance to racist ideologies and exclusions undermined not only black emancipation in the United States but the emancipation of humankind more generally. Anticipating the vulnerability and insecurity of contemporary American workers in general (and black and brown in particular) occurring in tandem with the exploitation of non-white labor in the so-called "developing" world as the result of Western deindustrialization, Du Bois's insight remains unimpeachable, though his language, derived from nineteenth-century Marxist thought, is clearly dated.

Du Bois argued that the Reconstruction era was not simply a battle between black and white races, or between master and ex-slave; it was also a vast labor movement galvanized by the promise of industrial democracy that was to eventually betray itself on the altar of racial apartheid at home and imperialism abroad. And the implications of that failure of democratic vision and will were felt everywhere. As historians since Du Bois have convincingly argued, one might rightly question the recasting of Civil War struggles in terms of a general strike or even the desire for a "dictatorship of the proletariat." But the fact remains that by 1876 the dream of political democracy in the United States was deferred indefinitely. As a result of ensuing decades of unchecked corporate and imperial power, the nation and the world were eventually plunged into economic depression and war. The hopes of Reconstruction dashed, Du Bois pondered the violence and carnage that followed in its wake, not just for black Americans, but for ordinary citizens the world over. His eloquent assessment is worth repeating at length:

God wept; but that mattered little to an unbelieving age; what mattered most was that the world wept and still is weeping and blind with tears and blood. For there began to rise in America in 1876 a new capitalism and a new enslavement of labor. Home labor in cultured lands, appeased and misled by a ballot whose power the dictatorship of vast capital strictly curtailed, was bribed by high wage and political office to unite in an exploitation of white, yellow, brown and black labor, in lesser lands and "breeds without the law." Especially workers of the New World, folks who were American and for whom America was, became ashamed of their destiny. Sons of ditch-diggers aspired to be spawn of bastard kings and thieving aristocrats rather than of rough-handed children of dirt and toil. The immense profit from this new exploitation and world wide commerce enabled a guild of millionaires to engage the greatest engineers, the wisest men of science, as well as pay high wage to the more intelligent labor and at the same time to have enough surplus to make more thorough the dictatorship of capital over the state and over the popular vote, not only in Europe and America but in Asia and Africa.

The world wept because within the exploiting group of New World masters, greed and jealousy became so fierce that they fought for trade and markets and materials and slaves all over the world until at last in 1914 the world flamed in war. The fantastic structure fell, leaving grotesque Profits and Poverty, Plenty and Starvation, Empire and Democracy, staring at each other across World Depression. And the rebuilding, whether it comes now or a century later, will and must go back to the basic principles of Reconstruction in the Unites States during 1867–1876.[7]

Du Bois's depiction of the age of rampant industrialization, robber barons, and racist exploitation thus challenges a form of contemporary common sense that equates a free market economy with democracy by invoking the power of capital to denigrate those values Americans hold most sacred— freedom, self-reliance, and a level playing field, as well as the maintenance and protection of family and community. The unfettered power of capital not only rendered free elections relatively meaningless through graft and corruption (or, in today's terms, though the management and distribution of everyday people's access to information and critical viewpoints); it also undid the bonds of family and community to the degree that it fostered identifications with the rich and powerful, however distant or remote, and a corresponding indifference to the plight of everyday people with little by way of resources or wealth and even less political leverage. But Du Bois's most startling insight is his prescient understanding of the global consequences of economic expansion and white racial domination in the interests of "nation building." Opposing images of "grotesque Profits and Poverty, Plenty and Starvation, Empire and Democracy" will no doubt resonate powerfully, if not eerily, for the twenty-first century reader. As U. S.-led global capitalism slowly recovers from its 2008 collapse, advancing unabated its neoliberal economic and social agenda and pauperizing vast non-white populations of the world, the clear majority of U.S. citizens continue to experience downward wage pressure and a rapidly declining standard of living, if not outright impoverishment and home foreclosure. Ordinary citizens bear the expense materially and psychologically as the military arm of the world's remaining superpower looks to widen the scope of its war on terrorism to protect American "freedoms." Though there is growing recognition of the role that oil plays in the current U.S. military occupation of Iraq, and its deepening concern with Iran, precious few intellectuals link historically racist Western attitudes towards Muslim populations to the "war on terror," preferring instead a more coded rhetoric of religious and civilizational conflict. An awareness of the forces at work in the global movement of capital and the ongoing commitment to racial domination and exclusion—separate forces, yet inseparable—seems to lie just beyond the consciousness of average American citizens, though the consequences of these abstract pressures insinuate themselves into nearly every aspect of their lives.

Du Bois's *Black Reconstruction*, however, was not written to workers black and white, then or now, who have been ongoing victims of rapacious capital or racist ideological subterfuge. It is preeminently a challenge to the chroniclers of official history, to intellectuals and academics who recklessly use "a version of historic fact in order to influence and educate the new generation along the way [they] wish."[8] In the final chapter of *Black Reconstruction*, Du Bois confronts those historians who, assuming as axiomatic the inferiority of the "Negro," participated in the "most stupendous" campaign "the world ever saw to discredit human beings" in the interests of economic and racial domination, an effort involving the pedagogical force of the entire culture, of "universities, history, science, social life and religion."[9] The sting of this indictment is surely felt today among progressives who wonder how the United States got so far afield of its reputed values of liberty, equality, and justice for all. And so the gauntlet is thrown down to intellectuals in and out of the academy who desire a more democratic future than the less and less hopeful present that is currently on offer. As Du Bois grasped so keenly, the revitalization of democratic politics is preeminently a pedagogical endeavor. Education in the university or informally circulating through earnest public debate may not be all that is required to counter the anti-democratic excesses of neoliberalism's most zealous advocates, to say nothing of their racially driven motivations, but its absence guarantees their brilliant success. As we take the measure of the damage wrought by four decades of conservative counterrevolution, it seems appropriate to pose, after Du Bois, the question of the color line again, in an effort to avoid what Charles Lemert recently termed, with not a little chagrin, "pastism," or "the error of failing to grant the real or virtual dead credit for having understood present matters better than present company . . . a refusal to grant that others knew the rules before [we] did."[10]

Looking Backward: Post–Civil Rights
and Post-Reconstruction (2008–1876)

Du Bois was uncannily accurate in his prediction that the rebuilding of American political democracy, "whether it comes now or a century later, will and must go back to the basic principles of Reconstruction in the United States during 1867–1876." Nearly a century after its initial attempts at black emancipation, a renewed civil rights movement attempted to rebuild a democratic society out of the ashes of Jim Crow. Throughout the decade of the 1960s, organized citizens agitated for and achieved the formal, legal repeal of segregation, the reenfranchisement of black voters, and the passage of legislation guaranteeing equal opportunity in school and the workplace and an assurance of welfare benefits for black families. Yet the full realization of these rights and protections was not forthcoming. On the heels of such long-awaited victories, the nation's citizenry was told that civil rights had simply gone too far. In the ensuing decades, successive Supreme Court rulings have quietly dismantled *Brown v. Board of Education*, creating rapidly resegregated and unequal schools more reminiscent of the *Plessy v. Ferguson* era. Attacks on affirmative action have similarly diminished black students' access to universities, as it un-leveled the playing field for black-owned businesses. Felony disenfranchisement, ongoing voter intimidation in the South, and the massive fraud perpetuated against black voters in the 2000 presidential election have rendered formal voting rights a partial accomplishment at best.[11] In the late 1960s, black women achieved the right to receive welfare benefits, but this, too, proved a pyrrhic victory. By the 1980s they had become the unwitting poster children for a propaganda campaign to dismantle the welfare state, as the federal government reneged on the provision of compassionate services and redoubled its repressive functions. In much the same way that historians, intellectuals, journalists, and others demonized Reconstruction, the political revolution of the 1960s that secured civil rights for blacks, women, the criminally accused, senior citizens, and others was immediately reframed in terms of a cultural revolution that emphasized permissiveness, lack of work ethic, moral relativism, and utter contempt for mainstream values.

The history of American apartheid and its ongoing effects having disappeared from public memory in this proudly "post–civil rights era," we have once again entered an Orwellian era in American life, a time in which, as Du Bois once remarked, "logical argument [is] all but impossible." The general presumption of the post–civil rights era, roughly from the mid-1970s to the present, is that the racial injury and injustice derived from centuries of enslavement, Jim Crow laws, and urban ghettoization have been both widely acknowledged and corrected by established powers, and that we, as a nation, have transcended race in the interests of colorblind public policy. What is left out of that reading of contemporary political culture, of course, is the enormity of the backlash that ensued in the wake of civil rights advancements. As in the days of post-Reconstruction, the terms of political discourse have been utterly subverted by conservative ideologues and pundits soft-pedaling racial reaction in various guises and for various purposes. From crude appeals to deviant black sexuality, criminality, and intellectual/moral inferiority, as in Bush Sr.'s Willie Horton campaign and the vogue of Charles Murray in the mid-1990s, to the more coded appeals to "colorblindness," and "race-transcendence" of the Bush years and their abrupt abandonment in the hysteria over Obama's birthplace and his alleged Muslim faith, right-wing intellectuals and experts from across a variety of cultural sites—corporations, think tanks, churches, universities, and especially the mass media—have successfully revived the anti-black and anti-immigration rhetoric and imagery of a century ago. For neoconservatives, the goal of the post–civil rights era has been to roll back the gains made by new social movements in the 1960s and to radically restrict immigration in the interests of cultural nationalism and the consolidation of the political and economic power of structural whiteness, while silencing any discussion of race in mainstream national politics by insisting on a colorblind public policy. For neoliberals, it has been to "free" the markets through the relentless privatization and deregulation of formerly public goods and services provided by the state. To garner support for such a nakedly corporate agenda, neoliberals have also adopted a populist platform to "free" citizens of an oppressive tax burden by dismantling the welfare state (now rendered as an archaic set of bureaucracies that largely fail the populations they are designed to serve by absorbing tax dollars to promote the dependency and debauchery of poor minorities), thus dissolving the language of public life and common good.

Having either bought into dominant ideologies or simply denied access to any other ideology, everyday people, whose jobs and health care and homes are increasingly vulnerable in a rapidly globalizing economy and whose safety is increasingly uncertain in a post-9/11 world, continue to be swayed by a two-party system dominated by corporate and imperial interests—the very elite who were responsible for the current financial meltdown and the decades of economic insecurity that led up to it, the ones responsible, in other words, for sending jobs and factories (and now soldiers and munitions) overseas to promote a more flexible workforce, secure scarce resources, and exempt themselves from all forms of accountability. Of the many achievements of this ongoing right-wing campaign carried out by Republicans and Democrats alike, the preeminent victory has been the near-impossibility of carrying on frank and reasonable discussion of what is happening in our communities, our country, and across the globe—which has been abetted by Obama's inability to take control of the conversation. It is a victory as much determined by the right's tight control over national political rhetoric as it is by their capacity to manage and contain public spaces of pedagogy—both informally in the media,[12] and formally through successive attacks on public education at all levels. In the latter case, the Obama administration, far from countering the assault on schooling, has embraced high-stakes testing and zero tolerance—to name but two utterly ineffectual and reactionary initiatives—as part of its own vision for educational improvement.

In the run-up to the election of 2004, progressives in the United States did eventually begin to rethink the public role of pedagogy as they attempted to arouse the citizenry to "Take Back America" from the apostles of free market fundamentalism with their own counter-narratives of life in the new millennium. Though that election was lost, one narrative of renewal was famously heard at the Democratic convention, and it made all the difference by 2008. Yet missing from these critical interventions, Obama's included, was a sophisticated treatment of racial politics in the post–civil rights era, particularly as it intersects with the interests of neoliberal and neoconservative policy makers. Even so, if we are to learn anything from Du Bois's life and work, it is surely that strategies for political and economic democratization require sophisticated theorization of how race and class politics—though discrete discourses—inform and influence each other both within the United States and on the global stage. Before I elaborate on the significance of *Black Reconstruction* for understanding the current political context, let me provide brief examples of three exemplary, though incomplete, efforts to challenge the right-wing juggernaut that make a similar recourse to history.

Though unsuccessful in "taking back America" in 2004, progressives did eventually find their voices and begin to push back against the entrenched free-market, anti-government ideologies of the right in ways that would prove decisive in the next election cycle. In a May 2003 issue of *The Nation*, William Greider mapped the "grand ambition" of the conservative forces guiding the second Bush administration. In a lead article titled "Rolling Back the Twentieth Century," he asserted that the right's primary objective was to recast the federal government under Bush Jr. in the likeness of what it was—quite literally—under William McKinley, who held the office of president from 1897 to 1901. This was the gilded era of government, when corporations and religious organizations reigned supreme, before any Progressive-era New Deal, before, as conservative tactician Grover Norquist put it, the ascendancy of "Teddy Roosevelt, when the socialists took over."[13] For Norquist and the conservative groups he has so masterfully organized in the last two decades, regaining paradise lost requires the demise of "big government." Though it has proven a popular catch-phrase among mainstream Americans, as Greider observes, the right's objectives are quite radical by any standard. They are, in short, the elimination of federal taxation of private capital; the phasing out of pension-fund retirement systems; the withdrawal of government from any direct role in housing, healthcare, and assistance to the poor; the restoration of the centrality of church, family, and private education to the nation's cultural life; the strengthening of business and market-based solutions to public concerns in areas like the environment; and, finally, the dismantlement of organized labor.

Similarly, in his opening speech at the "Take Back America" conference sponsored by the Campaign for America's Future a month later, Bill Moyers discussed the influence of the McKinley administration, and especially Mark Hanna, on Karl Rove, Bush's reputed brain. Hanna was the primary architect of McKinley's public persona and largely responsible for his successful bid for the governorship of Ohio and later the presidency—much as Rove enabled Bush's ascendency as governor in Texas and his transition to the White House. The political achievements of Mark Hanna, Karl Rove's hero, were largely the result of old-fashioned corporate shakedowns. Hanna, Moyers notes, "saw to it that first Ohio then Washington were 'ruled by business . . . by bankers, railroads and public utility corporations.'" This "degenerate and unlovely age," Moyers notes, is the "seminal age of inspiration for the politics and governance of America today."[14]

Then in the August 2003 issue of *Harper's* Lewis Lapham offered yet another scathing indictment of present-day chicanery by invoking days of future past. Lapham examines McKinley-era weapons of mass deception, which were used to preempt the threat of an emergent populist movement for social and political reform in the face of widespread economic inequality. "If by 1890 the Industrial Revolution had made America rich," Lapham writes, "so also it had alerted the electorate to the unequal division of the spoils. People had begun to notice the loaded dice in the hand of the railroad and banking monopolies, the tax burden shifted from capital to labor."[15] Reflecting the same instability as the boom and bust cycles experienced in the 1990s and currently, the economic depression and widespread unemployment in the winter of 1893–94 aroused the nation's citizenry, and the government literally reached for its guns. Looking for "'something,' in the words of an alarmed U.S. senator, to knock the 'pus' out of this 'anarchistic, socialist and populist boil,'" Lapham explains, "the McKinley administration came up with the war in Cuba, the conquest of the Philippines, the annexation of Puerto Rico, and an imperialist foreign policy. . . . Only by infecting the republic with the delusion of imperial grandeur could the nation . . . smother the republican spirit and replace the love of liberty with the love of the flag . . . [as] all political quarrels [were] suspended in the interests of 'the national security.'"[16] Moving between past and present, between steel interests and oil interests, a war in Cuba and a war in Iraq and Afghanistan, Lapham's indictment of the Bush administration and its propaganda machine is penetratingly clear. It would be a grave mistake, of course, to assume that U.S. military operations in the Middle East were merely a means to distract (or silence)

American citizens—though they may well function in this way—rather than part of a broader effort to secure resources, labor, and trade advantages from formerly colonized nations. What Lapham's analysis gestures toward, in spite of its shortcomings, is an opportunity to gauge the impact of unfettered corporate and imperial power on civilian populations both at home and abroad—and a crucial opportunity to challenge the racism that promotes complicity with such abuses.

If the project to "take back America" in the interests of substantive, participatory democracy eventually took root among everyday citizens, it was precisely because of committed intellectuals working in the public interest of the caliber of Moyers, Greider, and Lapham, whose acumen and courage in the face of a rising tide of jingoistic patriotism and the relentless merging of government with corporate power have been unflinching. They were helped, of course, by events like Katrina in 2005, which precisely exposed the dangers of a financially starved and ineffectual federal government about which these critics had warned the American people. What remains under the radar among the most outspoken proponents of democracy today, even under the Obama administration, is the existence of a "preemptive" war at home on black America, the domestic corollary to an expanding "nation-building" and securitizing agenda abroad. That the Bush administration emulated the McKinley era in its show of raw corporate and imperial power is surely correct. But the graphic juxtaposition of two eras of unprecedented political corruption explains the ascendancy of neither. Hence it is worth investigating another parallel to that brutal era that has been left unexamined, what Du Bois called "the American blindspot." If we are to draw any meaningful conclusions from the turn-of-the-twentieth-century hijacking of political democracy, if we are to truly take it back in our own time, we must expand our understanding of the racial politics of both that era and our own, as they are inextricably entwined with corporate and imperial agendas.

I would like to advance the argument, therefore, that the McKinley administration represents the culmination of a series of events set in motion in the aftermath of the Civil War and southern Reconstruction, just as the Bush administration reflects the organizational pinnacle of right-wing reaction to the civil rights revolution of the 1960s. The revolution of 1863–76 and the revolution that spanned the decade of the 1960s won, first for black men then for black men and women, the rights, responsibilities, and protections of democratic citizenship, at least in theory, for a time. Among the rights afforded citizens were those that vouchsafed the capacity for self-possession and self-determination—the right to paid labor, education, enfranchisement, as well as protections from state violence in its various forms—insult, humiliation, isolation, incarceration, starvation, disease, and murder. On the heels of each revolutionary victory, however, came a swift and pervasive counter-revolutionary response, and, as I will later detail, education would prove a primary battlefield throughout.

Following the southern Reconstruction experiment, the national Republican Party of the late 1800s, the party of Abraham Lincoln, eventually abandoned its efforts to achieve racial equality after it failed to win the support of Southern conservatives and faced potential political defeat. Rutherford B. Hayes, for example, secured his quite-controversial election in 1876 by promising to stop enforcing civil rights and promptly withdrawing federal troops from the South. The concessions to former Confederates came fast and furious, and all at the expense of newly manumitted slaves. By the year 1896, McKinley had won the presidential election and "separate but equal" had been rendered legal by the landmark *Plessy v. Ferguson* decision. Not only did black Americans suffer the formal loss of civil rights and legal protections as a result of the Supreme Court's ruling (most had experienced the actual loss of these in the two decades leading up to the decision), but they were increasingly subject to forms of domestic terrorism throughout the 1890s, with some two hundred lynchings occurring on average per year. A time of cynicism and deep despair among black intellectual leadership, it was an era marked by the ascendancy of black leaders like Booker T. Washington, who, in concert with majority white opinion, rejected civil rights struggle in favor of philanthropy and self-help.

Facing its own political crisis nearly one hundred years later, the contemporary advocates of civil rights, the Democrats, took note. After Republican presidential victories from 1968 to 1988, elections won by a virtually all-white party utterly opposed to civil rights, the Democrats followed suit and excised the rhetoric of racial justice from its national platform. The Democratic Leadership Council was formed in the mid-1980s by mostly white, male, largely southern Democratic politicians, corporate lobbyists, and fundraisers to counter the "liberal fundamentalism" of the party's base—principally blacks and other minorities, in addition to unionists, feminists, and Greens. The DLC quickly gained ascendancy on a platform (backed by corporate dollars) declaring that the Democratic Party had become too solicitous of African American and Latino political support, too respectful of workers' rights, and too responsive to the peace, justice, and environmental movements.[17] The success of the DLC culminated in the election of Bill Clinton, who had been the DLC-New Democrat candidate for president in 1992: it was a triumph that spelled a political disaster for black constituencies. For example, Bruce Dixon observes: "Rather than answer the Reaganite myth of the welfare queen, Clinton pandered to it and gave us a 'welfare reform' more punitive than anything Reagan-era Republicans could have wrested from Congress."[18] To assuage African American votes in light of such stark failures to serve that constituency, Dixon notes the appearance of a new class of "black Trojan horse Democrats," who, financed by corporate power, were being foisted on black communities to allegedly "represent" their interests. Had the strategy changed by 2009? Between the soaring rhetoric of Obama's stump speeches in the run-up to the presidential election and the many capitulations of his administration to the financials and other industries in the summer of 2009, his professed commitment to stand for "all America" and his much-noted unwillingness to address the calamitous impact of the recession on people of color in particular, which interests Obama serves remains at best an open question.

As the unprecedented corporate influence on the political system in both periods makes clear, the Post-Reconstruction era and the more recent, post–civil rights era were periods of unprecedented economic change, enabling the rapid consolidation of corporate power. The former was set in motion by the Long Depression after the panic of 1873. It was the bust that ended what Eric Hobsbawm called the "Age of Capital," the largest period of economic expansion in the early history of capitalism. Following a series of wage cuts among the nation's railway workers, who already suffered low wages and dangerous working conditions, and the scheming and profiteering of railroad companies, the year 1877 erupted in a series of tumultuous strikes extending from cities in the Northeast to St. Louis. As a result, the nation experienced a run on banks and the failure of thousands of businesses, which was followed by the collapse of half the nation's iron producers, and half its railroads, between 1873 and 1878; this led to the failure of other business and industries that had risen in tandem with heavy industrialization. While some concessions were made to working Americans, northern industrialists strengthened their position in collusion with southern planters. In addition, revolutionary breakthroughs in technology increasingly made manual labor redundant, as innovations in steam and electricity replaced human muscle. By the year 1877, the historian Howard Zinn writes,

The signals were given for the rest of the century: the black would be put back; the strikes of white workers would not be tolerated; the industrial and political elites of North and South would take hold of the country and organize the greatest march of economic growth in human history. They would do it with the aid of, and at the expense of, black labor, white labor, Chinese labor, European immigrant labor, female labor, rewarding them differently by race, sex, national origin, and social class, in such a way as to create separate levels of oppression—a skillful terracing to stabilize the pyramid of wealth.[19]

Although it is true that many black Americans have come to enjoy middle-class status in the post–civil rights era, their share of the economic pie has improved only slightly since the days of Reconstruction. Consider that in 1865, blacks owned 0.5 percent of the nation's net worth, and in 1990, their net worth totaled only 1 percent.[20] With the advent of postindustrialism, the United States witnessed a frenzy of breakneck deindustrialization, the weakening of organized labor, and an increase in joblessness, poverty, and decaying infrastructure, particularly in the nation's cities, as well as an attendant psychological fallout of fear, anxiety, and insecurity. In the face of increased competition from newly rebuilt industries in Europe and Japan, whose urban centers had been all but destroyed in World War II, as well as a series of wildcat strikes at home in the early 1970s, U.S. industries began to take flight, enabled by startling advances in information technologies. In the decades that followed, the nation would experience the loss of millions of jobs in manufacturing; there was a significant decline in wages as well, as corporations moved factories overseas to developing nations that offered cheap, non-unionized labor, tax holidays, and totally unregulated land beyond the reach of any environmental protection groups— sending a resounding message to American workers. Although blue-collar workers in general have suffered from the flight of industry overseas in the last thirty years, black Americans have been particularly squeezed—as is also the case in the present recession. Because pay for blacks historically has been higher in manufacturing than in many other fields, deindustrialization hit blacks disproportionately harder than whites. According to a 2003 article written by Louis Uchitelle of the *New York Times,* since 2001 the United States had lost 2.6 million jobs, nearly 90 percent of them in manufacturing. Uchitelle observes, "In 2000, there were two million black Americans working in factory jobs, or 10.1 percent of the nation's total of 20 million manufacturing workers." Since the recession began in March 2001, he adds, "300,000 factory jobs held by blacks, or 15 percent, have disappeared. White workers lost many factory jobs, too—1.7 million in all. But because they were much more numerous to begin with, proportionally the damage was less, just 10 percent."[21] While unemployment for black men has generally been double the rate for their white counterparts, 10.5 percent, according to one low estimate,[22] the jobless rate among minority teens is the highest in 55 years. According to the Children's Defense Fund, the 2003 jobless rates, five years prior to the current recession, were already "78.3% (the highest since 1983) for black teens and 68.4% for Latino teens, the highest reported for young Latinos."[23] In 2003, corporate analysts predicted that the nation's service sector and IT jobs would quickly follow suit: "3.3 million U.S. service industry jobs and $136 billion in wages [would] move offshore to countries like India, Russia, China, and the Philippines" in the next fifteen years, which would further stress an already tight labor market and continue to drive wages down as the cost of health care and education continued to spiral to outrageous heights.[24] That was the 2001–3 recession for black America; what they experienced in 2008 when many millions more jobs disappeared in less than a year was an all-out depression.[25]

Given the untoward vulnerability of American workers in both eras, the pervasive mood of the post-emancipation era, as W.E.B. Du Bois describes it in *Black Reconstruction,* is as apt a description as we'll find of our current situation: a pervasive and multivalent fear. The insecurity, anxiety, and uncertainty of citizens were aroused by many things, Du Bois wrote, "but usually losing their jobs, being declassed, degraded, or actually disgraced; of losing their hopes, their savings, their plans for their children; of the actual pangs of hunger, of dirt, of crime. And of all this, most ubiquitous in modern society is that fear of unemployment."[26] And fear is what propelled the mob violence and lawlessness that was in 1865–68 "spasmodic and episodic," only to become organized and systemic throughout the South in the decades that followed. "Lawlessness and violence filled the land," Du Bois reflected, "and terror stalked abroad by day, and it burned and murdered by night. The Southern states had actually relapsed into barbarism. . . . Armed guerrilla warfare killed thousands of Negroes; political riots were staged; their causes or occasions were always obscure, their results always certain: ten to one hundred times as many Negroes were killed as whites."[27] Today's culture of fear is, of course, the topic of much scholarly attention, having spawned what Mike Davis recently called "fear studies." From sophisticated theoretical analyses such as Ulrich Beck's *Risk Society* to Barry Glassner's more popular, eponymous investigation, *The Culture of Fear,* intellectuals in and out of the academy have taken up the perils of postmodern society, both real and manufactured for cynical exploitation and legitimation of lethal force. Politicians in both periods were able successfully to translate a generalized anxiety and uncertainty about unemployment, poverty, homelessness (and, in the new millennium, nuclear annihilation, terrorist attacks, environmental devastation), into a specific fear of crime and a personal concern over safety, as both periods witnessed the "official solidification of the centuries-old association of blackness with criminality and devious violence."[28] As the result of the successful mobilization of racially coded fears, the mob violence of over a century ago has been supplanted by the prevalence of profiling, harassment, brutality, even murder of black and brown populations by an increasingly paramilitarized police force, now the legitimate arm of the law. Yet earlier violent inclinations have not disappeared entirely. Indeed, the threat of mob violence, by the summer of 2009, appears all the more imminent, fueled in no small way by white resentment over Obama's victory, as the ongoing displays of defaced images of the president and other racist iconography at town hall meetings and various grass-roots protests would indicate.

The generalized instability and anxiety of the post-Reconstruction and post–civil rights eras were thus the result of dramatic shifts in the economy no less than dramatic shifts in the body politic, as black Americans demanded the rights and entitlements of full citizenship. In both instances, however, they found themselves on the bad end of public policies meant to bolster and appease a white citizenry discomforted by political, economic, and social upheaval. This is what Du Bois referred to as a "public and psychological wage" to compensate for the decline in real wages, which translated into turn-of-the-century protocols requiring that public deference and titles of courtesy be extended to white citizens because they were white—not to mention their being admitted to public parks and beaches, attending the best schools, having the right to vote, et cetera. Black Americans, conversely, suffered the spiritual and material weight of the color line with the establishment of Jim Crow laws and social practices. The brief period after the Civil War in which black men were allowed to vote, black representatives were elected to state legislatures and Congress, and all children in the South were allowed to attend public schooling, at the state's expense, was effectively over. Free and equal participation in democratic life gave way to racial domination, ghettoization, segregation, and disenfranchisement—conditions that still mark the lived experiences of black and brown Americans untouched by the election of Obama and were indeed exacerbated by the recession he inherited.

Like the backlash that followed Reconstruction, the response to the peaceful, nonviolent struggle for civil rights that spanned the decade of the 1960s was an escalation of war rhetoric on the part of the established order, coupled with real destruction and casualties, as Johnson's War on Poverty became Nixon's War on Crime, then Reagan's War on Drugs, which was expanded and folded into Bush Jr.'s War on Terrorism. As the stagnation of wages, growing unemployment, and an insufficient safety net only deepened poverty for Americans on the low end of the wage spectrum in the 1970s and 1980s, the field of wartime operations shifted from the conditions of impoverishment to the poor themselves, who became an increasingly racially defined population. Efforts to polarize the electorate along racial lines picked up speed with Nixon's so-called tax revolt of the late 1970s, which pitted taxpayers against "tax recipients" and fueled a dramatic attack on the welfare state. Reagan's 1980 campaign for president capitalized on this polarization, attacking racial quotas and food stamps, and extending its reach to a rejection of any government interference in the economy and an all-out assault on "big government." Racial management and containment no longer required the overt brutality of the klansmen of decades past. In post–civil rights America, particularly in the late 1970s and 1980s, a nightly battalion of conservative social scientists, legal scholars, educators, and preachers endowed with media omnipresence waged an ideological war against the "underclass," a term used to criminalize the poor by transforming them into a tangle of filth and human garbage. Their mantra: that big government's handouts had corrupted black and Latino communities by creating generations of cheats, who were characterized by laziness, drug addiction, sexual excess, and a general taste for criminality and violence. As a result of such coded rhetoric, white working-class and middle-class voters increasingly perceived the Democrats' civil rights agenda to be in the service of blacks as well as feminists, gays, and other marginalized groups. "Quotas," "preferential treatment," and "groups" were so many code words used by the Reagan administration that signaled to largely white suburban voters (who embraced the ideology of rugged individualism) that the era of big government handouts to minorities was now over.[29]

Whereas the turn-of-the-century recompense to white workers turned on appeals to white supremacy and the real material privileges of whiteness under Jim Crow, the more recent attempts to assuage the pain of white workers in the new economy came in the form of public recognition of, and vows to end, their alleged victimization by big government policies that favored racial set-asides and affirmative action, or, in the parlance of conservatives, "reverse racism," which was now challenged in the name of "fairness" and a "colorblind" public policy. "During the Reagan-Bush years," John Brenkman notes, "working class and middle class whites were willing to accept the massive shift of wealth from the middle class to the rich so long as they simultaneously perceived that Reagan's policies were transferring wealth *from blacks to whites*."[30] By the 1992 election year, it became clear to Democratic Party officials that they could not win an election without wooing back the so-called Reagan Democrats who had fled the party in the previous decade. In *Chain Reaction*, an incisive analysis of the impact of Reagan-Bush politics on the Democratic Party, Thomas and Mary Edsall argue that the Clinton campaign appropriated the slogans of the Reagan-Bush era and crafted an explicitly "race-neutral" platform, which "voters were known to interpret in strictly racial terms."[31]

What cannot be overemphasized here is the role that race has played in abetting neoliberalism's efforts to depoliticize popular constituencies and privatize all remaining public goods and services though the discourses of anti-statism and self-help. Repressive state institutions—the juvenile justice system, the police, the prison—were the only institutions left to tend to the increasingly racial poor. Tragically, as I've previously stated, the strategy of "race-neutrality" is one to which the Obama administration actively appeals.

As the history of the post-Reconstruction and post–civil rights eras reveals, there is a very short distance between blaming oppressed or excluded groups for their own misery, demonizing them for their poverty, and then criminalizing their behavior. All over the South, the passage of so-called Black Codes in the years after Reconstruction enabled the mass incarceration of former slaves for committing "crimes" such as vagrancy, absence from work, ownership of firearms, or violations of racial etiquette— in other words, practices that were quite legal if one were white. It is worth noting that during slavery there were no blacks in prison; punishment for any transgression was meted out by the master of the plantation. "On the morrow of Emancipation," Loïc Wacquant notes, "southern prisons turned black overnight. . . . The introduction of convict leasing as a response to the moral panic of crime presented the double advantage of generating prodigious funds for the state coffers and furnishing abundant bound labor."[32] It was for these reasons that Frederick Douglass referred to incarcerated blacks as "prisoners of war," rather than criminals.

Over one hundred years later, Douglass's insight still has teeth. In the midst of racial backlash in an allegedly "colorblind" era, the war on crime and the war on drugs shook loose from their metaphorical moorings and became a real war. The renewed interest in prison labor, prison privatization, and what Paul Street has called "correctional Keynesianism"[33] are the contemporary corollaries of earlier efforts to both contain and extract free labor from a potentially subversive, largely black prison population. Politicians looking to up one another on "get tough" crime policy militarized city spaces, armed police with paramilitary weaponry and surveillance equipment, and made lifers out of nonviolent offenders with "three strikes" laws, expanding what critics have called the prison-industrial complex. The prison population has grown from 196,000 inmates in 1972[34] to over 2.3 million today, making the United States, the land of the free and home of the brave, the world's largest jailer in the span of three decades and the *"first genuine prison society* in history."[35] Even in the early 1970s, before the mass incarceration frenzy accelerated, prisoners were predominantly black and Latino, and many were political activists who had organized resistance movements in their communities. Currently, as a result of a failed war on drugs and a radical rewriting of sentencing policy, one in three young black males is likely to spend some time in the criminal justice system, in spite of the fact that drug use is relatively the same across racial and ethnic groups. The race to incarcerate in turn broke up families, where parental rights weren't dissolved altogether; increased poverty and unemployment, as it denied ex-felons the right to public housing, food stamps, and veterans' benefits: thus, it led to yet more crime in poor communities.[36] The net result is to push young black men in particular a little closer to prison, the asylum, or the grave.

That objective conditions worsened for the majority of black Americans in both the post-Reconstruction and post–civil rights eras seems difficult to contest in the face of such overwhelming evidence, though right-wing politicians and pundits give altogether different rationalizations for such immiseration. To add insult to injury, Du Bois notes, the alleged faults and failures of southern Reconstruction were placed squarely on "Negro ignorance and corruption."[37] Citing literally dozens of accounts from children's history texts, Du Bois discovered an overwhelming chorus of agreement on this issue. "The South found it necessary to pass Black Codes," wrote one of these historians,

for the control of the shiftless and sometimes vicious freedmen. The Freedman's Bureau caused the Negroes to look to the North rather than the South for support and by giving them a false sense of equality did more harm than good. With the scalawags, the ignorant and non-property holding Negroes under the leadership of the carpetbaggers, engaged in wild orgy of spending in the legislature. The humiliation and distress of the Southern whites was in part relieved by the Ku Klux Klan, a secret organization which frightened the superstitious blacks.[38]

According to this historian, the Klan "frightened" blacks because blacks were "superstitious," not because the Klan was a terrorist organization that tortured and lynched at will, to say nothing of engaging in repeated acts of intimidation, threat, and arson. As a result of such organized ideological assault, Du Bois writes, "There is scarce a child in the street that cannot tell you that the whole effort was a hideous mistake . . . that the history of the U.S. from 1866 to 1876 is something of which the nation ought to be ashamed and which did more to retard and set back the American Negro than anything that has happened to him."[39]

As we saw in Chapter 3, the political history of the 1960s, similarly, is currently subject to a great deal of "revision," with similarly tragic consequence. These debates aren't merely academic, as these selective narratives have sanctioned drastic changes in, if not the shredding of, the social contract. One of the primary architects of the ideological campaign to roll back the welfare state was Charles Murray, who in his 1984 book *Losing Ground* recast the advances of civil rights in the 1960s as a veritable bargain with the devil:

The reforms of the 60s . . . discouraged poor young people, and especially poor young males, from pursuing this slow, incremental approach [to lifting themselves out of poverty] in four ways. First, they increased the size of the welfare package and transformed the eligibility rules so as to make welfare a more available and attractive *temporary* alternative to a job. Second, the reforms in law enforcement and criminal justice increased access to income from the underground economy. By the 1970s, illegal income (including that from dealing in drugs, gambling, and stolen goods, as well as direct predatory crime) had become a major source of income in poor communities. Third, the breakdown in inner-city education reduced job readiness. Acculturation to the demands of the workplace—arriving every day on time, staying there, accepting the role of a subordinate—diminished as these behaviors were not longer required in the schoolroom. Fourth, the reforms diminished the stigma associated with welfare and simultaneously devalued the status associated with working at a menial, low-paying job—indeed holding onto a menial job became in some communities a *source* of stigma.[40]

Thus Murray, the right-wing rhetorical alchemist, is able to reassign the blame of growing inner city joblessness and the rise of underground economies from deindustrialization to glam welfare lifestyles. Similarly, the evidence of failing schools does not indict the failure to enforce *Brown* or decreasing federal financial support for education, but leads to unsubstantiated claims about the disappearance of discipline from urban schools. Indeed, the political impact of such challenges to the legacy of the 1960s on a largely white electorate was, as we have seen, pure gold.

As the ongoing assaults on communities of color suggest, the transition from a political economy of slavery to that of industrialism and, much later, post-industrialism does not necessarily translate into a progressive movement from slavery to freedom, but rather signals a shift in racial definition and management, from brute force to the rule of law.[41] Given the increasing intolerance for overt physical violence, we should not be surprised by the government's relentless focus on legal structures in periods of racial reaction. As in the post-emancipation era, in the post–civil rights era the government responded to the challenge of equal, popular participation and power sharing by shoring up a new form of power: a reactionary Supreme Court was put in place to achieve what neither a divided Congress nor the presidency could do. In the earlier era, with the appointment of Morrison Waite as chief justice under President Ulysses S. Grant, the legal protections guaranteed by the Fourteenth and Fifteenth amendments were both "reinterpreted" and rendered innocuous. Racist exclusion was not rendered explicit; rather, it was implicitly upheld in the all-too-familiar rhetoric of "States' Rights." These and other mechanisms of systemic, violent exclusion remained in place until the 1960s, when black Americans fought for and won—again—the rights and entitlements they had garnered as citizens one hundred years prior. With the appointment of Antonin Scalia as justice and the promotion of John Rehnquist to chief justice under Reagan—and the subsequent addition of Clarence Thomas under Bush Sr.—the civil rights legislation that ensured equal opportunity in education and work and enfranchisement was substantially undermined. Though the discourse of States' Rights is alive and well, in the rush to repudiate explicit forms of racist oppression that were once legally sanctioned by *Plessy*, the courts inaugurated a new commitment to state racelessness—or colorblindness—as a means to camouflage the "post-racist racism" of the state while aiding the simultaneous advancement of market exclusions in the rapidly expanding private sector.[42] Nowhere was the influence of this decidedly conservative Supreme Court more keenly felt than around educational equality and access. To the degree that struggles for democratization require an educated and empowered citizenry, the right-wing attack on public education at all levels makes strategic sense.

Black Educational Exclusion in the Post–Civil Rights Era

Access to and influence upon educational institutions, in fact, were central to the revolutionary efforts of those short years post-1863 and post-1964 when black political power was a visible reality. According to Du Bois, newly manumitted slaves desired only two things: first, they wanted land to own and work for their own crops; second, they wanted to know not just "the cabalistic letters and numbers" but also the "meaning of the world,"—but more specifically, they wanted to know "what . . . had recently happened to them—this upturning of the universe and revolution of the whole social fabric."[43] Consumed with a desire for learning, black Americans poured themselves into organizing and they introduced free public schooling to the South, where none had existed before—one of many astounding results of the political will and social vision of former slaves turned critical and active citizens, not even a generation removed from bondage. Yet in the decades that followed, efforts to undermine the civil rights and entitlements of blacks would become equally organized, culminating in the 1896 *Plessy v. Ferguson* decision asserting the constitutionality of already "separate but (un)equal" transportation, school facilities, and the like. As a result of this landmark decision, blacks would not be denied educational access altogether as in the days of slavery, but, as Du Bois notes, there were innumerable ways to make such schools run considerably less efficiently:

. . . in the first place, the public school funds were distributed with open and unashamed discrimination. Anywhere from twice to ten times as much was spent on the white child as was on the Negro child, and even then the poor white child did not receive an adequate education. . . . The Negro schools were given few buildings and little equipment. No effort was made to compel Negro children to go to school. On the contrary, in the country they were deliberately kept out of school by the requirements of contract labor which embraced the labor of wife and children as well as of the laborer himself. The course of study was limited. The school term was made and kept short and in many cases there was the deliberate effort, as expressed by one leading Southerner, Hoke Smith, when two Negro teachers applied for a school, to "take the less competent."[44]

The significance of the attack on educational opportunity was underscored by Du Bois, who noted the preeminent role of education even in the midst of a counter-revolution: "Had it not been for the Negro school and college," he wrote, "the Negro would, to all intents and purposes, have been driven back to slavery."[45]

In the 1960s, black Americans agitated for and achieved not only the desegregation of the nation's public school system but also expanded access to higher education for all students of color and increased their influence over the curriculum, including black faculty appointments. Currently, countervailing strategies enjoy even broader range, and as a result black educational access at all levels of schooling is in jeopardy. To be sure, older tactics that mitigated the potential for children to learn in school were still in play—the wide disparities in school funding, the squalid conditions of most school buildings, the overcrowding, the lack of adequate resources, and the hiring of non-certified and unmotivated teachers that Du Bois details. But with the dawn of the twenty-first century, school reforms have made the experience of schooling, which is now compulsory, as painful as possible for certain populations of students, challenging even the most invested learners. Such measures include the militarization of schools, now complete with security guards, drug-sniffing dogs, see-through knapsacks, metal detectors, and zero-tolerance policies that threaten those who misbehave with not only expulsion but actual jail time. Add to this the hijacking of the curriculum in the name of test preparation, the culturally biased nature of such examinations, and the accountability measures under No Child Left Behind (NCLB), which pressure school administrators to get rid of those students who test poorly and might threaten the school's survival. The relentless instrumentalization of knowledge in the interests of testing and accountability has proved a venerable means of short-circuiting debate over the very substance of school curricula and the place of the student within the school. As a result of such reform efforts, the prospects for poor and minority youths to attain a higher education are rapidly worsening. This trend will likely continue as the current education secretary under Barack Obama, Arne Duncan, largely supports Bush's NCLB, and has extended its commitments to high-stakes testing and zero-tolerance protocols.[46] University of Illinois at Chicago education professor Kevin Kumashiro states that Secretary Duncan's Chicago policies had been "steeped in a free-market model of school reform" that worsened the drop-out rate, increased segregation, and did little if anything to enable student achievement. He also cites that, under Duncan's leadership, there was "less parental community involvement in school governance. Less support for teacher unions. Less breadth and depth in what and how students learn as schools place more emphasis on narrow high-stakes testing. More penalties for schools but without adequate resources for those in high-poverty areas."[47]

The roll-back of educational access for black students, once a central cause of the civil rights movement, has been met with near-total silence, both in the mainstream media and in the academy. Gary Orfield, former head of the Harvard Project on School Desegregation, notes that

during the civil rights movement, research on desegregation was abundant. Government and foundations pumped dollars into race relations work. It seemed as if the academic world was a strong resource for the . . . movement, but it turned out to be only a fair-weather friend. When the government was supporting civil rights, the issue became the central focus of research. Once politics changed and research funding dried up, so did most academic involvement. Part of the logic of resegregation is the cutoff of most of the information about segregation and its consequences. The federal government has published no basic statistics on national school segregation levels since the Carter administration.[48]

And as the university goes, so goes public discussion, it seems. In the post–civil rights era, local administrators and school boards, of course, never say that they are pursuing a separate but equal educational system. Rather, they discuss the need to move beyond "physical desegregation" or "racial balancing" or "numerical integration." In spite of such blatant, Orwellian mystifications, challenges to the resegregation of public schools are conspicuously absent in mainstream media. In fact, on educational policy issues, with the exception of affirmative action, the leaders of the Democratic and Republican parties enjoy a convergence of opinion and purpose, with support for standards, accountability, and school choice registering near-universal approval.

Although progressives were right to suport the Supreme Court's June 2003 affirmative action decision, there should be no mistaking that it was a shameful compromise. Nor should the decision be abstracted from decades of school-related decisions quietly denying black educational access. The fact remains that higher education continues to be out of reach for the vast majority of poor youth, who are subject to grossly inferior and rapidly resegregating elementary and secondary schools—schools which they are compelled by law to attend. All of which is to say that there might be no cause for a debate over alleged racial preferences, either now or in twenty-five years, as Justice Sandra O'Connor fancied, if the Rehnquist court had upheld and enforced the *Brown* verdict of 1954. But in a series of decisions since *Milliken v. Bradley* in 1974, the court, abetted by a largely silent academy, has quietly reversed the decree to desegregate that was established by the Warren court. With a team of graduate students, Gary Orfield, the head of the Harvard Civil Rights Project, documented Supreme Court decision after decision—*Milliken II* (1977), *Dowell* (1988), *Pitts* (1992), and *Jenkins* (1995)—which have enabled the resegregation of the nation's schools, such that they now resemble those of the *Plessy* era. In *Dismantling Desegregation*, Orfield observes:

> The common wisdom passed down by teachers through the generations is that *Brown v. Board of Education* corrected an ugly flaw in American education and American law. We celebrate *Brown* and Martin Luther King Jr. in our schools, even when these very schools are almost totally segregated by race and poverty. Millions of African American and Latino students learn the lessons of *Brown* while they sit in segregated schools in collapsing cities, where almost no students successfully prepare for college.[49]

Almost two decades ago, Jonathan Kozol attempted to awaken the conscience of the nation to the tragic denial of King's dream in *Savage Inequalities: Children in America's Schools*. Documenting in lurid detail the crushing inequalities between rich (predominantly white) and poor (predominantly nonwhite) school districts across the nation, Kozol exploded the prevailing common sense which characterized public schools as the "great levelers" of a democratic society. According to this mythology, schools provide the conditions for hardworking youth graced with a little native intelligence to achieve the much-vaunted American dream. Yet the presumption of equality is entirely misguided:

A typical wealthy suburb in which homes are often worth more than $400,000 draws upon a larger tax base in proportion to its student population than a city occupied by thousands of poor people. Typically, in the United States, very poor communities place high priority on education, and they often tax themselves at higher rates than do the very affluent communities. But even if they tax themselves at several times the rate of an extremely wealthy district, they are likely to end up with far less money for each child in their schools.[50]

The upshot of such "savage inequality" is that poor school districts have had to forgo (as they currently do) experienced, qualified teachers, up-to-date textbooks, let alone technologies like DVDs or computers, and quite often a safe and healthy school infrastructure. Yet all public school children have to take the same standardized tests to gain access to a post-secondary educational credential, now an essential ingredient (though hardly a guarantee) for transcending minimum wage work. In the mid-1990s, the General Accounting Office estimated that it would take $112 billion to bring the nation's public schools simply up to building code. That figure does not include monies for hiring good, qualified teachers, administrators, and support staff or providing school children with adequate resources like books and computers or "extras" like courses in art and music, busing, or extracurricular sports. Tragically, the state of public schools has only deteriorated further since the book's publication in 1991, in keeping with the general decline in public support for matters of racial justice, to be sure, but also as a result of the skyrocketing costs of two wars and a massive global recession that decimated state and school budgets. Gary Orfield notes that "among whites, though support for desegregation continued, the issue of racial justice went to the bottom of the list of national priorities. In 1995, 56 percent of whites thought that blacks were well off or better off than whites in terms of education in spite of massive gaps."[51] Explaining the contradiction between the perceived benefit and the actual state of black education, Orfield points to the rhetoric of race: "Conservative politicians won white voters by telling them that civil rights policies had gone too far and were hurting whites. No powerful defense of civil rights and no leadership helping the public understand the persisting inequality in educational opportunities for minority students existed."[52] Part of the reason for this ongoing crisis in American public schooling lies in federal cuts in education ongoing since the Reagan administration.

The stated rationale for such a shift in national priorities is that American public schools are bureaucratic, wasteful, and altogether ineffectual—the result of a big government monopoly on education. As a result of such inefficiency, the public school system poses a threat to U.S. national security and economic dominance in the world market. To be sure, some public schools really are ailing, but the reasons for this, according to David Berliner and Bruce Biddle, authors of *The Manufactured Crisis*, have to do with the grossly unequal funding of public education, residential segregation, and the astonishingly high poverty rates of U.S. school children relative to most other industrialized nations, coupled with inadequate health care and social services. Preferring the former diagnosis of general ineptitude, the Bush administration insisted that throwing money at schools would not cure public school ills and would no longer be tolerated. Although the Obama administration has pledged billions of dollars to aid the nation's schools, the actual delivery of that aid awaits budgetary approval by a Congress embattled over the president's "reckless" taxing and spending "socialist" agenda. Should the funding be approved, the infusion of cash from the federal government will undoubtedly mitigate some of the effects of the recession, curtailing for example some but not all teacher layoffs, but the broad vision of the administration remains largely in lockstep with prior administrations' emphases on accountability through high stakes testing and security through zero tolerance policies.

Given the present precarity of the Obama agenda on education, which at the time of this writing is merely aspirational, it seems prudent to focus on the conditions on the ground, so to speak, as defined by the prior Bush administration's policy initiatives. Rather than address the complexity of educational inequalities disproportionately impacting poor and minority students, the Bush administration sought solutions to troubled public schools in the much-touted No Child Left Behind legislation, which afforded certain key advantages to constituencies that were in favor of privatization, all the while appearing sympathetic to the plight of marginalized youth. Not only do they maintain the advantages accorded white students, who perform better on average than black and Latino students on standardized tests, the school reforms were also very business friendly. Renamed "No Child Left Untested" by critics, the reform places high priority on accountability, tying what little federal money schools receive to improvements in test performance. For additional financial support, public schools are left no other meaningful option than to engage in public-private partnerships, like the highly publicized deals schools cut with soft drink giants, which provide schools with needed revenue in exchange for soda machines in cafeterias. And clearly the media giants who own the major publishing houses stand to benefit from the 52 million-strong market of public school students now required to take tests every year from the third grade on. The impact of NCLB also proved highly televisable, visibility being a key factor in the art of persuading a public weaned away from political debate in favor of the spectacle. Thus the media provide routine reportage of school districts' grade cards and the public—often monetary—rewards given to schools that score high marks on achievement tests, liquidation of those that don't. Media preoccupation with school safety issues, moreover, ensured highly publicized expulsion, sometimes even felony incarceration, of troublemakers, typically students of color. In short, accountability for teachers and administrators and zero tolerance for students unwilling to toe the line are the new educational imperatives. All of which demonstrates that the federal government is "doing something" to assuage the public's fears about schools that it largely created through financial deprivation and policies favoring market-driven resegregation. As a result, the little federal aid that schools do receive is increasingly spent on testing and prep materials as well as new safety measures such as metal detectors, armed guards, security cameras, and fencing, in accordance with NCLB. In addition to draining public schools financially, both high-stakes testing and zero-tolerance policies have served to push out or kick out black and Latino youth in disproportionate numbers.[53] In stark contrast to their predecessors, President Obama and Secretary Duncan have plans to pump over 12 billion into the nation's schools—but the money will be used to support the kinds of projects that NCLB also prized, including privatization, militarization, and lots and lots of accountability through testing.

Most recently it has become evident, as Du Bois might have predicted, that eventually all children suffer from the systemic disinvestment in education and other public goods and services at the hands of a right-wing, pro-business, and anti-civil rights governing elite. For example, the disastrous state of California's economy can be traced back, in part, to draconian cuts in education since the 1970s. The key factor in rising spending in California in recent years—and the alleged reason for the state's budgetary woes prior to the 2008 recession—has been its efforts to rebuild a crumbling educational system. Economist Paul Krugman explains that the passage of Proposition 13 in 1978, which introduced a cap on property taxes, "led to a progressive starvation of California's once-lauded public schools. By 1994, the state had the largest class sizes in the nation; its reading scores on par with Mississippi's."[54] So it seems that the chickens came home to roost, as the infamous tax revolt of the 1970s, fueled by racist propaganda dressed up as fiscal populism, utterly devastated the state. According to Mike Davis, the famed author of *City of Quartz* and chronicler of Los Angeles's savage history, "As the Latino population soared, white voters—egged on by rightwing demagogues—withdrew support from the public sector. California became a bad school state in lockstep with becoming a low wage state. Overcrowded classrooms and dangerous playgrounds are part of a vicious cycle with sweatshops and slum housing."[55] As Californians sought to halt creeping "Mississippization," they passed, in addition to living wage ordinances and other legislation, Proposition 98, which allocated more money for schools. This is what conservatives are now deriding as "runaway government spending." What began as a mechanism to perpetuate racial exclusion in the post–civil rights era has led, in part, to the decline of the world's six largest economy. By the 2008 recession, California found itself over $24 billion in debt and in deep crisis—and thanks to Proposition 13 it had no feasible way to raise the necessary taxes.[56]

But America's youth have been paying the price not only of racial animus and political demagoguery at home, but also for the U.S. imperialist agendas abroad, particularly the military occupation of Iraq. Budgetary shortfalls in most states, a direct result of the cost of the Iraqi war and security measures post 9/11, have only exacerbated inequalities in funding, resulting the mass firings of teachers, the shortening of school years, the dismantling of extra-curricular programs, and the postponing of much-needed structural repair. Soaring deficits and the request of an additional $70 billion from Congress as early as September 2003 to aid the "peace" in Iraq signaled even more trouble for the nation's schools in the years that followed. Senator Robert Byrd reminded then-President Bush of his commitment to America's most vulnerable children in the following terms: "It is equally ironic that the Administration is seeking an estimated $60 to $70 billion in additional funding for Iraq from the American tax-payers at a time when the Senate is debating adding a fraction of that amount to an appropriations bill to provide critical funding—funding the President himself pledged to provide in his No Child Left Behind initiative—for schoolchildren in poor school districts."[57] Ironic indeed, as little mention was been made of repealing Bush's infamous tax cuts primarily for the wealthiest one percent of the population to offset federal expenditures. Seven years later, the economic picture is decidedly more grim. The Obama administration not only inherited the war in Iraq but expanded considerably troop levels in the war in Afghanistan, in addition to inheriting a global financial crisis that plunged the nation into severe recession and a slow, jobless recovery. As I have already argued, although the administration has reversed course with respect to Bush's notorious cuts in education and has pledged billions in federal aid and student load programs, the deficit remains in record high multi-trillion dollar territory and a gridlocked Congress has proven so far largely incapable of compromise on budgetary issues.

The tragic state of public education in America is not unrelated to the future of higher education. Clearly, children's K-12 experiences play a determining role in their access to and preparedness for post-secondary education. Within the last decade, the academy has come under fire for low retention rates among minority youth—more a pretense for another round of cuts in federal funding and student aid by the previous Bush administration than drawing public attention to a serious concern—yet few critics seem willing to acknowledge the obvious. Higher education is successful only to the degree that K-12 education is successful. Poor and minority youth who manage to survive the deplorable conditions of their K-12 education and still want to continue their schooling face skyrocket-ing college tuition rates, which have risen sharply in the last decade—and continue to do so as a result of recession-era cutbacks, particularly in the ravaged state of California. Moreover, the government revised the formula for financial aid for colleges which reduced the nation's largest primary award program, the Pell grant, by $270 million when it took effect in the 2004–5 academic year.[58] It remains to be seen, if Obama's proposals for educational stimulus do pass Congress, if the proposed funding for Pell grants will meet or exceed its prior inadequate endowment, which the relatively recent Bush cuts merely exacerbated. For youth unable to afford the costs, the Supreme Court's 2003 decision to uphold affirmative action was rather meaningless, as relatively few apply to the hundred or so selective colleges in the United States. A 2003 study by Anthony Carnevale, vice president of the Educational Testing Service, found that "74 percent of the students at the 146 most prestigious colleges and universities—where competition for admissions is most intense and where affirmative action is practiced—come from the top 25 percent of the nation's socioeconomic scale (as measured by income, educational attainment and occupation of parents. Only 3 percent come from the bottom 25 percent, and a total of 10 percent come from the bottom half."[59] Because college admissions officers tend to rely on hard variables like testing, and race and socioeconomic status especially are both more strongly correlated with high test scores than with intelligence or aptitude, the distribution of scarce slots at highly selective universities is skewed in favor of white youth whose parents have money. Hence, as Carnevale asserts, higher education, especially at public institutions, which are supported largely through tax dollars, has become "a gift the poor give to the rich."[60]

How was the Bush administration able to pass spending cuts on student loans and on higher education, given rising student need for financial assistance (and rising student debt) and rising educational costs, which would negatively affect already high tuition rates, thereby placing even more economic pressure on students and their families? According to a July 2003 article in the *Chronicle of Higher Education*, Bush planned to use the renewal of the Higher Education Act as an occasion to lambast universities for high tuition and dropout rates. Looking to revive his "compassionate conservative" image for the 2004 election cycle with an issue that would play well with the public, he could do that, political observers noted, "by empathizing with low-and middle-income families that are struggling to pay their college bills. He can also do that, they say, by scolding colleges for allowing so many disadvantaged students to drop out lacking the skills they need to improve their lives."[61] The White House was right to be concerned, but tuition had gone up partly in response to successive cuts in the federal budget that the president himself had signed into law. The anticipated report, "The College Cost Crisis," appeared in mid-September of 2003. Written by John Boehner and Howard McKeon, two Republicans on the House education committee, the report charged the university with "wasteful spending," the result in part of a woeful lack of accountability "to parents, students, and taxpayers—the consumers of higher education."[62] The answer, Congressman Boehner believed, was in a bill that would further cut federal financing to colleges whose tuition hikes were more than double the rate of inflation or the consumer price index. Rather than meeting the needs of struggling students, the bill was simply a means to withdraw more funds from universities already so financially strapped that they have had to compromise, as a matter of survival, the quality of education students received by closing departments, offering fewer courses, hiring more grad students and adjuncts to teach courses, skimping on advising, health, and counseling services, and disbanding sports teams. Stanley Fish, then dean of the College of Liberal Arts and Sciences at the University of Illinois at Chicago, objected to such logic. He argued that it was precisely because of diminished federal support for education that colleges and universities were becoming cost-prohibitive for the working and middle class families that the government seemed so eager to help. As applications for admissions continued to rise, financial support from the government had been withdrawn. Fish concluded: "If the revenues sustaining your operation are sharply cut and you are prevented by law from raising prices, your only recourse is to offer an inferior product. Those who say, as the state has said to the University of Illinois, 'We're taking $200 million from you but we expect you to do the job you were doing and do it even better,' are trafficking in either fantasy or hypocrisy."[63]

But there was one further irony. At the state level, monies were increasingly tied up in efforts to maintain the national shift in priorities from education to incarceration, particular for blacks and Latinos. If Bush had really wanted to aid the struggling poor and minority youth in their efforts to achieve a post-secondary degree, he would have considered a repeal of the Drug-Free Student Aid provision of the Higher Education Act of 1998, a roundabout line of attack in the infamous War on Drugs. Under this ruling, any student who has been convicted of the possession or sale of a controlled substance is either temporarily—or perhaps permanently, depending on the offense—ineligible for Stafford loans, Pell grants, or work-study programs. Students with one drug possession conviction lose their aid for a year from the date of conviction; with two convictions, they lose two years; a third offense results in permanent loss of aid. Sanctions for selling drugs are even stricter. The inherent unfairness of the law has been well documented by critics. Its primary impact is on minority students of lower income, who are disproportionately targeted in the war on drugs and are, unlike their middle-class counterparts, dependent on federal aid for schooling. Further, the law ignores any financial aid applicants who have committed crimes unrelated to drugs. For example, students found convicted of bombing a nursery school or shooting a teacher remain eligible for student loans; yet those who have been caught smoking a joint or two are refused, their life's ambition reduced to enticing customers to super-size their orders of fries. What the Drug-Free Student Aid provision made clear was the government's obvious preference for incarcerating black youth over educating them. It's well documented that drug war enforcement is racist. African Americans make up only 12 percent of the U.S. population and only 13 percent of drug offenders—about the same proportion as white drug users—yet, African Americans make up 62 percent of those with drug convictions. Like the Black Codes of post-Reconstruction, the punishment for drug violations is not well correlated with crime, but rather with race and class. In the 2000–2001 school year, the first in which the drug-free provision of the Higher Education Act was enforced, about 34,000 students and college applicants were denied financial aid, thus preventing these mostly poor and black students from exercising one of the most basic principles of empowerment in the country.

Again, it is not simply black and brown youth who pay for the drug war and mass incarceration, but all youth, the eventual inheritors of a $5 trillion deficit and an utterly divided, unequal society. In fact, the 2003 Supreme Court decision upholding affirmative action at the University of Michigan Law School cannot be abstracted from its "other" affirmative action decision regarding the legality of three-strikes laws in the criminal justice system, the only place, Angela Davis once quipped, with a robust affirmative action scheme. With 2.3 million inmates in a prison system whose sentences are now getting longer, and the cost of maintaining a single prisoner at about $26,000 a year (triple that if they're older, and age they will), the incarceration experiment costs about the same as an Iraqi war brought home—particularly when one adds on prison construction costs, medical costs, families reduced to welfare and children in foster care, and the loss of tax revenue at all levels. And that doesn't begin to gauge the destruction of poor and minority communities hardest hit by the prison boom. According to Marc Mauer, director of the Sentencing Project and author of *Race to Incarcerate*, there is a direct correlation between increases in state appropriations for criminal justice and decreases in spending on welfare, health care, and education—especially higher education.

Toward a New "New Deal": Resurrecting Educational Thought in the Interests of Racial Justice and Substantive Democracy

The reversal of democratic fortune described by Du Bois in the penultimate chapter of *Black Reconstruction*, titled "Back Toward Slavery," seems as relevant today as it did seventy-five years ago. He wrote:

The attempt to make black men American citizens was in a certain sense all a failure, but a splendid failure. It did not fail where it was expected to fail. It was Athanasius contra mundum, with back to the wall, outnumbered ten to one, with all the wealth and all the opportunity, and all the world against him. And only in his hands and heart the consciousness of a great and just cause; fighting the battle of all the oppressed and despised humanity of every race and color, against the massed hirelings of Religion, Science, Education, Law and brute force.[64]

Du Bois further lamented the utter lack of organized progressive response to the systemic degradation of black humanity, noting, "there is scarcely a bishop in Christendom, a priest in the church, a president, a governor, mayor, or legislature in the United States, a college professor or public school teacher, who does not in the end stand by War and Ignorance as the main method for the settlement of our pressing human problems. And this despite the fact that they deny it with their mouths every day."[65] The same silence on issues of racial equality and racial justice continues to dominate contemporary mainstream political culture. Nevertheless, the university remains a crucial site of struggle and one of the few remaining spaces where a generation of young people can learn to assume the responsibilities of democratic citizenship. By way of conclusion, I would like to engage, though briefly, the challenges confronting intellectuals who attempt to foster a critical, engaged anti-racist politics on campus, in spite of the university's much-celebrated and much-maligned "multicultural turn."

If the rollback of black educational access at all levels of schooling has been met with thunderous silence on the part of academics over the last two decades, so too have most reneged on their responsibility to engage students politically,[66] in order to recover an ethical dialogue rooted in a form of historical recovery that, in Du Bois's words, transcends "history for our pleasure and amusement, for inflating our national ego, and giving us a false but pleasurable sense of accomplishment."[67] This is not to suggest that racial politics were utterly avoided at a time in university history derided by conservatives as the Great Takeover of radical-tenured-anti-Americans. The "multicultural turn" in fields like literary studies offered, at least initially, a radical reformulation of the experiences of blacks, Latinos and other racially defined minorities in the United States, but the project reflects only a partial victory at best. When the history of African Americans becomes literary history, the privatization of racial experience reproduces not challenges, but the neoliberal emphasis on hyperindividualism and its depoliticizing effects. The upshot of such a relentless focus on identity politics remains nonetheless in keeping with the conservative ideology of colorblindness and its commitment to historical denial. By reconceptualizing racism as a private—as opposed to deeply social and structural—phenomenon, colorblind ideology displaces the tensions of contemporary racially charged relations to the relative invisibility and protectedness of the private sphere. But more immediately, racism remains invisible to most students, who are left alone to ponder why such privatized experiences, so removed from their own, should concern them. The consequences of efforts to "manage diversity" were not only that a generation or two of students have been without any sense of how race structures U.S. society, both currently and historically.[68] In addition, race has played a central role in a deepening disdain for "big government," "welfare," and programs for "special interests," resulting in a cynical political sensibility that begins and ends with how to keep the tax man out of one's pockets.

The task facing critical educators is not an easy one. Not only is the university itself under attack—facing pressure by the corporate sector to instrumentalize knowledge in the interests of profit and pressure by conservatives to cleanse humanities curricula of any untoward critique of American culture or political institutions, particularly those that challenge the much-vaunted "racial harmony" of the post–civil rights era or the desire of the government to bring democracy (as opposed to a form of neocolonial occupation) to the Middle East. But access to a post-secondary credential as well as social and cultural capital for growing numbers of working class and minority students is clearly becoming more questionable. Linking questions of pedagogy to political agency requires that educators mediate the fraught relations between knowledge and action, private concerns and public interests, and individual freedoms and the social contract. At the same time, any pedagogical project that seeks to revitalize questions of citizenship, community, and the public good must be attentive to not only the ways in which such notions have historically perpetuated racist exclusions, but also the degree to which they are currently under erasure in an era marked by the racial neoliberalism.

Over the nine decades in which he lived, W.E.B. Du Bois wrote passionately and eloquently on all issues educational. Though questions of access and equity remain—to this day—central issues for youth of color in the United States, in his later years, Du Bois's attention returned again and again to pressing debates in higher education. As depression-era hardship lessened, in part, through the stimulus that was World War II, as hot war morphed into cold war, and as the tide turned against FDR's "brain trust" and anti-intellectual backlash reached its fullest expression in the figure of Joseph McCarthy, Du Bois honed and refined, in particular, his defense of humanistic inquiry. As much as he feared the decline of black educational access, he feared the very disappearance of critical and comprehensive education itself even more.

In 1938, Du Bois returned to Fisk University on the occasion of the fiftieth anniversary of his graduation from that institution and was given the honor of delivering the commencement speech, which he titled, "The Revelation of Saint Orgne the Damned." I will spare my colleagues a frenzied search through ecclesiastical sources to discover who Saint Orgne was, and explain, as Du Bois did, that Orgne was a popular anagram of the term "Negro." As the Depression dragged to its unsteady conclusion, Du Bois expressed deep concern for the world that the young graduates—

descendants of the "Damned"—now assembled before him were about to inherit. He said:

The most distressing fact in the present world is poverty; not absolute poverty, because some folk are rich and many are well-to-do; not poverty as great as some lands and other historical ages have known; but poverty more poignant and discouraging because it comes after a dream of wealth, or riotous, wasteful and even vulgar accumulation of individual riches, which suddenly leaves the majority of mankind today without enough to eat; without proper shelter; without sufficient clothing.[69]

Seventy years later, in 2008, many millions of Americans, particular populations of color, found themselves facing a similar state of poverty as they lost their jobs, their health care, their homes, and the majority of their possessions. And the outlook for today's youth, who stand to inherit the debt from mounting trillion dollar bailouts and failed war, is even more dire. But Du Bois's insight does more than invite obvious connections to the contemporary. What he grasped so uncannily was that Americans then (as now) confronted poverty of a particular kind, which inflicted its own unique sense of privation and pain. This poverty happened seemingly without any notice—"suddenly," he writes—and in the immediate aftermath of an era of "riotous, wasteful and even vulgar" accumulation of wealth for the few, while their glittering riches, the very stuff of media frenzy, fueled the ever-bright fantasy lives of the rest. The sound of warning is unmistakable.

Recently, popular bromides have suggested that the economic downturn would provide an opportunity for Americans to simplify their lives, reconnect with what matters most like family and friends, and relinquish their taste for the extravagant—lessons that would serve them well leading into the recovery. Yet history offers little support for imagining this particular kind bust to be an occasion for pervasive social uplift and moral improvement. Rather, people feel cheated and they burn with resentment. Du Bois observed in *Black Reconstruction* that the recessions that followed periods of decadence in the post-Reconstruction decades of the 1880s and 1890s, and then again in the late 1920s and 1930s, saw dramatic increases in levels of violence, particularly against subordinated groups. This result could be anticipated from the nativist and racist efforts of demagogues—among them politicians, religious leaders, even academicians—to redirect of popular rage away from economic and political graft and corruption. Then, as now, the threat of mob violence returned, as events since the summer of 2009 have endlessly proven.

Facing the young graduates of the class of 1938, Du Bois proposed that "we black folk of America are faced with the most difficult problem of realizing and knowing the part we play in . . . our own salvation and that of the world."[70] He recognized that as a result of the "segregation of color" and the "domination of caste" he and they were cut off from the national recovery effort, even though they were sure to live out its consequences. But he offered the young people before him a way forward nonetheless, marking as he did, the pitfalls to avoid. "Nothing could be more fatal to our ideas and the better ideals of the world," he warned them, "than for us with unconscious ignorance or conscious perversity or momentary applause to join the forces of reaction; to talk as though the twentieth century presented *the same oversimplified path of economic progress which seemed the rule of the nineteenth: work, thrift, and wealth by individual effort no matter what the social cost.*"[71] Mercifully, there was no talk of post-partisanship here. He offered concrete, actionable advice so as not to allow "obvious opportunity to slip by during these awful days of depression."[72] He prevailed on them to participate in public life, to bolster their civic courage, to revive their sense of social entitlement, and to take advantage of available public housing and other forms of aid as they pushed energetically for the establishment of model villages for resettlement, socialized medicine, consumer protections, unemployment protections, and the like. Du Bois also sought a revolution in thought, encouraging the students to envision an even brighter future, what later Derrida would call "democracy to come," for themselves and their children: "We have got to think of the time when poverty approaches abolition; when men no longer fear starvation and unemployment; when health is so guarded that we may normally expect to live our seventy years and more, without excess of pain and suffering. In such a world life begins; in such a world we will have freedom of thought and expression.[73] Such a world is realizable, he insisted, when citizens are given educational opportunities of a most worldly and capacious kind, for it is in such pursuit that genuine political freedom is to be found. "Given a chance for the majority of mankind, to be educated, healthy and free to act," he insisted, "it may well turn out that human equality is not so wild a dream as many seem to hope.[74] But then, as now, it is precisely this kind of liberal education that is least valued and largely unavailable. Indeed, what he described then as "the central contradiction and paradox of the day" is even more pertinent now. He asserted:

It is the contradiction and paradox of this day that those who seek to choke and conventionalize art, restrict and censor thought and repress imagination are demanding for their shriveled selves, freedom in precisely those lines of human activity where control and regimentation are necessary; and necessary because upon this foundation is to be built the widest conceivable freedom in a realm infinitely larger and more meaningful than the realm of economic production and distribution of wealth. The less freedom we leave for business exploitation the greater freedom we shall have for expression in art.[75]

Under present conditions of neoliberal rule, markets have been granted unprecedented freedom, while citizens have been subject to every possible mode of surveillance, control, and regimentation that new technologies enable—with individual imagination and creativity and hope the predictable casualties. But the ruthless imperatives of the political economy were not solely responsible for unleashing the forces of repression. Strikingly, given today's resurgence of Christian fundamentalism, Du Bois located similarly repressive, corollary conditions at work in religious institutions and in higher education, with similarly corrosive effects on human capacities to think, judge, act, and hope. Of the church, he accused:

[Religion] has built up a body of dogma and fairy tale, fantastic fables of sin and salvation, impossible creeds and impossible demands for ignorant unquestioning belief and obedience. Ask any thorough churchman today and he will tell you, not that the object of the church is to get men to do right and make the majority of mankind happy, but rather that the whole duty of man is to "believe in the Lord Jesus Christ and be saved"; or to believe in the "one Holy and Catholic church," infallible and omniscient.[76]

The sharpness of his critique notwithstanding, Du Bois did not dismiss out of hand the importance of religious institutions and belief in the lives of everyday people. In place of the "impossible demands for ignorant unquestioning belief and obedience," Du Bois proposed an alternative and important social role for religious leaders and congregants that involved "hearty research into real ethical questions."[77] Rather than sacrificing democracy on the altar of blind obedience, religion could, he saw, play a role in forging the moral character of a citizenry. He listed among possible topics for discussion and debate, the most pressing moral and political questions of the day: "When is it right to lie? Do low wages mean stealing? Does the prosperity of a country depend on the number of its millionaires? Should the state kill a murderer? How much money should you give to the poor? Should there be any poor? And as long as there are, what is crime and who are the criminals?" He insisted that religious belief should not be sequestered in the private sphere—and thus protected—away from critical inquiry and engagement, but must be part of agonistic debates that would shape public morality and democratic commitment.

In similar fashion, he challenged the conventional higher educational wisdom of the day, which—like today, and more insistently so as a result of the global recession—prized scientific innovation and technical mastery over more humanistic forms of academic inquiry which encourage self-reflective, creative, and critical thinking. It is this kind of thinking that is precluded from the technical, vocational training that was, and is, the offspring of unquestioned faith in the marriage of progress and technology. Du Bois boldly asserted that "freedom is the path of art, and living in the fuller and broader sense of the term is the expression of art."[78] He elaborated:

The freedom to create within the limits of natural law; the freedom to love without limit; the freedom to dream of the utter marriage of beauty and art; all this men may have if they are sufficiently well-bred to make human contact bearable; if they have learned to read and write and reason; if they have character enough to distinguish between right and wrong and strength enough to do right; if they can earn a decent living and know the world in which they live.[79]

If men could only be "sufficiently well-bred to make human contact bearable"—that is indeed the educational challenge of our new century. As I argued in Chapter 3, the ongoing war on thought and evidence that is currently being waged both inside and outside of the university precisely presupposes a suffocated and suffocating reality—a misanthropic world where other human beings either don't exist or don't matter.

Of the kind of education that would "make human contact bearable" Du Bois would say much more. About six years later, in 1944, he delivered an address in keeping with this theme called, pithily, "The

Meaning of Education," which constitutes the most concise breakdown of his educational philosophy. Herbert Aptheker provides actually two possible dates—1944 or 1945—for this talk in the brief introduction to the unpublished manuscript, which was left to his care among other of Du Bois's papers. Whatever the actual date, the span of time between Du Bois's two addresses was a decidedly bleak one in both American and world history, and there can be little doubt that it informed his skepticism about the university's increasing allegiance to techno-scientific research over and against other forms of inquiry. Speaking to students again, he addressed the importance of "what we used to call the humanities"—a curious phrase indeed, and one that betrayed even then the humanities' twilight existence. In support of this fast-fading institution, he offered his young audience as evidence for his unorthodox educational views the compelling personal experience of a man approaching his eightieth year. He regaled them with tales of his studies and his travels:

Thus I began to study what had happened in the past in this world; the history of the United States, of England and something of Europe. I began the discipline of languages, of ancient languages which had been used by civilizations now partially dead. I studied their literature and English literature by reading essays and books. I began to learn about the lives of certain men, who had left their imprint upon the world. Of the things which I had learned I began to write in essays and statements. Then I had courses in natural sciences, in chemical laboratories and physical; algebra and geometry, in studying rocks and stars. With this went a rather unusual amount of travel so that I had a chance of comparing people with people and land with land. I listened to lectures by distinguished students of science and history, I heard music in wide variety. I saw most of the leading examples of painting and sculpture throughout Europe.[80]

Anticipating his audience's suspicion that such an expansive education was in the finally analysis "impractical," that it imparted no "useful" or saleable skills, or worse still that it represented, by virtue of these willful transgressions of educational common sense, an expensive over-indulgence for which neither they nor their families could afford to pay, he acknowledged some truth in their silent accusations:

Now at the end of these twenty years of study and travel which must have cost in the aggregate something like forty thousand dollars, I was not prepared to do any specific piece of work: I could not make a table or cook a meal or sew on a button. I could not carve or paint; and the art of writing and revealing my thought had not been developed. On the other hand, I did have a rather firm grasp, and idea of what this world was, and how it had developed in the last thousand years. I knew something of the kind of human beings that were on earth, and what they were thinking and what they were doing. I was able to reason rather accurately, and whatever there was that I had not been trained to do, the specific training that was necessary came rather easily because I had this general grasp.[81]

In short, he concluded that his education had enabled him to think, to reason, to judge, and to channel emotion—activities precluded from the prior list of technical achievements. But the full force of his argument relied not on personal experience, but on the weightiness of history. First, he set the stage. "As I came into the twentieth century," he averred, "I was aware of the widespread criticism of the sort of education which I had had, and the questioning in the minds of men as to how far that sort of education was really valuable and how far it could be applied to the youth of today."[82] The criticism "sharpened" and grew more insistent during the war years, he continued, during which time young people who had mechanical training could "easily get jobs that paid wages most fabulous."[83] Techno-scientific training, tied not only to the war effort but to a general increase in the nation's standard of living, further imperiled the viability of the kind of education Du Bois had received. Indeed, the argument against humanistic inquiry appeared unassailable:

This had made the people say and doubtless you have had it emphasized here, that what education ought to do, is to prepare young people for doing work of this sort; and that it is a great waste of time to study what we used to call the humanities and art and literature, over periods which counted up into decades, rather than in a few years of intensive work made a man a capable workman of some trade or art where he could get an immediate and comfortable salary.[84]

But then he up-ended what was (and remains) the educational common-sense of the day by revealing the paradox of both tragic and global proportions that had resulted from such myopic vision:

We have a world whose technological perfection makes most things possible. And yet, on the other hand, this world is in chaos. It has been organized twice in the last quarter of a century for murder and destruction on a tremendous scale, not to mention continual minor wars. There is not only this physical disaster, there is the mental and moral tragedy which makes us at times despair human culture.[85]

More than sixty years later, the chaos, violence, and tragedy have only deepened. We now have what Etienne Balibar calls "a number of hetero-geneous methods or processes of extermination . . . which have themselves become 'globalized.'"[86] Among these new heterogeneous methods, he, too, lists wars but adds to this: "communal rioting, with ethnic and/or religious ideologies of 'cleansing'"; "famines and other kinds of 'absolute' pover-ty produced by the ruin of traditional or nontraditional economies"; and "seemingly 'natural' catastrophes, which in fact are killing on a mass scale because they are overdetermined by social, economic, and political struc-tures, such as pandemics." All of these, Balibar notes, are considered "ra-tional" and "functional" from the point of view of market capitalism—but they can only be read as irrational and destructive from the point of view of "*communities of fate*," or communities of peoples "thrown together" by history, who cannot "spontaneously converge, but also cannot completely diverge without risking *mutual destruction* (or *common elimination* by ex-ternal forces)."[87] In short, as Kant stated in his 1796 essay "Toward Perpet-ual Peace," and as Du Bois would paraphrase centuries later in his com-mencement address, if humans are to survive, "they . . . must finally put up with being near one another."[88]

But what is the way out of such a paradoxical existence (and should we not hesitate to call it "life")? Du Bois offered the following assessment: "Now when we compare the technical mastery which man has over the world, with the utter failure of that power to organize happiness, and peace in the world, then we know something is wrong. Part of that is our conception of education."[89] He further elaborated on what he perceived to be a curiously bifurcated notion of education at work in the public imaginary. People have two very different things in mind when they talk about education, he advanced: "one is training for mastery of technique; the other is training the man who is going to exercise the technique and for whom the technique exists."[90] Problems emerge with the presumption that we only really require the former, at the expense of the latter, rather than understanding the necessity of attending to both of these conceptual ends. He proposed the following scenario, deftly exposing the limitations of technical mastery:

If, regardless of the man himself, we train his hands and nervous system for ac-complishing a certain technical job, after that work is done we still have the question as to why it is done, and for whom, and to what end. What is the work of the world for? Manifestly it is for the people who inhabit the world. But what kind of people are they? What they are depends upon the way in which they have been educated, that is, the way in which their possibilities have been developed and drawn out.[91]

Technical training precludes such nagging philosophical questions. One is tempted to say it precludes thought in general; without the language of politics and political responsibility, key decisions are made by "crunching the numbers." Education that focused on training and what Du Bois called the formation of "Character" provided the wherewithal to think through both the possibilities of technological advance and its obvious, even murderous, limitations. Du Bois argued:

But when you have human beings who know the world and can grasp it; who have their feelings guided by these ideals; then using technique in their hands they can get rid of the four great evils of human life. These four evils are ignorance, poverty, disease and crime. They flourish today in the midst of miraculous technique and in spite of our manifest ability to rid the world of them. They flourish because with all our technical training we do not have in sufficient quantity and for a long enough time the education of the human soul; the training of men to know and think and guide their feelings by science and art.[92]

This is indeed a bold claim. The evils of the world can be dealt a death blow through the kind of cosmopolitan "education of the human soul" Du Bois long advocated. Capacious, critical study in the liberal arts provided the conditions for students to know the world and the kinds of people who inhabit it, to know how to access knowledge in both scientific and artistic domains, as well as judge and evaluate their contents, and to know how to temper their feelings in accordance with an unwavering capacity to think. I have argued throughout this book that today's educational conditions do not favor the DuBoisian imperative to know the world or the kinds of people who live in it. I have insisted that humanistic inquiry is increasingly threatened with extinction, as has apparently been the case for nearly a century. I've even suggested that for many—those who have capitulated to one or another of the many forms of contemporary anti-intellectualism—thinking itself, allowing emotion to be tempered by patient and careful thought, has become an act of irreverence, and is even considered indecent. Perhaps no more so stridently than when we approach the question of race. Indeed the most difficult intellectual disposition, the greatest obstacle to overcome, is the one we imagine to have already removed. One of the greatest failings of our time, as of Du Bois's, is our confident insistence that race no longer matters. In 1938 he told the young graduates of Fisk University not to be fooled:

> But right here we have not simply little or no advance, *but we have attitudes which make advance impossible*. On the matter of race, for instance, we are ultra-modern. There are certainly no biological races in the sense of people with large groups of unvarying inherited gifts and instincts thus set apart by nature as eternally separate. We have seen the whole world reluctantly but surely approaching this truth. We have therefore hastened to conclude there is no sense in studying racial subjects or inculcating racial ideals or writing racial textbooks or projecting vocational guidance from the point of view of race. And yet standing in stark contradiction of all of this are the surrounding facts of race: the Jim Crow seats on the street cars every day, the Jim Crow coaches in the railways, the separate sections of the city where the races dwell; the discrimination in occupations and opportunities and in law; and beyond that the widespread division of the world by custom into white, yellow, and black, ruler and eternally ruled.[93]

Du Bois describes the degree to which the discrediting of one form of racist thought—the confident belief in biological races, the innate inhumanity or inferiority of some to others—effectively covers over the emergence of another form of racist belief—the necessary separation of different classes of human being in accordance with their developmental and cultural capacities. As David Goldberg has argued, as naturalist forms of racial conception are superseded by historicist forms, the problem of racism appears to be solved. Du Bois attests to the lived contradictions and modes of self-evasion such (non)thinking produces: We are no longer racists because we don't believe in biological races, and yet we live the conditions of American apartheid. The denial goes deeper still: we need not redress racial segregation, because we have just proven that we are not racist. So, too, as the historicist logic gives way to its ultimate raceless expression, we cannot fool ourselves again into believing that racism no longer exists, in spite of the evidence that confronts us. Behind the commitment to colorblindness is a pervasive evasion of reality, a prohibition on thought, and a surrender of political will, effectively summarized by Du Bois: "Do nothing, think nothing, become absorbed in the nation."[94] We would do well to listen to his advice to students:

We have got to do something about race. We have got to think and think clearly about our present situation. Absorption into the nation, save as a long, slow intellectual process, is unthinkable and while it may eventually come, its trend and result depends very largely upon what kind of a group is being absorbed; whether such racial integration has to do with poverty-stricken and half-starved criminals; whether with intelligent self-guided, independent acting men, who know what they want and propose at any civilized cost to get it. No, separated and isolated as we are so largely, we form in America an integral group, call it by any name you will, and this fact in itself has its meaning, its worth and its values.[95]

Racism, I have argued, remains integrally American, even in the age of Obama, call it by any name you will. And that truth offers one difficult solution: "We have got to think and think clearly about our present situation." It is past time we rose to this occasion.

By addressing the contemporary crisis of democracy through a rigorous historical and social analysis of the contradictory relation between democratic government and the market economy as well as the class, gender, and racial divisions of society (particularly in light of the official rhetoric of "colorblindness" that shapes much public policy), we can open up a space for imagining alternative futures for democracy. Specifically, our task as educators is to open up dialogue by resurrecting the public memory of racial oppression and exclusion in the interests of exploring more democratic arrangements for government, the economy, and civil society, as well as those changes in consciousness, culture, and education needed to sustain such reforms. In doing so, we can arrest the rhetorical transformation of the public sphere by once again invoking, after Du Bois, a language of critical historical inquiry, substantive democracy, and racial justice both at home and across the globe. In this way we can hope to reverse the desperate experience of fear, anxiety, uncertainty, and alienation that accompanies the painful erosion of individual and social agency. Du Bois's extensive educational writings remind us that the promise of political democracy can only be achieved by a sustained pedagogical engagement with the nation's most cherished values of freedom, justice, and equality, *situated in and challenged by* its history of racial exclusion and class exploitation. Through sustained historical analysis and ethical inquiry, we can begin to understand and challenge the racist policies and practices of the past as they continue to shape our present. But there is more to this legacy than the history of racism, there are also the hard-won struggles of those who opposed such racist history, and it is this aspect of public memory that must also be engaged and acted upon. That is Du Bois's message and I hope it will be our legacy for future generations.

Notes

INTRODUCTION

1. Du Bois, *Black Reconstruction*, 727.

2. Said, *Orientalism*, 206.

3. Young, *Colonial Desire*, 93.

4. For an elaboration of the racially shaped nature of modern states, see David Theo Goldberg's *The Racial State*.

5. Said, *Orientalism*, 207.

6. Goldberg, *The Threat of Race*, 334–35.

7. In brief, Goldberg defines "naturalist" expressions of racism as biologically determined, whereas "historicist" beliefs acknowledge the full humanity of populations that have been rendered racially distinct (as opposed to the sub-humanity of naturalist presumption). Historicists define racial differences in terms of developmental lag, not as innate. Thus, racially indexed populations are characterized, or rather reified, as "backward," "primitive," or "premodern." For a much more detailed analysis, see *The Racial State*, particularly chapter 4, 74–97.

8. Ibid., 221.

9. For analysis of a key distinction between "anti-racial" or "post-racial" practices and those that can readily be said to be "anti-racist," see Goldberg's *The Threat of Race*, particularly chapter 1.

10. Cited in Muhammad, "Obama and the Harsh Racial Reality," an unpaginated electronic work.

11. For an exceptional, probing analysis of everyday encounters with colorblind racism, see Eduardo Bonilla-Silva's *Racism Without Racists*.

12. Goldberg, *The Racial State*, 217.

13. Said, *Representations of the Intellectual*. See especially the chapter titled "Professionals and Amateurs."

14. Johnson, *My Hope for America*, 51.

15. Hagopian, "The Dog Eats Its Tail," unpaginated electronic work.

16. Goldberg, *The Racial State*, 229–33.

17. The dust jacket of Horowitz's *The Professors* is particularly revealing in the outlandishness of its claims: "Today's radical academics aren't the exception—

they're legion. And far from being harmless, they spew violent anti-Americanism, preach anti-Semitism, and cheer on the killing of American soldiers and civilians—all the while collecting tax dollars and tuition fees to indoctrinate our children. . . . Horowitz exposes 101 academics . . . who happen to be alleged ex-terrorists, racists, murderers, sexual deviants, anti-Semites, and al-Qaeda supporters."

18. Lowen, *Creating the Cold War University*, 2.

19. Ibid., 3.

20. For an elaborated examination of these threats to university autonomy, see Henry Giroux's *The University in Chains*.

21. Cited in Giroux, *The University in Chains*, 22.

22. Ibid.

23. Goldberg has not only observed the racial coding of the current war on terror, but also adds that "virtually every war conducted by the US throughout its history . . . (World War I may be a notable exception), has been coded, if not styled and shaped, at least partly in explicit racial terms: think of the Revolutionary War, the Mexican War, all those Indian wars, the Civil War, the occupation of Hawaii and the Philippines in the 1890s, World War II, Korea, Grenada, Panama, 'Desert Storm' (Iraq I), Serbia, Afghanistan, and 'Operation Enduring Freedom' (Iraq II)" Goldberg, *The Threat of Race*, 55–56.

24. Gilmore, *Golden Gulags*, 90.

25. Rudman and Berthelsen, cited in Gilmore, *Golden Gulag*, 88.

26. Gilmore, *Golden Gulag*, 118.

27. Ibid., 118. Emphasis added.

28. Ibid., 118.

29. See Loury, "Lecture 1: Ghettoes, Prisons and Racial Stigma," 2. This lecture was published, in modified form, as *Race, Incarceration and American Values*.

30. Ibid., 3.

31. Simon, *Governing Through Crime*, 216.

32. Ibid., 209.

33. Ibid., 231.

34. Foucault, *"Society Must Be Defended,"* 173.

35. Bauman, *Modernity and Ambivalence*, 1991.

36. Goldberg, *Racist Culture*, 4.

37. Foucault, *"Society Must Be Defended,"* 173; 178–79.

38. Fish, *Save the World on Your Own Time*.

39. Mills, *The Sociological Imagination*, 193.

40. See Derrida's "The Future of the Profession or the University Without Condition (Thanks to the 'Humanities,' What *Could Take Place* Tomorrow)," an address delivered at Stanford University in 1998, which is reprinted in *Jacques Derrida and the Humanities*. A later version, recast as an essay, was titled "The University Without Condition" and appears in Derrida's *Without Alibi*. In the former lec-

ture, Derrida returns to Kant's *The Conflict of the Faculties* and in particular to its imposition of a limitation, as he puts it "to say *publicly* all that one believes to be true and what one believes one must say, but only *inside* the university," which he argues "has never been . . . either tenable or respectable, in fact or by law." This, even as he recognizes that this prohibition is what permits Kant to guarantee the faculty of philosophy an unconditional freedom to say what is true, at least theoretically. And while he believes in an academic space protected by what he calls "absolute immunity," he recognizes that it is "never pure, can always develop dangerous processes of auto-immunity," and yet such possibility "must not prevent us from addressing ourselves to the university's outside, without any utopic neutrality" ("The Future of the Profession," 40–41).

41. Sanders, *Complicities*, 9.

42. Ibid., 1.

43. Asad, *On Suicide Bombing*, 2.

CHAPTER 1

1. I'm referring to Barack Obama's *Dreams from My Father: A Story of Race and Inheritance*, as well as his *The Audacity of Hope: Thoughts on Reclaiming the American Dream*. John McCain, similarly, penned *Faith of My Fathers: A Family Memoir*.

2. Douglas Kellner, *Guys and Guns Amok*, 61.

3. For an exceptional analysis of the exclusions black American suffered with the implementation of Franklin Delano Roosevelt's New Deal and Lyndon B. Johnson's War on Poverty, see Jill Quadagno, *The Color of Welfare*. For an analysis of the impact of post-industrial decline on urban centers and its impact on black youth in particular, see Robin D. G. Kelley's *Yo' Mama's DisFUNKional!* and Michael Eric Dyson, *Holler if You Can Hear Me*.

4. For a comprehensive analysis of the dismantling of the social state, see the recent work of the eminent sociologist Zygmunt Bauman, particularly *Society Under Siege* and *Liquid Love: On the Frailty of Human Bonds*.

5. Martin Luther King, Jr., *Where Do We Go From Here*, 170.

6. Ibid., 191 and 171.

7. Schwartz, "In Dreams Begin Responsibilities," 9. Italics in the original.

8. Hannah Arendt, *The Origins of Totalitarianism*, 474.

9. For comprehensive, book-length studies of the war on thought, see Al Gore, *The Assault on Reason*, and Susan Jacoby, *The Age of American Unreason*, among others. Though it was the hallmark of the recent Bush administration, these authors reveal the long and interrelated history of American anti-intellectualism.

10. King, *Where Do We Go From Here*, 182.

11. "Welcome Back," *Guardian*, Nov. 6, 2008.

12. For an extensive investigation of the plight of contemporary youth in North America, see Lawrence Grossberg, *Caught in the Crossfire,* and Henry A. Giroux, *The Abandoned Generation.*

13. From a transcript titled "Barack Obama's Speech on Race," March 18, 2008.

14. Chris Hedges, "America's Wars of Self-Destruction," not paginated.

15. King, *Where Do We Go From Here,* 275–76.

16. For a grim snapshot of the nation's schools and their efforts to deal with increasing homelessness and deepening poverty, see Sam Dillon's "Hard Times Hitting Students and Schools," which made the front page of the *New York Times* on September 1, 2008.

17. "Remaining Awake Through a Great Revolution," 277.

18. Here again we would do well to recall Hannah Arendt's warning, worth quoting at length: "it could be that we . . . will forever be unable to understand, that is, to think and speak about the things which nevertheless we are able to do. In this case, it would be as though our brain, which constitutes the physical, material condition of our thoughts, were unable to follow what we do, so that from now on we would indeed need artificial machines to do our thinking and speaking. If it should turn out to be true that knowledge (in the modern sense of know-how) and thought have parted company for good, then we would indeed become the helpless slaves, not so much of our machines as of our know-how, thoughtless creatures at the mercy of every gadget which is technically possible, no matter how murderous it is" (*The Human Condition,* 3).

19. Faust, "The University's Crisis of Purpose."

20. James Baldwin, "Notes on the House of Bondage."

CHAPTER 2

1. Morrison, *Playing in the Dark,* 5.

2. Ibid., 12.

3. See Goldberg, *The Racial State,* 200–238, for an elaborated critique of the discourse of colorblindness in the contexts of the United States, Canada, the European Union, South Africa, and Brazil.

4. Gilroy, *Against Race,* 244.

5. Harold Bloom, *The Western Canon,* 31.

6. Willis, "We Need a Radical Left," 18. See also Robin D. G. Kelley's *Yo' Mama's DisFunktional!,* 103–24, for an invaluable analysis of the shortcomings of this position.

7. Rorty, "The Inspirational Value of Great Works of Literature," 15.

8. Ibid., 13.

9. Said, *Representations of the Intellectual,* 77.

10. See Dorothy Roberts's trenchant analysis in her *Killing the Black Body*, especially 169–72.

11. Cited in Mauer, *Race to Incarcerate*, 67.

12. Gilroy, *Against Race*, 244.

13. Carby, "The Multicultural Wars," 192.

14. Goldberg, *The Racial State*, 2.

15. Ibid., 212.

16. Jeff Jacoby, "A Left-wing Monopoly on Campus," unpaginated online article.

17. Ibid.

18. Ibid.

19. Cited in Wilson, *Patriotic Correctness*, 61.

20. Ibid., 65.

21. Cited in ibid., 65.

22. Horowitz, "Academic Bill of Rights," unpaginated online document.

23. American Association of University Professors, "AAUP Statement on the Academic Bill of Rights."

24. Wilson, *Patriotic Correctness*, 62.

25. One need only consider the profound—and enduring—influence of conservative "classics" like Charles Murray's *Losing Ground* or Samuel Huntington's *Clash of Civilizations* on public policy or their more recent (and decidedly more racist) contributions, *The Bell Curve* and *Who We Are: The Challenges to America's National Identity*, respectively.

26. Morrison, *Playing in the Dark*, 44–45.

27. Ibid., 7.

28. Goldberg, *The Racial State*, 229.

29. Ehrenreich and Muhammad, "The Recession's Racial Divide."

30. David Roediger, "Obama's Victory and the Future of Race in the United States."

31. Roger Simon on NBC's *Meet the Press*, Feb. 11, 2007. Cited by Peter Hart in "Obamamania."

32. Goldberg, *The Threat of Race*, 21.

CHAPTER 3

1. Monbiot, "How These Jibbering Numbskulls Came to Dominate Washington."

2. Editor, "American Health Care: Keep It Honest."

3. Moyers, transcript from *Bill Moyers Journal*, Sept. 4, 2009.

4. Hofstadter, *Anti-Intellectualism in American Life*, 21.

5. Ibid.

6. Ibid., 119.

7. For a comprehensive analysis of these various fundamentalisms, see Henry A. Giroux's *Against the Terror of Neoliberalism: Politics Beyond the Age of Greed* (2008).

8. Cited in Hofstadter, *Anti-Intellectualism in American Life*, 147. Emphasis mine.

9. Ibid., 147–48.

10. Ibid., 149.

11. On the blog accompanying the website accompanying his 2009 publication, *The Threat of Race*, David Goldberg pointed out the racially driven differences in the ways in which relative political newcomers Barack Obama and Sarah Palin were embraced by the electorate. He notes: "More than half the whites polled registered harsher senses of blacks than they did of whites. While 50 percent of white respondents at least sometimes have had sympathy for blacks, nearly half had never or rarely. Similarly, more than 30 percent of white respondents have never or rarely admired blacks. Nearly half the respondents characterized blacks as at least moderately violent, and 38 percent as lazy. Lest one think that generally stated racial prejudice does not necessarily translate into bias against a particular person, the study also revealed that 47 percent characterized Obama as 'inexperienced' while just 4 percent did McCain, 17 percent as 'un-American' and just 2 percent did McCain, and only 29 percent 'patriotic' while 61 percent did McCain. Just under 20 percent consider Obama's religion 'a reason not to vote for him,' perhaps a less surprising fact considering that 14 percent still think he is a Muslim."

12. Cited in Muwakkil, "The 'Post-Racial' President."

13. Cited in Conason, "The Racist Truth About Beck and Limbaugh."

14. Cited in Muwakkil, "The 'Post-Racial' President."

15. Cited in Zeleny and Rutenberg, "As Race Debate Grows, Obama Steers Clear of It."

16. Goldberg, *The Racial State*, 211. My emphasis.

17. Goldberg, *The Threat of Race*, 23.

18. Goldberg, *The Racial State*, 228–29.

19. Goldberg, *Racist Culture*, 57.

20. Goldberg, *The Threat of Race*, 120.

21. Goldberg, *The Racial State*, 223.

22. Gordon, *Bad Faith and Anti-Black Racism*, 86.

23. Cited in ibid., 87.

24. Allan Bloom, *The Closing of the American Mind*.

25. For a penetrating analysis of Hurricane Katrina and the production of disposable populations see Henry A. Giroux, *Stormy Weather: Katrina and the Politics of Disposability* (2006).

26. See the new Pew Charitable Trusts report, "1 in 100: Behind Bars in America 2008."

27. Jacoby, *The Age of American Unreason*, 10.

28. For more richly detailed accounts of Republican efforts to galvanize white voters through the mobilization of racial resentments, see Kevin Phillips' *The Emerging Republican Majority* and Thomas Edsall and Mary Edsall's *Chain Reaction*.

29. Cited in Lamis, *Southern Politics in the 1990s*, 7–8.

30. Herbert, "Impossible, Ridiculous and Repugnant," 24.

31. Bauman, *Life in Fragments*, 150.

32. Ibid., 149.

33. Hofstadter, *Anti-Intellectualism in American Life*, 299.

34. Ibid., 300–301.

35. Ibid., 305.

36. Cited in ibid., 299.

37. Allan Bloom, *The Closing of the American Mind*, 334.

38. Arendt, *Crises of the Republic*, 120–21.

39. Susan Jacoby, *The Age of American Unreason*, 146.

40. Gordon, *Disciplinary Decadence*, 32.

41. Ibid., 30.

42. Ibid., 30–31.

43. Consider the comments made by Ohio state senator Larry Mumper, who introduced a version of Horowitz's academic bill of rights to the state legislature. He argued that the university system was clearly broken, thus prohibiting real intellectual diversity in the classroom. He insisted, as proof of this claim, that "if the system were fair, Rush Limbaugh and Sean Hannity would be tenured professors somewhere." Further, Mumper warned that funding cuts for universities were "always in the back" of his mind: "Why should we, as fairly moderate to conservative legislators, continue to support universities that turn out students who rail against the very policies that their parents voted us in for?" (cited in Wilson, *Patriotic Correctness*, 73). In the face of this threat, Ohio's college presidents quickly capitulated, utterly compromising academic freedom and intellectual integrity.

44. Gordon, *Disciplinary Decadence*, 29.

45. Ibid., 29.

46. In a Nov. 2008 *New York Times* article, "Professors' Liberalism Contagious? Maybe Not," Patricia Cohen reported on a handful of studies that found the presumption of a "liberal thugocracy" in colleges and universities to be a "fantasy." Cohen stated that "three sets of researchers recently concluded that professors have virtually no impact on the political views or ideologies of their students." Reported one researcher, "'Parents and family are the most important influence' followed by news media and peers," adding that "'professors are among the least

influential.'" Describing the consequences of this long-held article of faith among conservatives, one researcher asserted that "perhaps the most insidious side effect of assumptions of liberal influence has been the overall disengagement on campus from civic and political affairs, and a reluctance to promote serious debate on political issues. If anything, he added the problem is not too much politics, but too little." For a brilliant article that complicates the conservative commonsense that liberal professors dominate college campuses, see Donald Lazere's "The Contradictions of Cultural Conservatism in the Assault on American Colleges."

47. Fish, *Save the World on Your Own Time*, 33.

48. Ibid., 71.

49. Ibid.

50. Hofstadter, *Anti-Intellectualism in American Life*, 237.

51. Fish, *Save the World on Your Own Time*, 25.

52. Donald Lazere's "Stanley Fish's Tightrope Act," a review of *Save the World on Your Own Time*, offers a brilliant analysis of the "tightrope" Fish is here attempting to walk.

53. Derrida, *Eyes of the University*, 102.

54. Fish, *Save the World on Your Own Time*, 14.

55. Ibid., 27. Emphasis his.

56. Ibid., 25–26.

57. Bauman, *Life in Fragments*, 149.

58. Ibid., 149.

59. Ibid., 149.

60. Fish, "Psychology and Torture."

61. Ibid.

62. Bauman, *Life in Fragments*, 157.

63. Fish, *Save the World on Your Own Time*, 15.

64. Ibid., 15.

65. Derrida, *Eyes of the University*, 151.

66. Ibid., 153.

67. Ibid., 147.

68. Ibid., 153. My emphasis.

69. Ibid.

70. Ibid.

71. Ibid., 147. Emphasis mine.

72. Ibid.

73. Fish, *Save the World on Your Own Time*, 125.

74. Fish, "The Last Professor."

75. Ibid.

76. Michaels, *The Trouble with Diversity*, 49.

77. Ibid.

78. Ibid.

79. Goldberg, *The Racial State*, 217.

80. Goldberg, *The Threat of Race*, 10.

81. Michaels, *The Trouble with Diversity*, 19–20.

82. For a very enlightening and comprehensive analysis of the limits of tolerance talk, see Wendy Brown, *Regulating Aversion*.

83. Michaels, *The Trouble with Diversity*, 17.

84. Ibid., 18. Emphasis mine.

85. Ibid., 79.

86. I addressed this issue in "The Age of Irony?" *JAC* 22.4 (Fall 2002): 960–76.

87. See Henry A. Giroux and Susan Searls Giroux, *Take Back Higher Education*, particularly chapter 5.

88. A Jan. 16, 2009, article titled "Black Job Losses Alarming" cites a National Urban League call to action based on Labor Department figures which "show among the major race and ethnicity groups, Blacks had the highest job loss in the fourth quarter of 2008 with Black men leading the surge at 13.4 percent." The National Urban League reports that "the real state of Black unemployment is worse than current government figures indicate. Using the December 2008 seasonal adjusted national figure for Black unemployment of 11.9 percent, League officials estimate that real Black unemployment was 22.8 percent."

89. Goldberg, *The Threat of Race*, 84.

90. Gilroy, *Against Race*, 152.

91. Ibid.

92. Hedges, "America the Illiterate."

93. Ibid.

94. Ibid.

95. Butler, "Uncritical Exuberance."

96. Hedges, "America the Illiterate."

97. Hedges, *Empire of Illusion*, 89.

98. Ibid., 110, 111.

99. Ibid., 111.

100. Ibid.

101. Ibid.

102. Cited in Julian Boyd, *The Papers of Thomas Jefferson*, 526–27. Emphasis mine.

103. Graham Boyd, "The Drug War Is the New Jim Crow."

104. Peterson, *The Portable Thomas Jefferson*, 215.

CHAPTER 4

1. For one of the most comprehensive accounts of the militarization of higher education, see Henry A. Giroux, *The University in Chains: Confronting the Military-Industrial-Academic Complex* (2007).

2. Cited in Borradori, "Autoimmunity: Real and Symbolic Suicides: A Dialogue with Jacques Derrida," 94.

3. Ibid., 98.

4. Ibid., 97.

5. Derrida, *Eyes of the University*, 135.

6. Foucault, *"Society Must Be Defended,"* 173.

7. Nietzsche, *On the Future of Our Educational Institutions*, 13.

8. Ibid., 15.

9. Ibid., 14.

10. Ibid.

11. Ibid., 19.

12. Ibid., 69. For a spirited discussion of what it would mean to recreate the conditions necessary for thought in the university, see Readings's *The University in Ruins*, particularly chapters 10 and 11.

13. The Greek *paideuein*, from which we derive paideia, means both "to teach" and "to torment." On the question of paideia in Nietzsche's "On the Future of Our Educational Institutions," see Valerie Allan and Ares Axiotis, *"Pathein Mathein:* Nietzsche and the Birth of Education."

14. Allen and Axiotis, *"Pathein Mathein,"* 19.

15. Nietzsche, *On the Future of Our Educational Institutions*, 21. Emphasis in the original.

16. Ibid., 26–27.

17. Ibid., 28.

18. Ibid.

19. Ibid., 29.

20. Ibid., 31.

21. Ibid.

22. Allen and Axiotis, *"Pathein Mathein,"* 22.

23. In several letters written later in 1872 and early 1873, Nietzsche complained to Malwida von Meysenbug that the lectures were, variously, "primitive," a depthless "farce" of inferior invention, a promise that fails in the end to deliver: "One acquires a dry throat from these lectures and in the end nothing to drink!" (cited in Grenke, "Translator's Introduction," 2).

24. I say "seemingly" here in due recognition of the difficulty Derrida establishes between what constitutes the "inside" and the "outside" of the university in the famed essay, "Mochlos, or The Conflict of the Faculties," in *Eyes of the University*, in which he states:

No discourse would be rigorous here if one did not begin by defining the unity of the university system, in other words the border between its inside and its outside. Kant wishes to analyze conflicts proper to the university, those arising between the different parts of the university's body and its power, that is, here, the faculties. . . . Today however—and this is a first limit to the translation of the Kantian text in our politico-epistemological space—there can be very serious competition and border conflicts between nonuniversity research centers and university faculties claiming at once to be doing research and transmitting knowledge, to be producing and reproducing knowledge. . . . Today, in any case, the university is what has become its margin. (93–94)

It is this sense of university marginality—a condition to which it has in part given itself over—and one which is predicated on the victory of instrumental rationalities, of scientism, historicism, journalistic plain speaking, and self-evidences that, for Nietzsche, shapes contemporary culture and mitigates the possibility of Thought.

25. Nietzsche, *On the Future of Our Educational Institutions*, 26.

26. Bauman, *Freedom*.

27. Nietzsche, *On the Future of Our Educational Institutions*, 42.

28. Ibid., 112–23.

29. Ibid., 78–79.

30. Bauman, *Life in Fragments*, 141.

31. Ibid., 143.

32. Goldberg, "Killing Me Softly," 350.

33. Ibid., 341.

34. Ibid. Emphasis mine.

35. Clark, "Schelling's Wartime: Philosophy and Violence in the Age of Napoleon," 140.

36. Foucault, *"Society Must Be Defended,"* 178–79.

37. Foucault, "The Subject and Power," 222.

38. Derrida, *Eyes of the University*, 143.

39. Nietzsche, *On the Future of Our Educational Institutions*, 36–37.

40. With Henry Giroux, I have taken up such issues in *Take Back Higher Education*. For additional critical work, see as well Stanley Aronowitz, *The Knowledge Factory*, and Henry Giroux, *The University in Chains*.

41. Nietzsche, *On the Future of Our Educational Institutions*, 37.

42. Ibid.

43. Ibid.

44. Bauman, *Does Ethics Have a Chance in a World of Consumers?*, 144.

45. Ibid., 146.

46. Ibid., 173.

47. Miller, "The Prophet and the Dandy: Philosophy as a Way of Life in Nietzsche and Foucault," 871.

48. Readings, *The University in Ruins*, 175.

49. Arendt, *On Revolution*, 137. Emphasis mine.

50. Ibid., 138.

51. Bauman, *Freedom*, 38.

52. Mbembe, *On the Postcolony*, 30.

53. Bauman, *Freedom*, 38.

54. Nietzsche, *On the Future of Our Educational Institutions*, 47. This pedagogical appeal and its popularity remain alive and well today, as the reader will no doubt recognize. For the sake of example, we might look to the 2000 decision by the Canadian Council for the Advancement of Education to award a gold medal to the University of Western Ontario's "Major in Yourself" website campaign. Thanks to David Clark for reminding me of this event.

55. Ibid., 47–48.

56. Ibid., 48.

57. Ibid.

58. Gordon, *Disciplinary Decadence*, 33.

59. Nietzsche, *On the Future of Our Educational Institutions*, 48.

60. Ibid.

61. Ibid., 49.

62. Ibid., 108–9.

63. Ibid., 109.

64. Ibid., 111.

65. Ibid.

66. Ibid., 106.

67. Ibid., 106–7.

68. Ibid., 77.

69. Ibid., 78.

70. Ibid.

71. Ibid., 114.

72. The first association was founded in Jena in 1815 in opposition to reactionary government policies, and many other student organizations quickly formed across German universities. After the 1819 assassination of August von Kotzebue by one of the members of the *Burschenschaft*, the organization was banned and driven underground, where it grew even more radical and violent. By the second half of the century the *Burschenschaft* had become a union of highly nationalistic and anti-Semitic social clubs.

73. Ibid., 114.

74. Ibid., 115.

75. Ibid., 117.

76. Von Clausewitz, *Vom Kriege* [*On War*], 120.

77. Bauman, *Does Ethics Have a Chance in a World of Consumers?*, 182.

78. Ibid., 183. Italics in the original.

79. Allan Bloom, *The Closing of the American Mind,* 337.

80. Ibid., 75.

81. For a penetrating analysis of this absence see Henry A. Giroux, *The Abandoned Generation.*

82. Kellner, *Guys and Guns Amok,* 61.

83. Derrida, *Eyes of the University,* 143.

84. On the question of university complicity with militarization and torture, see Henry A. Giroux, *The University in Chains.*

85. As is the case for Stanley Fish, who insists that academics have no moral duty to educate youth to be productive and engaged citizens, thus invoking the very positivistic presumption of moral neutrality that Nietzsche castigated as a betrayal of Thought.

CHAPTER 5

1. De Vries and Sullivan, *Political Theologies,* x–xi.

2. Ibid., xi.

3. Asad, *On Suicide Bombing,* 2.

4. Ibid., 38.

5. Butler, "Critique, Coercion, and Sacred Life in Benjamin's Critique of Violence," 201.

6. De Vries and Sullivan, *Political Theologies,* 48.

7. We might trace these lines of argument from the famous sixteenth-century debates of Las Casas and Sepúlveda to twentieth-century ruminations on notions of statecraft and the il/legitimacy of violence by Hannah Arendt, Frantz Fanon, and C.L.R. James.

8. Goldberg, *The Racial State.*

9. Although I would relish an opportunity to explore at length the troubling similarities between the Weimar republic and the political culture of the contemporary United States, to do so is beyond the scope of this chapter.

10. Gordon, *Bad Faith and Anti-Black Racism,* 53, 86.

11. Hanssen, *Critique of Violence,* 18.

12. Benjamin, "Critique of Violence," 297.

13. Ibid.

14. Habermas, *The New Conservatism,* 137.

15. Derrida, "The Force of the Law," 62.

16. Butler, "Critique, Coercion, and Sacred Life in Benjamin's Critique of Violence," 205.

17. Ibid., 206.

18. Ibid.

19. Goldberg, *The Racial State*, 4.

20. Ibid., 5.

21. Ibid., 9.

22. Ibid., 39.

23. Gordon, *Her Majesty's Other Children*, 166. Emphasis mine.

24. Benjamin, *Illuminations*, 257.

25. Gordon, *Her Majesty's Other Children*, 166–67.

26. Gordon, *Existentia Africana*, 45.

27. Ibid.

28. Ibid., 45. Emphasis mine.

29. Ibid., 46.

30. Ibid.

31. Ibid., 47.

32. Ibid., 48.

33. Ibid., 48–49. Emphasis mine.

34. Ibid., 49.

35. Butler, "Critique, Coercion, and Sacred Life in Benjamin's Critique of Violence," 204–5.

36. Ibid., 208.

37. Ibid.

38. Arendt, *The Origins of Totalitarianism*, 461–62. Emphasis mine.

39. Goldberg, *The Racial State*, 140.

40. Ibid.

41. Ibid.

42. Ibid., 143.

43. Ibid., 155.

44. Ibid.

45. Gordon, *Existentia Africana*, 52.

46. Gordon, *Bad Faith and Anti-Black Racism*, 101.

47. Douglass, *My Bondage and My Freedom*, 149.

48. Benjamin, "Critique of Violence," 295.

49. Douglass, *My Bondage and My Freedom*, 151–52.

50. Gordon, *Existentia Africana*, 60.

51. Benjamin, "Critique of Violence," 298.

52. Ibid., 298–99.

53. Cited in Gordon, *Existentia Africana*, 56.

54. Ibid.

55. Benjamin, "Critique of Violence," 298.

56. Gordon, *Fanon and the Crisis of European Man*, 81.

57. Benjamin, "Critique of Violence," 297–98. Emphasis mine.

58. Orlando Patterson has written extensively on the nature of slavery, and of U.S. southern slavery in particular, as imposing a kind of social death. What Patterson has to say about the role of religion in this regard is fascinating in light of our discussion of political theology. He writes: "Among more advanced slaveholding systems religion played an even greater role in the ritual process of incorporating the slave to his marginal status. Most ritual activities became the specialized preserve of religious institutions. And in both its structural and ritual aspects religion reflected the more centralized nature of political power. In the same way that the state had to develop a specialized set of laws to deal with the secular problems of the slave, so the state cult needed to develop a more specialized set of rules and beliefs to represent the condition of slavery" (*Slavery and Social Death,* 66).

59. Gordon, *Existentia Africana,* 61.

60. Benjamin, "Critique of Violence," 286. Emphasis mine.

61. This unpublished work was revised and published as the first chapter, "Signs," of their new book, *Of Divine Warning: Reading Disaster in the Modern Age.* The citations that follow are from the book.

62. Gordon and Gordon, *Of Divine Warning,* 8.

63. Gordon, *Existentia Africana,* 61.

64. Gordon and Gordon, *Of Divine Warning,* 9.

65. Ibid., 11.

66. Ibid.

67. Ibid., 12.

68. For an extensive analysis of the vagaries of media coverage of New Orleans post-Katrina, see *Stormy Weather: Katrina and the Politics of Disposability,* by Henry A. Giroux.

69. Gordon and Gordon, *Of Divine Warning,* 19.

70. Ibid., 26.

71. Ibid.

72. De Vries, "Introduction," 1.

73. Goldberg, *The Threat of Race,* 254.

74. Asad, *On Suicide Bombing,* 30.

75. Gordon, *Her Majesty's Other Children,* 174.

76. Ibid.

77. Gordon, *Bad Faith and Anti-Black Racism,* ix.

CHAPTER 6

1. Dedrick Muhammad, "Obama and the Harsh Racial Reality."

2. Michael Powell. "Bank Accused of Pushing Mortgage Deal on Blacks."

3. George D. Squires, "Scapegoating Blacks. Again."

4. See Henry A. Giroux and Kenneth Saltman, "Obama's Betrayal of Public Education? Arne Duncan and the Corporate Model of Schooling."

5. W.E.B. Du Bois, *Black Reconstruction in America,* 377.

6. Ibid., 346.

7. Ibid., 634–65.

8. Ibid., 714.

9. Ibid., 727.

10. Lemert, *Dark Thoughts,* 223.

11. I would like to thank David Goldberg for reminding me just how far the rolling back of civil rights victories has gone.

12. In place of rational argumentation, the public is bombarded with the cartoonish rantings of right-wing extremists such as Ann Coulter, Michael Savage, Bill O'Reilly, Dinesh D'Souza, and Rush Limbaugh. At the same time conservatives bemoan the power of the "liberal" media.

13. William Greider, "Rolling Back the Twentieth Century."

14. Bill Moyers, "This Is Your Story: The Progressive Story of America. Pass It On."

15. Lewis Lapham, "Yankee Doodle Dandy," 10.

16. Ibid.

17. Dixon, "Muzzling the African American Agenda with Black Help: The DLC's Corporate Dollars of Destruction."

18. Ibid., 3.

19. Howard Zinn, *A People's History of the United States,* 247.

20. Conley, *Being Black, Living in the Red, 25.*

21. Uchitelle, "Blacks Lose Better Jobs Faster as Middle-Class Work Drops," C14.

22. Ibid.

23. Children's Defense Fund, "June Jobless Rate Among America's Teens Highest in 55 Years."

24. Mark Gongloff, "U.S. Jobs Jumping Ship."

25. This is the conclusion of Barbara Ehrenreich and Dedrick Muhammad in their *New York Times* op-ed, "The Recession's Racial Divide."

26. Du Bois, *Black Reconstruction,* 678.

27. Ibid., 674.

28. Wacquant, "From Slavery to Mass Incarceration: Rethinking the 'Race Question' in the U.S.," 56.

29. For an elaborated analysis of the racially coded rhetoric of the right, see Thomas Edsall and Mary Edsall's *Chain Reaction.*

30. Brenkman, "Race Publics," 17. Emphasis added.

31. Ibid., 16.

32. Wacquant, "From Slavery to Mass Incarceration.," 53. For further analysis of the linkages between slavery, convict leasing, or the use of a largely black in-

carcerated population as free labor, and present-day mass incarceration, see Angela Davis's "From the Convict Lease System to the Super Max" and "Racialized Punishment and Prison Abolition." Though the Thirteenth Amendment of the U.S. Constitution abolished slavery, Davis observes, it also legalized it as a form of punishment.

33. Paul Street, "Race, Prisons, and Poverty," 25.

34. Mauer, *Race to Incarcerate*, 19.

35. The Sentencing Project offers the most recent rates of U.S. incarceration. See: http://www.sentencingproject.org/template/page.cfm?id=107; Wacquant, "From Slavery to Mass Incarceration," 60.

36. For an analysis of the "hidden punishments" of incarceration, see *Invisible Punishment*, edited by Mark Mauer and Meda Chesney-Lind.

37. Du Bois, *Black Reconstruction*, 713.

38. Ibid., 712.

39. Ibid., 717.

40. Charles Murray, *Losing Ground*, 443–44.

41. David Goldberg, *The Racial State*.

42. Ibid.

43. Du Bois, *Black Reconstruction*, 123.

44. Ibid., 697.

45. Ibid., 667.

46. For a critique of the affinities between the Bush and Obama administrations' vision for education, see Henry A. Giroux and Kenneth Saltman, "Obama's Betrayal of Public Education: Arne Duncan and the Corporate Model of Schooling," and Henry A. Giroux, "Obama's View of Education Is Stuck in Reverse."

47. Kumashiro, "Duncan Wrong Education Choice."

48. Gary Orfield, Susan Eaton, and the Harvard Project on School Desegregation, *Dismantling Desegregation*, 341.

49. Ibid., 23.

50. Jonathan Kozol, *Savage Inequalities*, 55.

51. Orfield et al., *Dismantling Desegregation*, 339.

52. Ibid.

53. See Henry Giroux's recent book, *The Abandoned Generation*.

54. Paul Krugman, "State of Decline," A21.

55. Mike Davis, "Cry California."

56. For more in-depth analysis of the antecedents leading to California's fiscal disaster, see David Theo Goldberg, "The State We Are In."

57. Byrd, "From Bad to Worse . . . Billions for War on Iraq, A Fraction for Poor Kids."

58. Greg Winter, "Tens of Thousands Will Lose College Aid, Report Says."

59. Quoted in Hentoff, "Sandra Day O'Connor's Elitist Decision: Another Three Card Monty," 1.

60. Quoted in Guinier, "Saving Affirmative Action and a Process for Elites to Choose Elites," 2–3.

61. Burd, "Bush's Next Target?," A20.

62. Cited in Fish, "Colleges Caught in a Vise," A31.

63. Ibid.

64. Du Bois, *Black Reconstruction in America*, 708.

65. Ibid., 678.

66. I would like to thank John Camoroff for bringing this point home in a personal exchange.

67. Du Bois, *Black Reconstruction in America*, 714.

68. For a brilliant analysis of managing diversity, see Goldberg, *The Racial State*.

69. Du Bois, "The Revelation of Saint Orgne the Damned," 110.

70. Ibid., 112.

71. Ibid. My emphasis.

72. Ibid., 124.

73. Ibid., 116.

74. Ibid., 119.

75. Ibid., 116.

76. Ibid., 114.

77. Ibid.

78. Ibid., 116.

79. Ibid., 117.

80. Du Bois, "The Meaning of Education," 250.

81. Ibid.

82. Ibid.

83. Ibid., 250–51.

84. Ibid., 251.

85. Ibid.

86. Balibar, *We, The People of Europe?*, 126.

87. Ibid., 131–32.

88. Kant, "Toward Perpetual Peace," 329.

89. Ibid., 251.

90. Ibid.

91. Ibid.

92. Du Bois, "The Meaning of Education," 252.

93. Du Bois, "The Revelation of Saint Orgne the Damned," 121.

94. Ibid., 122.

95. Ibid.

Bibliography

Agamben, Giorgio. *State of Exception*. Chicago: University of Chicago Press, 2005.

Allen, Valerie, and Ares Axiotis. "*Pathein Mathein*: Nietzsche and the Birth of Education." In *Nietzsche's Legacy for Education: Past and Present Values*. Edited by Michael Peters, James Marshall, and Paul Smeyers, 19–34. Westport, CT: Bergin & Garvey, 2001.

American Association of University Professors. "AAUP Statement on the Academic Bill of Rights." Posted Dec. 2003. http://www.aaup.org/statements/Spch-State/Statements/billofrights.htm.

Arendt, Hannah. *The Human Condition*. Chicago: University of Chicago Press, 1958.

———. *The Origins of Totalitarianism*. New York: Harcourt Brace. 1973 [1951].

———. *On Revolution*. New York: Penguin, 1963.

———. "On Violence." In *Crises of the Republic* by Hannah Arendt. New York: Harcourt Brace Jovanovich, 1969.

Aronowitz, Stanley. *The Knowledge Factory: Dismantling the Corporate University and Creating True Higher Learning*. Boston: Beacon, 2001.

Asad, Talal. *On Suicide Bombing*. New York: Columbia University Press, 2007.

Baldwin, James. "Notes on the House of Bondage." *Nation*, Nov. 1, 1980. http://www.thenation.com/doc/19801101/19801101baldwin.

Balibar, Etienne. *We, The People of Europe? Reflections on Transnational Citizenship*. Translated by James Swenson. Princeton, NJ: Princeton University Press, 2004.

Bauman, Zygmunt. *Does Ethics Have a Chance in a World of Consumers?* Cambridge, MA: Harvard University Press, 2008.

———. *Freedom*. Minneapolis: University of Minnesota Press, 1988.

———. *Life in Fragments: Essays in Postmodern Morality*. Oxford: Blackwell, 1995.

———. *Liquid Love: On the Frailty of Human Bonds*. Cambridge: Polity, 2003.

———. *Modernity and Ambivalence*. Cambridge: Polity, 1991.

———. *Society Under Siege*. Cambridge: Polity, 2002.

Benjamin, Walter. "Critique of Violence." In *Reflections: Essays, Aphorisms, Autobiographical Writings*. Edited and with an introduction by Peter Demetz. Translated by Edmund Jephcott. New York: Harcourt Brace & Jovanovich, 1978.

————. *Illuminations*. Edited with an introduction by Hannah Arendt. Translated by Harry Zorn. New York: Schocken Books, 1969.

Bérubé, Michael. *What's Liberal About the Liberal Arts? Classroom Politics and "Bias" in Higher Education*. New York: Norton, 2007.

"Black Job Losses Alarming." Jan 16, 2009. *Blackvoicesnews.com*. http://www.blackvoicenews.com/content/view/42922/3/.

Bloom, Allan. *The Closing of the American Mind*. New York: Simon & Schuster, 1988.

Bloom, Harold. *The Western Canon*. New York: Harcourt Brace, 1994.

Bonilla-Silva, Eduardo. *Racism Without Racists: Color-Blind Racism and the Persistence of Racial Inequality in the United States*. Lanham, MD: Rowman & Littlefield, 2003.

Borradori, Giovanna. "Autoimmunity: Real and Symbolic Suicides: A Dialogue with Jacques Derrida." Translated from the French by Pascale-Anne Brault and Michael Nass. In *Philosophy in a Time of Terror: Dialogues with Jürgen Habermas and Jacques Derrida*. Edited by Giovanna Borradori, 85–136. Chicago: University of Chicago Press, 2003.

Boyd, Graham. "The Drug War Is the New Jim Crow." NACLA Report on the Americas. July 31, 2001. http://www.aclu.org/drugpolicy/racialjustice/10830pub20010731.html.

Boyd, Julian P. *The Papers of Thomas Jefferson*. Volume 2: *1777 to 18 June 1779*. Princeton, NJ : Princeton University Press, 1950.

Brenkman, John. "Race Publics." *Transition* (66) 1995: 4–36.

Brown, Wendy. *Regulating Aversion: Tolerance in the Age of Identity and Empire*. Princeton, NJ: Princeton University Press, 2006.

Burd, Stephen. "Bush's Next Target?" *Chronicle of Higher Education*, July 18, 2003, A18–20.

Butler, Judith. "Critique, Coercion, and Sacred Life in Benjamin's Critique of Violence." In *Political Theologies: Public Religions in a Post-Secular World*. Edited by Hent De Vries and Lawrence E. Sullivan, 201–19. New York: Fordham University Press, 2006.

————. "Uncritical Exuberance." Blog. Nov. 5, 2008. http://www.indybay.org/newsitems/2008/11/05/18549195.php.

Byrd, Robert. "From Bad to Worse . . . Billions for War on Iraq, A Fraction for Poor Kids." Senate Floor remarks. Sept. 5, 2003. http://www.commondreams.org/views03/0906– 09.htm.

Carby, Hazel. "The Multicultural Wars." In *Black Popular Culture*. Edited by Gina Dent. Seattle, WA: Bay Press, 1992.

Children's Defense Fund. "June Jobless Rate Among America's Teens Highest in 55 Years." Press release. http://www.childrensdefense.org/release030708.php.

Clark, David L. "Schelling's Wartime: Philosophy and Violence in the Age of Napoleon." *European Romantic Review* 19 (April 2008): 139–48.

Cohen, Patricia. "Professors' Liberalism Contagious? Maybe Not." *New York Times,* Nov. 3, 2008. http://www.nytimes.com/2008/11/03/books/03infl.html.

Conason, Joe. "The Racist Truth About Beck and Limbaugh." Sept. 24, 2009. *Truthout.* http://www.truthout.org/092409I.

Conley, Dalton. *Being Black, Living in the Red.* Berkeley: University of California Press, 1999.

Davis, Angela Y. "From the Convict Lease System to the Super Max." In *States of Confinement.* Edited by Joy James. New York: St. Martin's Press, 2000.

———. "Racialized Punishment and Prison Abolition." In *The Angela Davis Reader.* Edited by Joy James, 96–107. Malden, MA: Blackwell, 1998.

Davis, Mike. "Cry California," *Common Dreams.* Sept. 3, 2003. http://www.commondreams.org/views03/0903–10.htm.

Derrida, Jacques. *Eyes of the University: The Right to Philosophy 2.* Translated by Jan Plug et al. Stanford: Stanford University Press, 2004.

———. "Force of the Law: The 'Mystical Foundations of Authority.'" In *Deconstruction and the Possibility of Justice.* Edited by Drucilla Cornell, Michel Rosenfeld, and David Gray Carlson, 3–67. New York: Routledge, 1992.

———. "The Future of the Profession or the University Without Condition (Thanks to the 'Humanities,' What *Could Take Place* Tomorrow)." In *Jacques Derrida and the Humanities: A Critical Reader.* Edited by Tom Cohen, 24–57. Cambridge: Cambridge University Press, 2001.

De Vries, Hent. "Introduction: Before, Around and Beyond the Theologico-Political." In *Political Theologies: Religion in a Post-Secular World.* Edited by Henry De Vries and Lawrence E. Sullivan, 1–90. New York: Fordham University Press, 2006.

De Vries, Hent, and Lawrence E. Sullivan, "Preface." In *Political Theologies: Religion in a Post-Secular World.* Edited by Henry De Vries and Lawrence E. Sullivan, ix–xii. New York: Fordham University Press, 2006.

Dillon, Sam. "Hard Times Hitting Students and Schools." *New York Times,* Sept. 1, 2008, A1.

Dirlik, Arif. "Bringing History Back In: Of Diasporas, Hybridities, Places, and Histories." *Review of Education, Pedagogy & Cultural Studies* 21 (1999): 95–131.

Dixon, Bruce D. "Muzzling the African American Agenda with Black Help: The DLC's Corporate Dollars of Destruction." *Black Commentator.* http://www.commondreams.org/views03/0612–08.htm.

Douglass, Frederick. *My Bondage and My Freedom.* Edited with an introduction by William L. Andrews. Urbana: University of Illinois Press, 1987.

Du Bois. W.E.B. *Black Reconstruction in America: 1860–1880.* New York: Atheneum, 1992 [1935].

———. "The Revelation of Saint Orgne the Damned." In *The Education of Black People: Ten Critiques, 1906–1960.* Edited by Herbert Aptheker, 103–26. New York: Monthly Review Press, 1973.

———. "The Meaning of Education." In *Against Racism: Unpublished Essays, Papers, Addresses, 1887–1961.* Edited by Herbert Aptheker, 249–52. Amherst: University of Massachusetts Press, 1985.

Dyson, Michael Eric. *Holler if You Can Hear Me: Searching for Tupac Shakur.* New York: Basic Books, 2001.

Editor. "American Health Care: Keep It Honest." *Economist,* Aug. 20, 2009. http://www.economist.com/opinion/displaystory.cfm?story_id=14258877.

Editor. "A Sampling of Statements on Race and Obama." *New York Times,* Sept. 17, 2009, A3. http://www.nytimes.com/2009/09/17/us/politics/17racequotesweb.html.

Edsall, Thomas, and Mary Edsall. *Chain Reaction: The Impact of Race, Rights and Taxes on American Politics.* New York: Norton, 1992.

Ehrenreich, Barbara, and Dedrick Muhammad. "The Recession's Racial Divide." *New York Times.* Sept. 13, 2009. WK17. http://www.nytimes.com/2009/09/13/opinion/13ehrenreich.html.

Essed, Philomena. *Understanding Everyday Racism: An Interdisciplinary Theory.* Newbury Park, CA: Sage, 1991.

Faust, Drew Gilpin. "The University's Crisis of Purpose." *New York Times,* Sept. 6, 2009, BR19. http://www.nytimes.com/2009/09/06/books/review/Faust-t.html.

Fish, Stanley. "Aim Low." *Chronicle of Higher Education,* May 13, 2003. http://chronicle.com/job/2003/05/2003051601.chtm.

———. "On Balance." *Chronicle of Higher Education,* April 1, 2005. http://chronicle.com/jobs/200504/2005040101c.htm.

———. "Colleges Caught in a Vise." *New York Times,* Sept. 18, 2003, A31.

———. *Is There a Text in This Class?* Cambridge, MA: Harvard University Press, 1980.

———. "The Last Professor." *New York Times,* Jan. 18, 2009. http://fish.blogs.nytimes.com/2009/01/18/the-last-professor/.

———. *Professional Correctness: Literary Studies and Political Change.* New York: Clarendon, 1995.

———. "Psychology and Torture." *New York Times,* Nov. 9, 2008. http://fish.

blogs.nytimes.com/2008/11/09/psychology-and-torture/.

———. *Save the World on Your Own Time.* Oxford: Oxford University Press, 2008.

Foucault, Michel. *"Society Must Be Defended": Lectures at the Collège de France, 1975–1976.* Edited by Arnold I. Davidson. Translated by David Macey. New York: Picador, 2003.

———. "The Subject and Power." In *Michel Foucault: Beyond Structuralism and Hermeneutics.* Edited by Hubert L. Dreyfus and Paul Rabinow, 208–26. 2d edition. Chicago: University of Chicago Press, 1983.

Gilmore, Ruth Wilson. *Golden Gulag: Prisons, Surplus, Crisis, and Opposition in Globalizing California.* Berkeley: University of California Press, 2007.

Gilroy, Paul. *Against Race: Imagining Political Culture Beyond the Color Line.* Cambridge, MA: Belknap, 2000.

Giroux, Henry A. *The Abandoned Generation: Democracy Beyond the Culture of Fear.* New York: Palgrave, 2004.

———. *Against the Terror of Neoliberalism: Politics Beyond the Age of Greed.* Boulder, CO: Paradigm, 2008.

———. "Obama's View of Education Is Stuck in Reverse." *Truthout,* July 24, 2009. http://www.truthout.org/072409A.

———. *Stormy Weather: Katrina and the Politics of Disposability.* Boulder, CO: Paradigm, 2006.

———. *The University in Chains: Confronting the Military-Industrial-Academic Complex.* Boulder, CO: Paradigm, 2007.

———. *Youth and the Suspect Society: Democracy or Disposability.* New York: Palgrave, 2009.

Giroux, Henry A., and Susan Searls Giroux. *Take Back Higher Education: Race, Youth and the Crisis of Democracy in the Post–Civil Rights Era.* New York: Palgrave, 2004.

Giroux, Henry A., and Kenneth Saltman. "Obama's Betrayal of Public Education? Arne Duncan and the Corporate Model of Schooling." *Truthout,* Dec. 17, 2008. http://www.truthout.org/121708R.

Giroux, Susan Searls. "The Age of Irony?" *JAC* 22:4 (Fall 2002): 960–76.

Goldberg, David Theo. "Killing Me Softly": Civility/Race/Violence. *Review of Education, Pedagogy & Cultural Studies* 27 (Oct.–Dec. 2005): 337–66.

———. "The Presidential Race" blog comment. Posted Oct. 27, 2008. http://www.threatofrace.org/blog/comment/195/.

———. *The Racial State.* Oxford: Blackwell, 2002.

———. *Racist Culture: Philosophy and the Politics of Meaning.* Oxford: Blackwell, 1993.

———. "The State We Are In." *Truthout*, June 9, 2009. http://www.truthout. org/060909T.

———. *The Threat of Race: Reflections on Racial Neoliberalism*. Malden, MA: Wiley-Blackwell, 2009.

Gongloff, Mark. "U.S. Jobs Jumping Ship." *CNNMoney*, July 22, 2003. http:// cnnmoney.printthis.clickability.com/pt/cpt?action=cpt&expire=&url ID=6989886& fb=Y&partnerID=2200.

Gordon, Lewis. *Bad Faith and Anti-Black Racism*. Atlantic Highlands, NJ: Humanities Press, 1995.

———. *Disciplinary Decadence: Living Thought in Trying Times*. Boulder, CO: Paradigm, 2006.

———. *Existentia Africana: Understanding Africana Existential Thought*. New York: Routledge, 2000.

———. *Fanon and the Crisis of European Man: An Essay on Philosophy and the Human Sciences*. New York: Routledge, 1995.

———. *Her Majesty's Other Children: Sketches of Racism from a Neocolonial Age*. Lanham, CO: Rowman & Littlefield, 1997.

Gordon, Jane Anna, and Lewis R. Gordon. *Of Divine Warning: Reading Disaster in the Modern Age*. Boulder, CO: Paradigm. 2009.

Gore, Al. *The Assault on Reason*. New York: Penguin, 2008.

Greider, William. "Rolling Back the Twentieth Century." *Nation*, May 12, 2003, 11–19.

Grenke, Michael W. "Translator's Introduction." In *On the Future of Our Educational Institutions* by Friedrich Nietzsche (1872). Edited and translated by Michael W. Grenke, 1–9. South Bend, IN: St. Augustine's Press, 2004.

Grossberg, Lawrence. *Caught in the Crossfire: Kids, Politics and America's Future*. Boulder, CO: Paradigm, 2005.

Guinier, Lani. "Saving Affirmative Action and a Process for Elites to Choose Elites." *Village Voice*, July 2–8, 2003. http://www.villagevoice.com/print/issues/0327/guinier.php.

Habermas, Jürgen. *The New Conservatism: Cultural Criticism and the Historians' Debate*. Cambridge, MA: MIT Press, 1989.

———. *Philosophical-Political Profiles*. Translated by Frederick G. Lawrence. Cambridge, MA: MIT Press, 1983 [1971].

Hagopian, Jesse. "The Dog Eats Its Tail: Oversized Classes, Overpopulated Prisons." *Commondreams*, March 7, 2009. http://www.commondreams.org/view/2009/03/07–2.

Hanssen, Beatrice. *Critique of Violence: Between Poststructuralism and Critical Theory*. London: Routledge, 2000.

Hart, Peter. "Obamamania: How Loving Barack Obama Helps Pundits Love Themselves." *Extra! Fairness & Accuracy in Reporting,* March-April 2007. http://www.fair.org/index.php?page=3094.

Hedges, Chris. "America the Illiterate." *Truthdig,* Nov. 10, 2008. http://www.truthdig.com/report/item/20081110_america_the_illiterate/.

———. "America's Wars of Self-Destruction." *Truthout,* Nov. 17, 2008. http://www.truthout.org/111708D.

———. *Empire of Illusion: The End of Literacy and the Triumph of the Spectacle.* New York: Nation Books, 2009.

Hentoff, Nate. "Sandra Day O'Connor's Elitist Decision: Another Three Card Monty." *Village Voice,* July 18, 2003.

Herbert, Bob. "Impossible, Ridiculous and Repugnant." *New York Times,* Oct. 6, 2005, 24. http://select.nytimes.com/2005/10/06/opinion/06herbert.html?_r=1.

Hofstadter, Richard. *Anti-Intellectualism in American Life.* New York: Vintage, 1963.

Horowitz, David, "Academic Bill of Rights." http://www.studentsforacademic-freedom.org/.

Huntington, Samuel. *Clash of Civilizations and the Remaking of the New World Order.* New York: Simon & Schuster: 1998.

———. *Who We Are: The Challenges of America's National Identity.* New York: Simon & Schuster, 2004.

Ivie, Robert L. "A Presumption of Academic Freedom." *Review of Education, Pedagogy, & Cultural Studies* 27 (2005): 53–85.

Jacoby, Jeff. "A Left-wing Monopoly on Campuses." *Boston Globe,* Dec. 2, 2004. http://www.boston.com/news/globe/editorial_opinion/oped/articles/2004/12/02/a_left_wing_monopoly_on_campuses/.

Jacoby, Russell. "The New PC." *Nation,* April 4, 2005. http://www.thenation.com/doc.mhtml?i=20050404&s=jacoby.

Jacoby, Susan. *The Age of American Unreason.* New York: Pantheon, 2008.

Johnson, Lyndon Baines. *My Hope for America.* New York: Random House, 1964.

Kant, Immanuel. "Toward Perpetual Peace." In *Practical Philosophy.* Translated and edited by Mary J. Gregor. In *The Cambridge Edition of the Works of Immanuel Kant.* Edited by Paul Guyer and Allan W. Wood. Cambridge: Cambridge University Press, 1996.

Kelley, Robin D. G. *Yo' Mama's Disfunktional! Fighting the Culture Wars in Urban America.* Boston, MA: Beacon, 1997.

Kellner, Douglas. *Guys and Guns Amok: Domestic Terrorism and School Shootings from the Oklahoma City Bombing to the Virginia Tech Massacre.* Boulder, CO: Paradigm, 2007.

King, Martin Luther. "Remaining Awake Through a Great Revolution." In *A Tes-*

tament of Hope: The Essential Writings and Speeches of Dr. Martin Luther King, Jr.* Edited by James M. Washington, 268–78. New York: Harper Collins, 1991.

———. *Where Do We Go From Here: Chaos or Community?* Boston: Beacon, 1967.

———. "The World House." In *Where Do We Go From Here: Chaos or Community?*, 167–91. Boston: Beacon, 1967.

Kozol, Jonathan. *Savage Inequalities: Children in America's Schools.* New York: Harper Perennial, 1992.

Krugman, Paul. "State of Decline." *New York Times,* Aug. 1, 2003, A21.

Kumashiro, Kevin. "EQUAL TIME: Duncan Wrong Education Choice." *Atlanta Journal-Constitution.* Dec. 23, 2008. http://www.interversity.org/lists/arn-l/archives/Dec2008/msg00171.html.

Lamis, Alexander P. "The Two Party South: From the 1960s to the 1990s." In *Southern Politics in the 1990s.* Edited by Alexander P. Lamis, 1–49. Baton Rouge: Louisiana State University Press, 1999.

Lapham, Lewis. "Yankee Doodle Dandy." *Harpers,* Aug. 2003, 9–11.

Lazere, Donald. "'The Closing of the American Mind' 20 Years Later." *Inside Higher Ed,* Sept. 18, 2007. http://insidehighered.com/layout/set/print/views.2007/09/18/lazere.

———. "The Contradictions of Cultural Conservatism in the Assault on American Colleges." *Chronicle of Higher Education,* July 2, 2004. http://chronicle.com/weekly/v50/i43/43b01501.htm.

———. "Stanley Fish's Tightrope Act." *College English* 71 (May 2009): 528–38.

Lemert, Charles. *Dark Thoughts: Race and the Eclipse of Society.* New York: Routledge, 2002.

Loury, Glenn C. "Lecture I: Ghettos, Prisons and Racial Stigma." The Tanner Lectures, April 4, 2007. http://www.econ.brown.edu/fac/Glenn_Loury/loury-homepage/teaching/Ec%20137/Ec%20137%20spring07/LECTURE%20I.pdf.

———. *Race, Incarceration and American Values.* Boston: MIT Press, 2008.

Lowen, Rebecca S. *Creating the Cold War University: The Transformation of Stanford.* Berkeley: University of California Press, 1997.

Mauer, Mark. *Race to Incarcerate.* New York: New Press, 1999.

Mauer, Mark, and Meda Chesney-Lind, eds. *Invisible Punishment: The Collateral Consequences of Mass Imprisonment.* New York: New Press, 2003.

Mbembe, Achille. *On the Postcolony.* Berkeley: University of California Press, 2001.

McCain, John (with Mark Salter). *Faith of My Fathers: A Family Memoir.* New York: Harper, 2008.

Michaels, Walter Benn. *The Trouble with Diversity: How We Learned to Love Identity and Ignore Inequality.* New York: Metropolitan, 2006.

Miller, James. "The Prophet and the Dandy: Philosophy as a Way of Life in Nietzsche and Foucault." *Social Research* 65 (Winter 1998): 871–96.

Mills, C. Wright. *The Sociological Imagination.* London: Oxford University Press, 1959.

Monbiot, George. "How These Jibbering Numbskulls Came to Dominate Washington." *Guardian,* Oct. 28, 2008. http://www.commondreams.org/view/2008/10/28.

Morrison, Toni. *Playing in the Dark: Whiteness and the Literary Imagination.* Cambridge: Harvard University Press, 1992.

Moyers, Bill. "This Is Your Story: The Progressive Story of America. Pass it On." Speech given at the Take Back America conference, sponsored by the Campaign for America's Future, on June 4, 2003. Washington, D.C. http://www.commondreams.org/views03/0610-11.htm.

———. Transcript. *Bill Moyers Journal,* Sept. 4, 2009. http://www.pbs.org/moyers/journal/09042009/transcript4.html.

Muhammad, Dedrick. "Obama and the Harsh Racial Reality." *Counterpunch,* May 28, 2009. http://www.counterpunch.org/muhammad05282009.html.

Murray, Charles. *Losing Ground: American Social Policy, 1950–1980.* 10th anniversary edition. New York: Basic Books, 1995 [1985].

Murray, Charles, and Richard J. Herrnstein. *The Bell Curve: Intelligence and Class Structure in American Life.* New York: Free Press, 1996.

Muwakkil, Salim. "The 'Post-Racial' President." *In These Times,* Aug. 24, 2009. http://www.inthesetimes.com/article/4750/the_post-racial_president/.

Myrdal, Gunnar. *The American Dilemma: The Negro Problem and Modern Democracy.* New York: Harper & Bros., 1944.

Nietzsche, Friedrich. *The Birth of Tragedy* (1872). Translated by Shaun Whiteside. New York: Penguin Classics, 1994.

———. *On the Future of Our Educational Institutions* (1872). Edited and translated by Michael W. Grenke. South Bend, IN: St. Augustine's Press, 2004.

Obama, Barack. *The Audacity of Hope: Thoughts on Reclaiming the American Dream.* New York: Vintage, 2006.

———. *Dreams from My Father: A Story of Race and Inheritance.* New York: Three Rivers Press, 2004 [1995].

———. "Transcript of Barack Obama's Speech on Race." *New York Times,* March 18, 2008.

Orfield, Gary, Susan E. Eaton, and the Harvard Project on School Desegregation. *Dismantling Desegregation: The Quiet Reversal of* Brown v. Board of Education. New York: New Press, 1996.

Patterson, Orlando. *Slavery and Social Death.* Cambridge, MA: Harvard University Press, 1982.

Peters, Michael, James Marshall, and Paul Smeyers. *Nietzsche's Legacy for Educa-*

tion: Past and Present Values. Westport, CT: Bergin & Garvey, 2001.

Peterson, Merrill D. *The Portable Thomas Jefferson*, New York: Penguin, 1975.

Pew Charitable Trusts report. "1 in 100: Behind Bars in America 2008." http://www.pewcenteronthestates.org/uploadedFiles/One%20in%20100.pdf.

Phillips, Kevin P. *The Emerging Republican Majority.* New Rochelle, NY: Arlington House, 1969.

Powell, Michael. "Bank Accused of Pushing Mortgage Deal on Blacks." *New York Times,* June 6, 2009. http://www.nytimes.com/2009/06/07/us/07baltimore.html?_r=1.

Quadagno, Jill. *The Color of Welfare: How Racism Undermined the War on Poverty.* Oxford: Oxford University Press, 1994.

Readings, Bill. *The University in Ruins.* Boston, MA: Harvard University Press, 1996.

Rich, Frank. "Awake and Sing." *New York Times,* April 12, 2009. http://www.nytimes.com/2009/04/12/opinion/12rich.html.

Roberts, Dorothy. *Killing the Black Body: Race, Reproduction, and the Meaning of Liberty.* New York: Vintage, 1997.

Robespierre, Maximilien. "Principles of Revolutionary Governments" (1793). *Oeuvres.* 3 volumes. Laponneraye, 1840.

Roediger, David. "Obama's Victory and the Future of Race in the United States." *Counterpunch,* Nov. 10, 2008. http://www.counterpunch.org/roediger11102008.html.

Rorty, Richard. "The Inspirational Value of Great Works of Literature." *Raritan* (Summer 1995): 8–17.

Said, Edward. *Orientalism.* New York: Vintage, 1978.

———. *Representations of the Intellectual: The 1993 Reith Lectures.* New York: Pantheon. 1994.

Sanders, Mark. *Complicities: The Intellectual and Apartheid.* Durham, NC: Duke University Press, 2002.

Schwartz, Delmore. "In Dreams Begin Responsibilities." In *In Dreams Begin Responsibilities and Other Short Stories,* 1–9. New York: New Directions, 1978.

Simon, Jonathan. *Governing Through Crime: How the War on Crime Transformed American Democracy and Created a Culture of Fear.* Oxford: Oxford University Press, 2007.

Snow, C. P. *The Two Cultures.* 1959. Reprinted Canto edition. Cambridge: Cambridge University Press, 1993.

Squires, George D. "Scapegoating Blacks. Again." *ColorLines Magazine,* summer web issue 1. http://www.colorlines.com/article.php?ID=513.

Street, Paul. "Race, Prison, and Poverty: The Race to Incarcerate in the Age of

Correctional Keynesianism." *Z Magazine*, May 2001, 25–31. http://www.zcom-munications.org/race-prison-and-poverty-by-paul-street.

Uchitelle, Louis. "Blacks Lose Better Jobs Faster as Middle-Class Work Drops." *New York Times*, July 12, 2003, C14.

Virilio, Paul. *Desert Screen: War at the Speed of Light*. New York: Continuum, 2005.

Von Clausewitz, Carl. *Vom Kriege* [*On War*]. 2d edition. Volume 3. Berlin: Ferd. Dümmlers Verlagsbuchandlung, 1853

Wacquant, Loïc. "From Slavery to Mass Incarceration: Rethinking the 'Race Question' in the U.S." *New Left Review* 13 (Jan.–Feb. 2002): 41–60.

"Welcome Back." *Guardian,* Nov. 6, 2008.

Willis, Ellen. "We Need a Radical Left." *Nation*, June 29, 1998, 18–21.

Wilson, John K. *Patriotic Correctness: Academic Freedom and Its Enemies*. Boulder, CO: Paradigm, 2006.

Winter, Greg. "Tens of Thousands Will Lose College Aid, Report Says." *New York Times*, July 18, 2003.

Woodson, Carter G. *The Miseducation of the Negro* (1930). Reprint. New York: Classic House Books, 2008.

Young, Robert. *Colonial Desire: Hybridity in Theory, Culture and Race*. New York: Routledge, 1995.

Zeleny, Jeff, and Jim Rutenberg, "As Race Debate Grows, Obama Steers Clear of It." *New York Times*, Sept. 17, 2009. http://www.nytimes.com/2009/09/17/us/politics/17obama.html.

Zinn, Howard. *A People's History of the United States: 1492–Present*. Revised and expanded edition. New York: Harper Perennial, 1995.

Index

Abu Ghraib, 42, 89

Academic Bill of Rights (student), 68–70, 80–82, 114, 251n43

academic freedom: crisis of, 28, 147–49, 246n20; for students, 67–70, 147, 149–50, 159

academy, 3, 11; anti–intellectualism of, 96–118; casualization of labour in, 51, 61, 145; labeled as liberal/left, 65–71, 251n46; labor in, 3, 15, 48, 51, 145; rise of managerial class in, 51, 145; and tenure, 51. *See also* intellectuals; university

affirmative action: attacks on, 100, 201; neoliberalism versus, 94; Supreme Court decision in 2003 on, 220–21, 227, 229

Afghanistan: war in, ix, 35, 46, 89–90, 205, 226

African Americans: criminalized and imprisoned, 10, 118–20, 126, 211, 214, 228–29; and economic inequality, 5; impact of the recession on, 192–93; 118–19; racism towards, 68; and second–class citizenship, 126; studies, 53, 64, 231; voters, 208

Against Race (Gilroy), 120

"Against Theory" (Michaels and Knapp), 113

Agamben, Giorgio, 167

Age of American Unreason (Susan Jacoby), 82

American Association of University Professors (AAUP), 69

American Council of Trustees and Alumni (ACTA), 66

American dream, 25, 35, 126, 221

American literature, 53–54

American Renaissance (Matthiessen), 53

Angelus Novus (Klee), 168

anti-intellectualism, 74–126, 240; American, 26–27, 116, 247n9; of corporate logic, 103–4; and folksiness, 81; as historical amnesia, 116–17; pundits of, 193

antiracialism: compared to antiracism (Goldberg), 73, 115, 245n9. *See also* racialism

anti-semitism, 168

antiwar movement, 15

apartheid: American, 119, 198, 201, 241; South African, 25

Aptheker, Herbert, 237

Arendt, Hannah, 43, 98–99, 109, 116, 119, 139, 147–48, 154, 161, 167, 177, 248n18

Aronowitz, Stanley, 61

Asad, Talal, 163, 164, 166, 188

Assault on Reason, The (Gore), 81

Associated Press, 186

Atwater, Lee, 91

Ayers, William, 12, 80

Bad Faith and Anti–Black Racism (Gordon), 167

Baldwin, James, 50

Balibar, Etienne, 239

Ball State University, 69